PARALEGALS
AND
SUCCESSFUL LAW PRACTICE

Robert G. Kurzman, J.D., LL.M.
and
Rita K. Gilbert, J.D., LL.M.

Institute for Business Planning
IBP PLAZA, ENGLEWOOD CLIFFS, N.J. 07632

© 1981 *by*

Institute for Business Planning, Inc.
IBP Plaza, Englewood Cliffs, N.J. 07632

*All rights reserved. No part of this book
may be reproduced in any form or by
any means, without permission in writing
from the publisher.*

Library of Congress Cataloging in Publication Data

Kurzman, Robert G.
  Paralegals and successful law practice.

  Includes bibliographical references and index.
  1. Legal assistants—United States.   I. Gilbert,
Rita K.   II. Title.
KF320.L4K87   349.73'023   81-13157
ISBN 0-87624-426-6 347.30023   AACR2

"This publication is designed to provide accurate and authoritative information in regard to the subject matter covered. It is sold with the understanding that the publisher is not engaged in rendering legal, accounting or other professional service. If legal advice is required, the services of a competent professional person should be sought."

—From a Declaration of Principles jointly adopted by a Committee of the American Bar Association and a Committee of Publishers and Associations.

Printed in the United States of America

ISBN 0-87624-426-6

Paralegals
and
Successful Law Practice

Dedication

From: Robert G. Kurzman

To my understanding and patient wife, Carol, for her tolerance in accepting my being incommunicado during the many hours in preparing this book. Also, to my secretary, Anne Kahn, my appreciation for her cooperation in typing as well as editing portions of the manuscript as well as to Linda Meyer, an outstanding paralegal in my office, for her advice and editing assistance.

From: Rita K. Gilbert

> To Bruce, Mom, Lloyd and Lonya
> With All My Love
> To Dad, Who Was My Inspiration,
> But Did Not Live to
> See Its Publication

About the Authors

Robert G. Kurzman is a partner in the firm of Goldschmidt, Fredericks, Kurzman & Oshatz (New York City). In addition to active participation in local bar associations, Mr. Kurzman is a member of the ABA Tax Section, Probate and Real Property Section and Family Law Section. He is also a member of the Trusts and Estates Section and Special Committee on the Integration of the Uniform Probate Code, within the New York State Bar Association.

Mr. Kurzman has been coordinator of the Estates and Trusts Division of the Paralegal Institute at Manhattanville College and Adjunct Assistant Professor of Law and Taxation, New York University, S.C.E. He has also been a member of the Advisory Board at Southern Methodist University School of Law Estate Planning Institute, and is a Fellow of the American College of Probate Counsel.

Mr. Kurzman has been very active in seminars, primarily on estate and taxation work, and particularly during the last several years. In connection with some of these seminars, he has published "Estate Planning Considerations on the Organization of Business: Proprietorships, Partnerships, Corporations," 34th New York University Institute on Federal Taxation; and "Far Away Places—Estate Tax Haven or Pitfall?," 11th Annual Institute on Estate Planning, University of Miami (Matthew Bender & Co.).

Mr. Kurzman received his J.D. from Cornell University in 1957, and has been admitted to practice in the U.S. Supreme Court, U.S. Court of Claims, U.S. District Court Southern and Eastern Districts, and the U.S. Court of Appeals. He now resides in New Rochelle with his wife, Carol, and their children, Marc, Nancy and Amy.

Rita K. Gilbert is an Associate in the firm of Campbell & Hyman, in New Rochelle, New York. The scope of Mrs. Gilbert's business and educational backgrounds reflects a wide variety of interests and experience. As a paralegal (Certificate, New York University, 1975) she worked for Danziger,

Markhoff and Feigert in the area of estate administration. As a law student, she served an internship in the U.S. Attorney's Office, Southern District of New York. She has also worked as a stockbroker with the firm of Hodgen, Haight & Co., in Washington, D.C.

Among her academic endeavors, Mrs. Gilbert can list: participation in the Washington Seminar Honors Program, American University; exchange student to both the University of Edinburgh, and later to the University of Puerto Rico; recipient of a Fulbright Fellowship to Guatemala. After receiving her A.B. from Hunter College, Mrs. Gilbert continued her studies, earning an M.A. in Advanced International Studies from Johns Hopkins University in 1966.

Mrs. Gilbert earned her J.D. degree in 1979 as a member of Pace University's first Law School graduating class. She is currently a member of the N.Y. Bar Association, Tax and Estate & Trust field, as well as a member of the Florida Bar Association, Westchester Bar Association, Tax Section, the Westchester Women's Bar, and the N.Y. Women's Bar Association.

Mrs. Gilbert is admitted to practice in the U.S. District Court Southern and Eastern Districts of New York. Her contributions to this book may be seen to reflect clearly the unique dual viewpoint of one who has participated in the legal profession both as a paralegal and as an attorney.

Mrs. Gilbert resides in New Rochelle, New York with her husband and two children.

What This Book Will Do for You

The following remark, made by a prominent attorney to a third-year law school class, provides our theme in this book: "The key to success for an attorney today is hiring a top-notch paralegal."

With overhead costs skyrocketing for most firms, the American Bar Association, back in 1968, established a Special Committee on Legal Assistants, which promulgated as part of its credo the following resolution:

> (T)he legal profession recognizes that there are many tasks in serving a client's needs which can be performed by trained non-lawyer assistants working under the direction and supervision of a lawyer.

Still, more than a dozen years later, we continue to face growing public criticism that the cost of competent legal services is escalating beyond the reach of the average citizen. You owe it to yourself and to your clients to become more aware of the many advantages to be gained by delegating non-lawyer tasks, so often performed by a lawyer, to a legal assistant. *Paralegals and Successful Law Practice* clearly demonstrates those advantages, and shows you how you can build them into your practice.

Your authors are two experienced attorneys, one of whom entered the legal profession initiallly as a paralegal. We have endeavored to examine here the broad range of legal services that a trained paralegal is competent to perform with skill and independence. Such services are within the framework of the professional canon of ethics and other promulgated guidelines.

Our first chapter details the benefits—in terms of cost reduction, profit increase, and office productivity—that are yours if you introduce an efficient system, utilizing paralegals, into your office. Following this we discuss and demonstrate the most effective means of locating (Chapter 2), hiring (Chapter 3), and training (Chapter 4) legal assistants. This coverage features a review of paralegal training programs currently available.

Also within Chapter 4, on training, we discuss and illustrate successful methods for integrating the trained paralegal as a valuable adjunct in the contemporary law firm. And, in the following chapter (Chapter 5), we detail further how you can increase your profits and productivity by developing efficient systems within which you, your paralegal(s), and all your staff will function as a well-coordinated team—whether you are a specialist, or in general practice.

The synergistic effect of a lawyer/paralegal team is to provide the lawyer with more time to exercise special professional skills, through delegation of the somewhat more mechanical legal functions to the trained paralegal. Paralegals have proven particularly valuable in the areas of estate planning and probate administration, litigation, real estate, corporate practice, domestic relations, employee benefit plan work, and many other areas. For each of the areas listed, and some others as well, we examine the work that paralegals could and should be doing. This specific coverage, used in conjunction with the systems demonstrated in Chapter 5, will help you determine and implement the best methods for employing paralegals at your work.

Chapter 10 highlights the valued services that legal assistants render to U.S. Government agencies and offices, legal aid offices, financial institutions, title insurance companies, and corporate law departments. Again, this material along with the systems in Chapter 5, provides you with tools and plans for enhancing productivity and profits. Chapter 11 rounds out the coverage of paralegal systems by telling you how to evaluate and improve the performance of your staff members—attorneys, staff supervisors, paralegals, clerks, secretaries—and the system itself.

In addition, there are two more chapters. A nationwide look at paralegal compensation and fringe benefits packages, through a series of local surveys, offers you some valuable help with budget preparation. Finally, we review guidelines and opinions already rendered on the ethical uses of paralegals, and recommend sources for further clarification should you need them.

Effective use of paralegals involves more than hiring of a new employee. Rather, it represents a commitment to a system designed to be a cost-saving device. A paralegal should not be hired or used as a replacement for a lawyer. Central to the success of a paralegal system is the ability to have work and responsibility delegated effectively. This book has been tailored to be a practical working tool, to show you how to achieve maximum control and efficiency from the employment of legal assistants.

You'll find a number of extensive, practical discussions, illustrating procedures and strategies. For example:

- Five Steps to Increase Your Enjoyment of the Practice of Law
- Where to Locate Paralegals With Prior Training
- Examining Paralegal Institutions Throughout the United States
- How to Evaluate Paralegal Programs and Courses
- Put Paralegal Training Curricula to Work for You
- Four-Step Procedure for Hiring Paralegals
- Who Should Be Your Supervising Attorney or Legal Assistant Coordinator?
- How to Restructure Work Assignments for Maximum Effectiveness
- How to Train the Paralegal in Your Own Office
- Benefits and Methods of Developing an Effective Office manual
- How to Avoid Friction in Adding Paralegals to Your Staff
- Mixing Paralegals With Systems: Game Plan for a Rewarding Experience
- Three Essential Steps to Beginning a System to Increase Your Law Office Profits
- Benefits of Using the Systems Approach
- Three Pitfalls the Systems Approach Avoids
- Benefits of Using Paralegals in Estate Planning and Administration
- What Kinds of Work Are Paralegals Capable of—and Permitted to Do—in Estate Planning and Probate Administration?
- How Paralegals Help Make Preparation for Trial a Less-Pressured, More Manageable Endeavor
- Utilizing the Real Estate Paralegal
- Utilizing the Paralegal in Corporate Practice
- Benefiting by Use of Paralegals in Employee Benefit Plan Practice
- The Paralegal is Your Greatest Public Relations Asset
- Paralegals Gain Invaluable Experience Working for Government Agencies

- Tap the Ever-Deepening Pool of Paralegal Experience
- Three-Step System for Rating Your Use of Paralegals
- How to Assess Your Needs and Plan to Improve Your System
- Free-Lance Paralegals Can Handle Specific Work for You
- A Close Look at Paralegal Compensation via Eight Regional Surveys
- Ethical and Accepted Uses of the Paralegal

In addition, we have included a great many checklists, guides, forms, schedules, and other useful working aids. For example:

- Criteria Summary Chart to Guide the Decision Between Hiring From Without or Promoting From Within
- Checklist of Desirable Qualities in a Supervising Attorney or Legal Assistant Coordinator
- Plaintiff Investigation and Preparation Checklist for Use by the Paralegal in a Personal Injury Case
- Task Inventory for Paralegal Work Assisting Practitioners in Criminal Cases and With Legal Research
- Sample Job Description for Paralegals in Several Title Insurance Company Positions
- Sample Job Descriptions for Paralegals Assisting Corporate Counsel
- Sample Form for Evaluating Paralegal Employees

It is our hope that *Paralegals and Successful Law Practice* will help improve the delivery of legal services in the near future, and remain a helpful reference tool over the long run. We are confident that it will, because we show precisely how proper employment of trained legal assistants can be a significant means for *you* to achieve greater productivity, increased profits, and cost savings for you and your clients.

In the chapters that follow, you will find our step-by-step outline to guide you and your staff in streamlining your work into the smoothest and most profitable practice possible. Those who have pioneered these ideas, and made the most of them, have seen their firms' productivity more than double.

In many instances, you can use our material exactly as presented. Other times you'll want to adapt our guidelines to fit your particular practice. Combine these approaches, and *Paralegals and Successful Law Practice* will be your first step on the road to a less stressful and more rewarding practice.

Acknowledgments

The authors wish to take this opportunity to thank the following paralegals who gave so much of themselves in agreeing to be interviewed for this book:

Dolores Scott Whittle	David French
Kathryn A. Albertson	Monica Schlesinger
Carole Murphy	Susan Jason
Linda Meyer	Denise Zahralban Kaback
Patricia Schwartz	Mary Kanian
Mary Hedley	Kathleen M. Commins
Kathleen Statler	Elizabeth McKeever
Joe Canillo	Loretta May
Sandra Ray	Astrid Garcia
Margaret Metz	Anita Kramer
Mary Korth	Ellen Klutch

A very special thank you to three paralegals who not only agreed to be interviewed but were of invaluable assistance throughout the writing of this book:

Mary Guinan
Nancy Siegel
Linda Harrington

To those paralegals who preferred not to be named, we both want to say thank you for all of your efforts on behalf of the paralegal profession.

Contents

Dedication v
About the Authors vii
What This Book Will Do for You ix
Acknowledgments xiii

PART ONE: ESTABLISHING A PARALEGAL SYSTEM IN YOUR OFFICE

1	**Legal Assistants—What Can They Do for You?**	
101	Introduction: We All Want Our Money's Worth	3
101.1	What Is a Legal Assistant?	4
102	Make the Most of Your Time: Achieve Efficiency and Flexibility Through the Skillful Use of Paralegals	5
102.1	Give Your Clients Emotional Support Without Infringing on Your Time	6
103	Reduce Your Legal Fees While Earning Greater Profits	7
104	Effective Use of Legal Assistants Will Lessen the Possibility of Legal Malpractice Suits	8
105	How to Integrate the Paralegal Into Your Present Office Infrastructure	9
105.1	How to Turn Your Present "Old-Fashioned" System of Law Office Management Into a Progressive One	10
106	Delegation is the Economics of the Law Today	10
107	Five Steps to Increase Your Enjoyment of the Practice of Law	12

2 How to Locate Qualified Paralegals

201	Where to Locate Paralegals With Prior Training	13
201.1	Recruiting Through Employment Agencies	13
201.2	Recruiting Through Classified Advertising	16
201.3	Recruiting Through Placement Offices at Paralegal Schools	16
201.4	Other Valuable Recruiting Sources	17
202	Examining Paralegal Institutions	18
202.1	Some Paralegal Training Programs in the Eastern United States	18
202.2	Some Paralegal Training Programs in Middle America	22
202.3	Some Paralegal Training Programs on the West Coast	24
203	How to Evaluate Paralegal Programs and Courses	26
203.1	Guidelines for Coverage in Courses for Corporate Paralegals	28
203.2	Guidelines for Coverage in Courses for Probate Paralegals	28
203.3	Guidelines for Coverage in Courses for Litigation Paralegals	29
203.4	Guidelines for Coverage in Courses for Real Estate Paralegals	30
203.5	Guidelines for Courses for Matrimonial Paralegals	30
203.6	Guidelines for Coverage for Courses in Pension, Profit Sharing and ERISA	31
203.7	Guidelines for Coverage in Courses on Effective Use of Legal Materials	32
203.8	Guidelines for Courses in Administrative Law	33
203.9	Put Paralegal Training Curricula to Work for You	33
204	Benefits and Pitfalls of On-the-Job Training for You and the Paralegal	34
204.1	One Benefit of On-the-Job Training—Availability of Simultaneous Training in Substance and Procedure	35
204.2	Higher Based Salaries or Less Experience?	35
204.3	Familiarity With General Office Procedures	36
204.4	Ensuring Competence in Your Field of Specialization	37
204.5	One Benefit of Many Outside Training Programs— Legal Research Training	37

204.6	Job Transition	37
205	Deciding Which Route You Should Take in Hiring	38
206	Summary	40

3 Hiring the Paralegal

301	Introduction to a Four-Step Procedure for Hiring Paralegals	42
302	Step One: Establish Criteria for Employment	43
302.1	Criteria Satisfaction Table for Prospective Employees	43
302.2	Develop a Job Description Manual	44
303	Step Two: Assemble Job Candidates for the Time-saving Group Interview	45
303.1	Announce the Job Openings	46
303.2	How to Process the Resumes You Receive	47
304	Step Three: The Mechanics of the Group Interview	49
304.1	"Testing" the Candidates to Ensure the Hiring of a Top-Notch Paralegal	50
304.2	Closing the Interview—Success Formula Completed	52
305	Step Four: How You Make Your Hiring Decisions	54
305.1	Your Staff Can Help You	54
305.2	Let Your Staff Help You Decide	55
306	The Bottom Line of the Group Interview: Saving Money and Attorney's Time for the Firm	56

4 Training the Paralegal to Function Effectively in Your Office

401	Introduction: Getting Your Paralegal Started	57
402	Who Should Be Your Supervising Attorney or Legal Assistant Coordinator?	58
402.1	Checklist of Desirable Qualities in a Supervising Attorney or Legal Assistant Coordinator	58
402.2	Sample Job Description: Law Office Administrator	59
402.3	Where Do You Find a Qualified Legal Assistant Coordinator or Law Firm Administrator?	62
403	Educating and Training Paralegals	63
403.1	Your Best Approach—Defined Responsibility in a Team Setting	64

404	Coordinating and Blending the Paralegal with Your Staff	67
404.1	How to Achieve Lawyer Acceptance of Paralegals	67
404.2	How to Restructure Work Assignments for Maximum Effectiveness	68
404.3	Assuring Lawyer Responsibility for Paralegals' Work Product	69
405	Basic Internal Education and Communication (Feedback) Help Paralegals Improve Office Procedures	70
405.1	Acknowledge the Paralegal's Work	71
405.2	Reinforce Your Appreciation and Increase the Challenge	71
405.3	The Whole Staff Benefits From Communication	72
406	How to Offer Complete Training for the Paralegal in Your Own Office	72
406.1	Training Should Be Thoroughly Planned and Evenly Paced	73
406.2	Introduce Paralegals to Your Forms and Start Them Solving Problems	74
406.3	Give Paralegals Complete Assignments—and Always Offer Feedback	74
407	The Six Do's for Effective Paralegal Training	75
408	The Most Effective Paralegal Training Can Occur in a Systematized Office	76
408.1	Law Office Systemization Provides Multiple Function and Benefits	77
409	Benefits and Methods of Developing an Effective Office Manual	78
409.1	Materials Necessary to Set Up an Office Manual	79
409.2	Actual Steps in Setting Up Your Manual	79
409.3	Training Benefits Provided by Office Manuals	80
410	Basic Contents of a Sample Office Manual Office Procedures Section That Can Be Tailored to Your Requirements	80
411	How to Avoid Friction in Adding Paralegals to Your Staff	83
411.1	Know How Your Whole Staff Feels	83
411.2	Have Well-Defined Promotion Standards	84
411.3	Always Anticipate the Consequences of Your Decisions	84
411.4	Don't Forget Space and Supply Considerations	85
412	Training the Paralegal for Work in Your Specialized Areas of Practice	85

PART TWO: EFFECTIVE UTILIZATION OF LEGAL ASSISTANTS IN THE MAJOR SPECIALIZED AREAS OF PRACTICE

5 How to Increase Your Law Office Profits

501	Why You Should Develop and Implement a Smoothly Functioning System in Your Office	91
501.1	Defining Systems Management	93
501.2	How Paralegals and Systems Interface to Benefit the Firm	93
502	Three Essential Steps to Building Your System	94
502.1	Identify Areas of Law for Systemization	95
502.2	Assemble Pertinent Information	95
502.3	Organize and Sequence All Information and Documents for System Utilization	96
502.4	Maintaining Control of System Development	98
503	Step One: Identify Areas of Law for Systemization	99
504	Step Two: Assemble All the Procedural Information, General Facts and the Full Variety of Documents You Require for Each Specific Job	99
504.1	Prepare a Preliminary List of Every Step and Task Involved in Completing All the Work in the Area You've Chosen to Systematize	100
504.2	Organizing, Assembling and Redrafting "Universal" Versions of Documents	101
504.3	Prepare a List of Important Dates	102
505	Step Three: Organize and Sequence the Procedures, Facts, and Documents for Systematized Use	103
505.1	Drafting a Master Information List	103
505.2	Creating Reference Numbers for MIL Information	104
505.3	Converting Your "Universal" Documents for Use With the MIL Information	106
505.4	Maintaining Integrity of Documents in the System	106
505.5	Eventual Use of the MIL	107
505.6	Preparing the Procedural Outline and Checklist	107
506	Putting It All Together	108
507	Summary of Steps in Developing a System	108
508	Benefits of Using the Systems Approach	110

508.1	Systems Give You Centralized Control Over Work	110
508.2	You'll Gain the Flexibility to Adapt to Changes Readily	110
508.3	You Gain Continuity of Style and Procedures	111
508.4	You'll Always Be Able to Accumulate Knowledge and Develop New Methods	111
509	Three Pitfalls the Systems Approach Avoids	112
509.1	You Can Reduce Spiraling Legal Costs (While Improving Your Firm's Income)	112
509.2	You Can Cut Down on Loss of Legal Business to Other Professions	113
509.3	You Can Eliminate Problems Stemming From Inadequate Client Contact	113
510	Conclusion—A System is the Obvious Choice for Long-Term Efficiency	114
511	Selection of Samples for Reference As You Build Your Law Office System	115
512	Using Systems and Paralegals Profitably in Your Firm	131

6 Utilizing the Estates and Trust Paralegal

601	Benefits of Using Paralegals in Estate Planning and Administration	132
601.1	What Kinds of Work Are Paralegals Capable Of and Permitted to Do—in Estate Planning and Probate Administration?	133
602	Integrating Your Paralegal Into Estate Planning Work	136
602.1	Inventory and Fact Sheet for Effective Estate Planning	137
602.2	Paralegals Can Compute Model Estate Taxation for Various Potential Occurrences	163
602.3	Completing the Estate Plan	163
603	Paralegals Can Perform a Great Deal of Work in Estate Administration	164
603.1	Liberating the Attorney to Practice Law	164
603.2	Estate Progress File	165
603.3	Teamwork Triumphs	167
604	Summary	167

7 Utilizing the Litigation Paralegal

701	Introduction	168
701.1	Get Paralegals Involved Early in Each Case	169
701.2	How Paralegals Help Make Preparing for Trial a Less-Pressured, More Manageable Endeavor	169
701.3	Paralegal Capabilities in Litigation Support	170
702	Where Paralegals Should Supplant Attorneys in Pre-Trial Work	172
702.1	Activity Documentation Chart for Litigation Team	173
702.2	One Attorney's System for Success	173
703	Paralegals Can Be Particularly Useful During Discovery	175
703.1	Paralegal Activities Upon Receipt of a New Case—Plaintiff	175
703.2	Personal Data Sheet to be Completed During Interview Between Personal Injury Client and Legal Assistant	176
703.3	Plaintiff Investigation and Preparation Checklist for Use by Paralegal in Personal Injury Case	182
703.4	A Tip on Billing Your Paralegal's Time	184
703.5	Paralegal Activities Upon Receipt of a New Case— for the Defendant	185
703.6	Paralegals Can Draft Competent Pleadings	187
703.7	Paralegals Should Handle All Incoming Interrogatories	187
703.8	Paralegals Can Also Reduce Your Time Managing Depositions	188
704	The Paralegal is Indispensable at Trial Preparation	189
704.1	Paralegals Can Assist in Preparing an Appeal	189
705	Other Litigation-Related Functions	191
706	Benefiting by Use of Paralegals in Domestic Relations Practice	192
706.1	The Paralegal is an Excellent Source of Contact	192
706.2	Paralegals Should Be Responsible for Preparation of Financial Data	195
706.3	The Paralegal Can Interview Witnesses Skillfully	203
706.4	You Can Entrust the Paralegal With Preparation of Notices to Creditors and Financial Institutions	203
706.5	Preparation of Pleadings Can Be Handled by the Paralegal	203
706.6	Checklist of Supplemental Matters Your Paralegal Can Also Handle Well	205

8 Utilizing the Real Estate Paralegal

801	Introduction	207
802	Paralegals Can Effectively Draft and Review Residential and Commercial Leases and Agreements of Sale	210
803	Paralegals Will Carefully Review Title Reports and Surveys	210
804	Paralegals Should Draft and Review Mortgage and Other Financing Documents	211
805	Paralegals Should Draft and Review Deeds	211
806	Paralegals Can Be Responsible for Dealing With Title Companies	212
807	Paralegals Should Prepare Closing Statements and Attend Closings	213

9 Utilizing the Paralegal in Corporate Practice

901	Introduction	222
902	Paralegals Should Have Responsibility for Preparing and Filing Documents Relating to Incorporation and Dissolution	223
903	Paralegals Should Prepare Minutes, Agenda, Notices and Proxy Materials for Corporate Meetings	226
903.1	Give Paralegals Official Corporate Functions	245
904	Paralegals Can Maintain the Stock Transfer Ledger	245
905	Have Paralegals Gather Information and Draft and File Government Reports	245
906	Paralegals Should Be Responsible for Assembling "Blue Sky" Materials	247
907	Paralegals Can Provide Extremely Valuable Assistance in the Preparation of Registration Materials	248
908	Benefiting by Use of Paralegals in Commercial Practice	248
909	Benefiting by Use of Paralegals in Employee Benefit Plan Practice	255
909.1	Types of Plans	255
910	Paralegals Can Research Eligibility and Vesting Requirements for Various Plans Under ERISA	255
911	How Your ERISA Paralegal Will Spend the Day	256

912	The Paralegal is Your Greatest Public Relations Asset	257
913	Summary Regarding Use of Paralegals in the Law Office	258

10 Benefiting From Utilization of Paralegals Outside of the Private Law Sector

1001	Paralegals Gain Invaluable Experience Working for Government Agencies	259
1001.1	The U.S. Attorney's Office Offers a Wide Range of Duties to Paralegals	260
1001.2	Paralegals' Litigation Work is About the Same as for a Private Firm	260
1001.3	The Paralegal as "Intelligence Analyst"	261
1001.4	Paralegals' "Trial Work" for the U.S. Attorney's Office	261
1002	Other Values of the Paralegal to Government Employers	262
1003	Summary—Another Look at the Wide-Ranging Work Paralegals Do for the Government	262
1004	Paralegals Have Very Broad Responsibilities in Many Legal Aid Offices	264
1004.1	It's a Fact—Paralegals Reduce the Cost of Effective Legal Services, No Matter Who They Work for	264
1005	Paralegals Are Valued Employees of Financial Institutions	265
1005.1	Paralegals and Finance-Related Work	266
1006	Paralegals Perform Important and Diverse Work in Title Companies	267
1006.1	Sample Job Descriptions for Paralegals in Several Title Insurance Company Positions	268
1007	Use of Paralegals by Insurance Companies	271
1008	Corporate Use of Paralegals is Increasing	271
1008.1	Sample Job Descriptions for Paralegals Assisting Corporate Counsel	272
1008.2	How Does the Corporate Paralegal's Role Differ From the Law Firm Legal Assistant	275
1008.3	Similarities Between Law Firm and Corporate Paralegals	276
1009	Tap the Ever-Deepening Pool of Paralegal Experience	276

PART THREE: EVALUATING AND REFINING THE PARALEGAL SYSTEM IN YOUR OFFICE

11 Evaluating Your Paralegal Program

1101	Assessing the Accomplishments of the Paralegal System is Necessary Maintenance	279
1102	Three-Step System for Rating Your Use of Paralegals	280
1102.1	Step One: Evaluate Employees With This Sample Form	280
1102.2	Step Two: Evaluate Yourself and/or Your Supervisory Staff With the Following Criteria	284
1102.3	Step Three: Evaluate How the System Itself Works	285
1103	How to Assess Your Needs and Plan to Improve Your System	286
1103.1	Improving Case Handling Procedures—Work Flow Changes	287
1104	New Trends in the Profession May Benefit You	287
1104.1	Temporary Paralegal Service Agencies Are Increasingly Useful	287
1104.2	Free-Lance Paralegals Can Handle Specific Work for You	288
1104.3	More and More Legal Clinics Have Large Paralegal Staffs	288
1105	A Plea for Continuing Education	289

12 Compensation and Fringe Benefits

1201	Determining Compensation and Fringe Benefits for Your Paralegal	290
1202	Nationwide Look at Paralegal Compensation	291
1202.1	Survey of Paralegal Compensation in the Eastern United States	291
1202.2	Survey of Paralegal Compensation in the Midwestern United States	292
1202.3	Survey of Paralegal Compensation in the Western United States	292
1203	Some Additional Factors of Importance in Paralegal Compensation and Status	292
1203.1	Training and Education	297
1203.2	Period of Employment as Paralegals	297
1203.3	Fringe Benefits	297

1203.4	Paralegals' Status and Participation in the Firm	298
1203.5	Billing Paralegal Time	298
1203.6	Professional Development of Legal Assistants	299
1203.7	Who Are Paralegal Employers?	299
1204	Budgeting for Your Paralegal Cost Savings	300
1204.1	How to Bill Your Paralegals' Time	301
1204.2	Sample Budget	302
1205	Provide Incremental Salary Increases Based Upon Merit and Inflation	303
1206	Evaluating Your Compensation Program	303

13 Ethical and Accepted Uses of the Paralegal

1301	Introduction	305
1302	Prohibitions: The Four Don'ts	306
1302.1	You May NOT Put a Paralegal's Name On Your Letterhead—Except in New York	307
1302.2	A Paralegal Cannot Assume the Role of a Lawyer	307
1302.3	A Paralegal May Never Be a Partner in Law Firm	308
1303	The Three Do's	308
1303.1	Paralegals May Use Business Cards That Connect Them With Their Firm	308
1303.2	Recognition Can Be Given on Legal Documents to Paralegals Involved in Their Preparation	309
1303.3	In Certain States the Paralegal May Sign Correspondence for the Firm	309
1304	Conclusions Regarding Ethics	310
1305	Mixing Paralegals With Systems: Game Plan for a Rewarding Experience	310

APPENDICES

A.	Paralegal Schools and Training Programs	315
B.	State and Local Paralegal Associations in the United States	335
C.	Alternate Letters of Rejection for Paralegal Position Applicants	341

D. National Federation of Paralegal Associations (NFPA), *Affirmation of Responsibility*; National Association of Legal Assistants (NALA), *Code of Ethics and Professional Responsibility* .. 345

E. Forms and Documents That Paralegals May Draft or Complete in Assisting the Attorney With Corporate Work 351

ILLUSTRATIONS

Figure 1.1	Division of Labor in Insurance Defense Litigation	6
Figure 1.2	Time and Cost Experience in Providing Legal Services	7
Figure 2.1	Summary of Criteria for Choosing Between Promoting From Within or Hiring From Without	39
¶402.1	Checklist of Desirable Qualities in a Supervising Attorney or Legal Assistant Coordinator	58
Figure 4.1	Summary of Steps in Training	75
Figure 5.1	Benefits From Combining Use of Systems and Paralegals	94
Figure 5.2	Sample "Universal" Letter	115
Figure 5.3	Sample "Universal" Letter	117
Figure 5.4	Sample "Universal" Letter	118
Figure 5.5	Sample "Universal" Pre-prepared Standard Form	119
Figure 5.6	Sample "Universal" Pre-prepared Standard Form	120
Figure 5.7	Samples of Common Variations in a Document—"Universal" Version	121
Figure 5.8	Sample Master Information List (MIL) Questionnaire	122
Figure 5.9	Sample Master Information List (MIL) Questionnaire	123
Figure 5.10	Sample Letter With MIL Reference Numbers	124
Figure 5.11	Sample Letter With MIL Reference Numbers	125
Figure 5.12	Sample Letter With MIL Reference Numbers	126
Figure 5.13	Sample Pre-prepared Standard Form With MIL Reference Numbers	127
Figure 5.14	Sample Pre-prepared Standard Form With MIL Reference Numbers	128
Figure 5.15	Samples of Common Variations in a Document—MIL Version	129

Figure 5.16	Sample Procedural Outline and Checklist	130
Figure 6.1	Task Inventory for Paralegals in Estate Planning, Probate, Estate Administration and Conservatorships	133
¶602.1	Inventory and Fact Sheet for Effective Estate Planning	137
Figure 6.2	Stock Data Form	158
Figure 6.3	Bond Data Form	159
Figure 6.4	Securities Valuation Form	160
Figure 6.5	Stock Notification Letter	161
Figure 6.6	Stock Inquiry Letter	162
¶603.2	Estate Progress File	165
Figure 7.1	Task Inventory for Paralegals in Litigation Work	170
Figure 7.2	Litigation Chart	174
Figure 7.3	Personal Data Sheet	177
Figure 7.4	Investigation and Preparation Checklist	182
Figure 7.5	Task Inventory for Paralegals: Investigation Work	186
Figure 7.6	Task Inventory for Paralegals: Domestic Relations Work	193
Figure 7.7	Affidavit of Net Worth—New York Specimen Form for Use in Matrimonial Action	196
Figure 7.8	Chart for Recording Notice to Creditors and Financial Institutions	204
Figure 8.1	Task Inventory for Paralegals in Real Estate Work	208
Figure 8.2	Sample Closing Statement—Simple Transaction	215
Figure 8.3	Sample Closing Statement—Complex Transaction	217
Figure 9.1	Task Inventory for Paralegals in Corporate Work	224
Figure 9.2	Waiver of Notice of Organization Meeting	227
Figure 9.3	Certificate of Election of Directors	228
Figure 9.4	Waiver of Notice of First Meeting of Board	231
Figure 9.5	Minutes of First Meeting of Board of Directors	232
Figure 9.6	Minutes of Regular Meeting of the Board	236
Figure 9.7	Notice of Special Meeting of the Board	237
Figure 9.8	Written Consent of the Sole Shareholder in Lieu of a Meeting	238
Figure 9.9	Written Consent to Action of the Board of Directors Without a Meeting	240
Figure 9.10	Minutes of Special Meeting of the Board	242
Figure 9.11	Minutes of the Annual Meeting of Shareholders	243

Figure 9.12	Resolution Re Qualification in Foreign State	244
Figure 9.13	Stock and Bond Transfer Record	246
Figure 9.14	Form of U.C.C. Security Agreement	250
Figure 10.1	Task Inventory for Some Paralegal Work in Banking Areas	266
¶1006.1	Sample Job Descriptions for Paralegals in Several Title Insurance Company Positions	268
¶1008.1	Sample Job Descriptions for Paralegals Assisting Corporate Counsel	272
Figure 11.1	Sample Employee (Paralegal) Evaluation Form	280
Figure 12.1	Nationwide Look at Paralegal Compensation	293
Figure 12.2	Billing Comparison for Office With and Without Paralegal Staff	302
Figure 12.3	Sample Budget for a Legal Assistant	303

Also, see Appendix E for a list of 31 more forms that paralegals may draft or otherwise use.

Part 1
Establishing a Paralegal System in Your Office

1

Legal Assistants—
What Can They Do for You?

"A lawyer's time and advice are his stock in trade."
ABRAHAM LINCOLN

[¶101]   **INTRODUCTION:**
WE ALL WANT OUR MONEY'S WORTH

The attorney finds his "stock in trade" severely limited as the clock on the wall refuses to add the necessary hours to keep up with the demands on his time. This book is designed to help the attorney become more efficient by first recognizing the difference between "legal counsel" and "legal mechanics" and then presenting methods for delegating the mechanics to lesser-paid members of the office staff. And if the goal of efficient operations is not sufficiently attractive, the economic benefits should be altogether convincing.

    We live in an era of consumerism. The public, our clients, now insist upon receiving the greatest possible value for their dollars spent on legal services. Consumers are beginning to recognize the difference between "legal counsel" and "legal mechanics." This must inevitably lead to dissatisfaction when a partner charging $125 per hour performs a task readily accomplished by a $30 an hour paralegal.

The need that paralegals fill is largely an economic one: a competent paralegal saves both the client and the attorney time and money (as you'll see quite clearly in ¶103).

Training a paralegal to assist a lawyer is one thing; training a lawyer to utilize the skills of a legal assistant effectively is another matter. The crucial point that must be made at the outset is that a firm's legal assistant program will be no better than the ability of the members of the firm to utilize the talents and skills of the legal assistants.[1]

We will demonstrate that well-trained legal assistants enable the attorney to apply his creative energies toward the essential practice of law, i.e., negotiations, drafting complex documents and instruments, and the art of advocacy.

[¶101.1] What is a Legal Assistant?

There are as many definitions of a "legal assistant" as there are writers on the subject. However, few have been able to improve upon the one contained in the American Bar Association's Status Reports:[2]

> *Legal Assistant:* Under the supervision and direction of the lawyer, the legal assistant should be able to:
>
> apply knowledge of law and legal procedures in rendering direct assistance to lawyers engaged in legal research;
>
> design, develop or plan modifications of new procedures, techniques, services, processes or applications;
>
> prepare or interpret legal documents and write detailed procedures for practicing in certain fields of law;
>
> select, compile and use technical information from such references as digests, encyclopedias or practice manuals;
>
> and analyze and follow procedural problems that involve independent decisions.

A more succinct definition whose impact will become greater as the attorney becomes committed to modern law office management techniques is the following:

---

[1] Kline Strong, *Utilization of Legal Assistants by Law Firms in the United States*, Special Committee of Legal Assistants, American Bar Association, June, 1971, Preliminary Draft at page 2.
[2] *Training and Use of Legal Assistants: A Status Report*, ABA Special Committee on Legal Assistants, 1974 at page 17.

Legal Assistants—What Can They Do for You? 5

"A paralegal is a nonlawyer who uses a system.[3]"

In this volume, the terms paralegal and legal assistant are used interchangeably and if the authors lapse into the bad habit of referring to these persons in the feminine gender, it is not due to a lack of recognition of the male members of the profession, but rather only that the majority of legal assistants are female. Similarly, if the attorney is referred to by a masculine pronoun, one of your authors, a recent female law school graduate, will try to rectify these momentary lapses.

Whether it is possible to handle a legal matter at a profit may indeed depend largely on who does it, lawyer or paralegal, and often on how it is done, manually or on automated equipment. Both of these factors, increased capacity and lowered threshold of profitability are built into systems utilizing paralegals. Such systems can enable you to serve more clients and earn more money.[4]

[¶102] MAKE THE MOST OF YOUR TIME: ACHIEVE EFFICIENCY AND FLEXIBILITY THROUGH THE SKILLFUL USE OF PARALEGALS

The legal assistant concept did not originate with the organized Bar. Rather, it evolved as a result of the requirements of the profession in modern times.

The key to efficiency in the modern law firm is to eliminate repetitive routines by the attorney at the established hourly rate, and to consolidate these routines into a procedure which is then transcribed into written form. It is both necessary and profitable to train legal assistants to perform routine tasks which do not require legal judgments. Techniques for accomplishing this streamlined approach are thoroughly discussed in Chapter 8. A preview however is the following:

Example: Much attorney dictation is no longer necessary. Many pleadings can be totally prepared by a paralegal using initial interview checklists. The result is a quality legal document prepared faster and at lower cost than a comparable document written solely by an attorney.

---

[3] Bernard Sternin, "Ten Most Frequently Asked Questions About Paralegals," *Legal Economics*, Winter, 1978 at 36.
[4] Id. at 34.

Another example of efficient division of labor principles can be readily seen from the Insurance Defense Litigation Chart below:[5]

Figure 1.1
Division of Labor in Insurance Defense Litigation

Function	Senior Lawyer	Younger Lawyer	Legal Assistant (Investigator)	Secretary
Client interview on receipt of file	X	May assist in some cases		
Examination of file	X	X		
Prepare checklist	X			
Acknowledge receipt of file	X			
Notice of retainer	X			
List of assignments	X			
Depositions	X	X		Control Appointments
Legal research	X	X	X	
Retain experts	X		X	
Investigation				
Evidence of record nature			X	
How the accident occurred			X	
Medical analyses			X	
Preparation	X	X		
Negotiating (team evaluation)	X	X		
Trial	X	X		

[¶102.1] Give Your Clients Emotional Support Without Infringing on Your Time

It is a known fact that many clients visit attorneys at times of deep emotional stress. Whether involved in a marriage which has fallen apart or mourning a recently deceased spouse, clients in this agitated state must be handled gently, with great patience and understanding. Many attorneys try to do the necessary "hand-holding" and fail dismally because they are thinking of that court appearance just one short hour away, or the answer to a complaint which must be prepared, or a myriad of other legal matters which demand prompt attention. Is it even necessary for the attorney to attempt this "hand-holding" when many more vital matters should be

---

[5] Checklist provided by Foley & Capwell, and reprinted in the Nov. 1972 issue of *The Practical Lawyer* at p. 49.

Legal Assistants—What Can They Do for You?

occupying his time? We maintain that it is unnecessary. By keeping his finger in every pie, the attorney is traveling down the highway of his profession at 25 mph instead of 55.

The paralegal often makes a better listener than the attorney. The paralegal is less harried and more understanding. Much of what clients discuss when they come to a lawyer revolves around their emotional crises, rather than the legal steps necessary to solve their problem. A trained legal assistant can sympathetically and diplomatically filter out purely emotional considerations and channel items of legal significance on to the attorney.

An important reason for freeing up attorneys from these hand-holding chores is to enable them to increase their available time for essential legal work. If you do not have to perform support tasks, you probably won't leave the office any earlier; rather, you'll take on a more productive workload. And this will translate into greater profits for you and better service for your clients.

[¶103] REDUCE YOUR LEGAL FEES WHILE EARNING HIGHER PROFITS

You don't have to drop your hourly rate and work a twenty-hour day to increase your profits. If you delegate work to legal assistants whose services are billed at considerably lower rates than the attorney-employer, you can handle more clients. The combination of paralegal and attorney billing on a greater number of clients is guaranteed to increase your profits. This fact can be readily illustrated by the following chart:[6]

Figure 1.2
Time and Cost Experience in Providing Legal Services

Traditional Office:
Lawyer Providing all Legal Counseling
Daily Experience:
        6 Billable hours (2 cases)
$100 per hour   = 3 hours per case
$600 billable hours per day   = $300 per case

---

[6] This chart originally appeared in the article by Edward J. Reisner, "Legal Assistants: New Future for the Practice of Law," 48 *Wisconsin Bar Bulletin* 7 (1975) but we have increased the dollar amounts to take into account inflation and the ever increasing spiral of fees charged by attorneys.

Figure 1.2 (Cont'd)
Time and Cost Experience in Providing Legal Services

Paralegal office:
Lawyer Supervising Two Legal Assistants
Daily Experience:

    Lawyer—6 hours (5 cases)
 $100 per hour   = 1.2 hours per case
 $600 per day   = $120 per case

Two Legal Assistants:
 12 hours per day (5 cases) = 2.4 hours per case
 $ 30 per hour   = 3 hours per case
 $360 per day

           Total:
 $960 per day   = 3.6 hours per case
            $192 per case

Therefore:

 Firm Billing Increased 80 percent
 Time per case increased 20 percent
 Cost to client decreased 36 percent

PRACTICAL HINT: Use this visual device to demonstrate to your clients your firm's extreme sensitivity to costs and quality of service.

[¶104] EFFECTIVE USE OF LEGAL ASSISTANTS WILL LESSEN THE POSSIBILITY OF LEGAL MALPRACTICE SUITS

When the legal assistant is properly trained in the use of:

1. Office manuals (e.g., on calendar control, document preparation, see ¶409 ff.);
2. Preprinted forms and checklists (Chapter 5);
3. Educating client: How client's case will proceed, what the client has to do, and the expected timetable:

your chance of being sued for malpractice will be greatly diminished.

 A survey conducted by a large insurance company listed errors involving Statute of Limitations lapses, missed court appearances, and misfiled documents as the cause of legal malpractice suits in 45 percent of such actions. With a systematized paralegal staff, this problem can be largely eliminated.[7]

[¶105] HOW TO INTEGRATE THE PARALEGAL INTO YOUR PRESENT OFFICE INFRASTRUCTURE

In the past, legal assistants have been underutilized, inefficiently utilized, or not utilized at all, and quite expectably they've been greatly frustrated by this. Many young associates have these very same complaints. However, once you have developed a system similar to that in Chapter 5, you will be well on your way towards the effective use of paralegals.

For optimum results, you should put paralegals to the "highest and best use." This can only be accomplished by proper training and motivation of the paralegal.[8] While we offer you an overview here, you'll find a broad and thorough treatment of this topic in Chapter 4.

As each new paralegal joins your firm, lines of responsibility may have to be redrawn requiring administrative and clerical adjustments. If the updating and upgrading of the administrative system fails to occur, the 8:30–10:00 a.m. migraine which many of you may have experienced becomes more the norm than the exception. Your office then falls prey to the crisis-administration syndrome that translates into a reactionary system of office management. This means you are being controlled by outside forces rather than *you* being in control at all times. You must act to limit any crisis rather than allow it to overwhelm you. The key is choosing to create the desired environment rather than allowing neglect to generate a crisis in which it is only possible to react.[9]

When the two-attorney office becomes the ten-attorney office using the same administrative systems that were utilized in the two-attorney set-up, breakdowns and crises may arise with increasingly greater frequency.

---

[7] *U.S. News and World Report*, June 7, 1971.

[8] Nancy E. Chadwick, "Progressive Use of Paralegals is Good Business," *The Retainer Supplement*, November 8, 1978 at page 12.

[9] Patricia M. Martin, "Goldilocks Syndrome: Crisis Administration in Law Office Management," *Law Office Economics and Management* (Spring 1979) at page 173.

[¶105.1] How to Turn Your Present "Old-Fashioned" System of Law Office Management Into a Progressive One

- ☐ STEP ONE: Begin to discuss administrative problems in terms of solutions, rather than excuses. This means that time must be spent in diagnosis and ultimately in the implementation of a well-designed system which should alleviate the 8:30-10:00 a.m. migraine of helplessness.
- ☐ STEP TWO: The system must be designed and implemented to:
    (1) establish consistent tests for hiring new personnel;
    (2) develop training programs and manuals for each job category;
    (3) initiate a program of review that will regularly evaluate employee performance, call attention to needed improvement, and reward special achievement.
- ☐ STEP THREE: The system must be designed and implemented to:
    (1) title all files appropriately;
    (2) review files routinely;
    (3) create an index and cross references that will catalog past and current research.
- ☐ STEP FOUR: The system must be designed to implement the *team approach*. Authority must be delegated to a paralegal coordinator so that:
    (1) no employee is ever idle;
    (2) no employee is ever asked to do more than he or she can reasonably be expected to accomplish;
    (3) maximum use is made of existing equipment;
    (4) new equipment is purchased whenever it will increase productivity and reduce operating costs.[10]

[¶106] DELEGATION IS THE ECONOMICS OF THE LAW TODAY

Unlike other professions, attorneys persist in refusing to delegate all but the most simple tasks to non-lawyers. This reluctance, motivated by a desire to

---

[10] Id. at page 177.

provide professional service is understandable, if not commendable, but nonetheless mistaken. In a critical self-appraisal, you will discover that many jealously guarded tasks can be performed equally well by non-lawyer legal assistants.

Once a task is identified as within the capabilities of a paralegal, it should be delegated. What tasks should be delegated? Any job which does not require legal judgment may be delegated. Indeed, the decision of what constitutes a legal judgment is itself a professional decision and must be made by you, the attorney. However, once you delineate the various areas of your practice and make checklists for the office manual (for example, in the estate administration field, see Chapter 6), the attorney or paralegal may initial the steps upon completion and go on to the next procedural step as outlined in the checklist.

In 1972, the Tennessee State Bar conducted an economic survey which suggested that use of legal assistants increases lawyers' income, in many cases by as much as 50 percent. You can use the basic chart in ¶103 to extrapolate the possibilities for your own firm. In offices where paralegals were not used, median lawyer income was $25,000. Where legal assistants were effectively utilized, the median lawyer income was $37,000.[11]

Altman & Weil, in their 1979 *Survey of Law Firm Economics* showed the median income of lawyers not using paralegals at $48,213, while those employing one paralegal per four attorneys enjoy a median income of $55,493. While the increase is not as dramatic as the previous survey discussed, the difference is not insubstantial.

One author recently suggested that a legal assistant program functions most effectively when there is the greatest possible decentralization and delegation of responsibility. This is accomplished through effective management-by-objective as opposed to management-by-exception. The former is the strategy of planning and obtaining desired results while meeting the goals and satisfaction of all concerned. The latter simply emphasizes preventing the lawyer from becoming involved in details, and permits him or her to concentrate on situations requiring the greatest attention.[12]

---

[11] "Progress in Tennessee—The Report of the 1972 Economic Survey of the Bar of Tennessee," 8 *Tennessee Bar Journal* 74–75 (1972).
[12] Paul G. Ulrich and Suzanne P. Clarke, "Building Your Firm's Legal Assistant Program," *Law Office Economics and Management* (March 1978) at page 127.

[¶107] FIVE STEPS TO INCREASE YOUR ENJOYMENT OF THE PRACTICE OF LAW

To summarize the goals of the chapters to follow, we have devised a five-step process which if followed should significantly increase your enjoyment of the practice of law as well as your profitability. These steps are:

1. Utilize a legal assistant to increase your caseload productivity.
2. Reduce your overhead on each case, while earning greater legal fees through increased workload.
3. Enjoy the benefit of skilled assistance, especially in the repetitive areas of your practice.
4. Develop standardized forms, checklists, and procedures to minimize the pressures of a busy law practice.
5. Sit back, and enjoy the benefits of a system designed to allow your law office to advance to the modern era in efficient law office management.

How does all the progress come about? Through proper training of your new paralegal, the subject of Chapter 2 which follows.

2

How to Locate Qualified Paralegals

**[¶201]   WHERE TO LOCATE PARALEGALS
              WITH PRIOR TRAINING**

The sources from which the attorney, corporation, or government entity may obtain a paralegal are extensive. As both the public and private sectors of our society grow with their attendant expansion of rules and regulations, trained paralegals fill the need for skilled personnel to deal with interpretation and application of legal matters at an economic level below the cost of licensed attorneys. Paralegals may be recruited by the employer through:

1. Employment agencies;
2. Advertising;
3. Direct contact with paralegal training institutes.

[¶201.1]   Recruiting Through Employment Agencies

If you use an employment agency, fees may vary. For example, in the New York area it is approximately 1 percent per thousand dollars of the paralegal's first year's salary. In San Francisco, the fee might be 80 percent of the paralegal's first month's salary.

Many agencies also provide a guarantee of partial fee rebatement if the employment of the paralegal terminates within a ninety-day period, although some guarantees are as short as four weeks. If there is a severance of employment within a ninety-day period, the fee owed the agency is the number of days over ninety (90), i.e., a paralegal who stayed on the job for five days would cost the employer $5/90$ of the fee due the employment agency.

PRACTICAL TIP: An employment agency provides the service of screening all prospective employees and attempts to match your requirements with the candidates who answer the advertisements they place in newspapers on your behalf. This service is usually included in their fee, but be certain to check with the respective agency in your own city.

[¶201.2] Recruiting Through Classified Advertising

If you prefer to avoid an agency fee by placing an advertisement directly with a newspaper, the larger publications generally charge in the range of $7.00 to $8.00 a line. This might include an average of thirty-one characters per line with a minimum of three to five lines, depending on the publication involved.

If you live in a large city, it is quite likely that the classified ad sections of your major newspapers currently feature numerous listings similar to the ones on pages 16 and 17:

PRACTICAL TIP: An employment agency provides the service of screening all prospective employees and attempts to match your requirements with the candidates who answer the advertisements they place in newspapers on your behalf. This service is usually included in their fee, but be certain to check with the respective agency in your own city.

[¶201.3] Recruiting Through Placement Offices at Paralegal Schools

Another source for recruiting paralegals is the placement offices of the better paralegal schools throughout the United States. Many schools are happy to place their graduates with no fee to the employer, but many others will charge a substantial fee for this placement service. The rationale for the fee is that the school is vouching for the quality of its student body and deserves some remuneration for its efforts. It is also claimed that the fee paid by the employer allows students to pay a lower tuition than would otherwise be necessary.

At the Institute for Paralegal Training in Philadelphia, Pennsylvania, a pioneer in the field of paralegal training, an employer pays the school a *tuition subsidy* ($1,800 at the time of this writing) for each graduate that is hired directly. However, if an employer sends an employee to the school, the tuition and tuition subsidy/placement fee is higher ($2,175 as of 1979). The Institute for Paralegal Training has a nationwide placement service.

Adelphi University, another ABA approved institution located in New York, does not charge the prospective employer for its placement service, nor does it charge the student. It is important to check with the placement office of the schools in your area to learn of their placement policy.[1]

[¶201.4]   Other Valuable Recruiting Sources

Other fruitful sources for your future paralegal personnel may be your national or state bar association and local paralegal associations. Many local bar associations maintain a permanent listing of paralegals seeking employment in the area. For example, the Rockland County Bar Association and the Westchester County Bar Association, both located in New York, maintain this service for their members. Check with the bar association in your area to ascertain whether this service is available.

Lastly, there are forty-four local and state paralegal associations located throughout the United States.[2] Many of these associations provide placement services for their members, or send resumes of their members seeking employment to the local bar association so as not to jeopardize their non-profit organizational status. This service is usually provided gratis to the prospective employer, and the latter is usually assured of an employee who expresses a professional attitude concerning the job as evidenced by membership in the paralegal association.

---

[1] A list as of 1979 of paralegal schools in the United States can be found in Appendix A.

[2] A list of these paralegal associations as of the time we went to press can be found in Appendix B.

ESTABLISHING A PARALEGAL SYSTEM

Typical Newspaper Ads for Paralegals

PARALEGAL
OFFICE OF THE ATTORNEY GENERAL
STATE OF ▬▬▬

Litigation Division of the ▬▬▬ Attorney General's Office is looking for a capable paralegal. Challenging work is offered in the field of Governmental regulation and enforcement activities. Congenial environment. Salary commensurate with experience and ability. Excellent benefits.

Mr. ▬▬▬▬▬▬▬

HELP WANTED

PARALEGAL SPECIALISTS

BLUE SKY — $20K
International Corp seeks 2 yrs exp.

REAL ESTATE — $19K
Expanding law firm seeks paralegal to develop department.

ERISA — $20K
Prestigious law firm seeks pension specialist.

TRUSTS & ESTATES — $23K
Accounting + Estate administration. Supervisory responsibilities.

PARALEGAL
With at least 2 yrs estate admin & drafting exper for trusts & estates dept of ▬▬ Ave law firm.

PARALEGAL FEE PAID
Blue Sky experience for major midtown LF; excellent salary/benefits.
▬▬▬ Agency

PARALEGALS f/pd $18-20K
Real Estate. Hvy commercial exp, independent work. Superior oppty
▬▬▬ ASSOC agency

Paralegals. Immed hire for expd R/E professional. Appt only. Call ▬▬
▬▬▬ Golden Agency, ▬▬

PARALEGALS f/pd agency
Our prestige clients demand that we fill these positions at once:
Trusts/estates .... to $30,000
Real estate .... to $25,000
Corporate/Conn .... to $25,000
Corp trust, spk Hebrew. to $20,000
Trusts/estates .... to $17,000
Corp. securities ...... to $15,000

PARALEGAL FEE PD $25K
REAL ESTATE
Prominent partner of midtown law firm seeks paralegal capable of handling associates level and administrative duties.

▬▬▬ AVE/Agency

PARALEGAL
Growing tax & financial firm sks estate & trust paralegal w/2-3yrs experience in fiduciary income tax prep., Indv inc tax prep., record-keeping for securities & invstmnts. Gd bnfts. Attrac ofcs. Sal open w/exp. ▬▬▬

PARALEGALS
Major NY & NJ law firms seeking Paralegals in all areas of law.
FROM $15,000-$25,000

PARALEGAL
Medium size midtown law firm seeks graduate of accredited paralegal program w/at least 3 yrs exper in estate administration. Submit resume & salary requirements: ▬▬▬

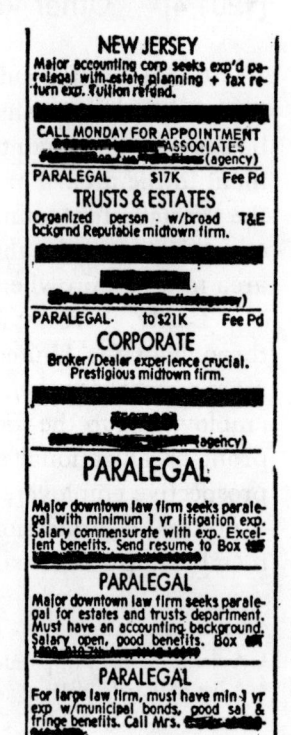

NEW JERSEY
Major accounting corp seeks exp'd paralegal with estate planning + tax return exp. Tuition refund.

CALL MONDAY FOR APPOINTMENT
▬▬▬ ASSOCIATES (agency)

PARALEGAL $17K Fee Pd
TRUSTS & ESTATES
Organized person w/broad T&E bckgrnd Reputable midtown firm.

PARALEGAL to $21K Fee Pd
CORPORATE
Broker/Dealer experience crucial. Prestigious midtown firm.

▬▬▬ (agency)

PARALEGAL
Major downtown law firm seeks paralegal with minimum 1 yr litigation exp. Salary commensurate with exp. Excellent benefits. Send resume to Box ▬▬

PARALEGAL
Major downtown law firm seeks paralegal for estates and trusts department. Must have an accounting background. Salary open, good benefits. Box ▬▬

PARALEGAL
For large law firm, must have min 3 yr exp w/municipal bonds, good sal & fringe benefits. Call Mrs. ▬▬▬

How to Locate Qualified Paralegals

Case Mgr $25,000+
Outstanding opportunity. D.C. law firms seek 5+ yrs litigation paralegal exper. Supervisory exper & knowledge of in-house computerization req'd.

Japanese $12,500+++
MAJOR MIDTOWN LAW FIRM seeks fluency in Japanese for paralegal position. Salary commensurate w/exper.

Entry $14,000
ONLY GRADUATES W/SUPERIOR ACADEMIC HISTORY will be considered for promising entry-level paralegal position. 4 wks vacation.

Corporation To $25,000
Fortune 500 co seeks 5+ yrs general corp housekeeping exper for Corporate Secretarial office. Tuition reimbursement plus other liberal benefits.

Corporate To $21,000
THREE LAW FIRMS seek experienced corp paralegals. Blue sky or SEC exper pref'd, but not required. Liberal benefits plus bonus.

Boston To $18,000
Major Boston law firm seeks experienced CORPORATE paralegals. Liberal benefits include bonus.

These are just a few of the many paralegal positions we have available. Call us for professional career guidance
Contact: ▬▬▬▬▬

LAW SERVICES

Paralaw-Long term oppty $18-25M+
TRADEMARK-Suburb Co.
2-15 yrs TM exp at corp or film Top corp, excel benefits, Nice boss
▬▬▬▬ Agency F/Pd

Real Estate $20,000
Prestigious Park Ave law firm seeks individual with commercial experience & desire to further their career.

Corporate $19,000
Corporate housekeeping, blue sky and SEC experience needed for large midtown firm. Your abilities will be rewarded.

Docket Clerk $13,000
Your patent & trademark experience will open the door to this downtown law firm. Ability to type own correspondence required.

Trust & Estates $16-20,000
Several positions available in either banks, corporations or law firms. Salary depends upon experience.

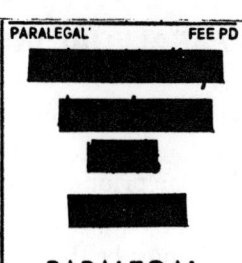

PARALEGAL FEE PD

PARALEGAL SPECIALISTS

LITIGATION $20K
Major corporation seeks specialist with excellent research and writing skills.

TRUSTS & ESTATES $24K
Administrative position. Prestigious midtown firm.

COMMERCIAL LIT $22K
New Jersey. Fortune 500. Seeks 2 years experience. Knowledge of maritime helpful.

REAL ESTATE $18K
1 year co-op experience.

CORPORATE $21K
Generalist with blue sky and syndicated experience.

PENSIONS $18K
Career opportunities in major corps.

▬▬▬ Ave/Agency

PARALEGAL FEE PD $25K
CALIFORNIA
West coast division of Fortune 500 company seeks experienced commercial litigation paralegal. Excellent benefits.

▬▬ Ave/Agency

PARALEGAL F/pd agency
to $25,000
Thoro corp law exp & contract writing ability req. Sophisticated pos, large firm, easily accessible suburb.

PARALEGAL f/pd agency
$30,000+
Thoro trusts/estate admin exp, incl fiduciary acctg req. An exclusive

PARALEGAL IMMIGRATION
Opportunity. Experience & knowledge of labor cert. helpful
Paralegal Fee Pd $12,700-13,500+
Coll grad. Some litigatn exp/course
▬▬▬ Agency ▬▬ St

PARALEGAL
Large Stamford law firm seeks corporate paralegal with 5-10 yrs exp. Salary commensurate w/exp. Send resume to: TIMES

PARALEGAL

EMPLOYEE BENEFITS PARALEGAL

Suburban ▬▬ Bank with national recognition seeks Employee Benefits Paralegal w/min of 2 yrs exp for position as Trust Officer. Responsibilities of this position include Administrative authority for Corporate pension & profit sharing plans, participant record keeping, gov'n'mt compliance procedures, familiarity w/investments & strong client contact. Career position with excel Bfts package. Please send resume & Sal history, in confidence, to:

TRUST CO.
▬▬▬▬ EOE

PARALEGAL
Trusts & Estates
Midtown office of major N.Y. City law firm seeks legal assistant with a minimum of 3 years of related experience. Salary commensurate with background.

Qualified applicants should submit resume with salary history to:
Box ▬▬▬
Equal Opportunity Employer M/F

PARALEGAL
City Hall area, bilingual (Spanish/English) for plaintiff negligence firm Exp pref. Heavy client contact. Practical knowl of NY State no-fault law desired. Call ▬▬

PARALEGAL
Expanding Park Avenue firm needs exp'd corporate legal assistant willing to take on responsibilities. Salary commensurate w/exp. Reply ▬▬
TIMES

Paralaw-Long term oppty $18-25M+
TRADEMARK-Suburb Co.
2-15 yrs TM exp at corp or firm
Top corp, excel benefits, Nice boss
▬▬▬ F/Pd

PARALEGAL
Established midtown law firm seeks paralegal w/1-3 yrs corp/securities exp. Salary open. Call ▬▬

PARALEGALS F/PD SAL OPEN
LITIGATION & REAL ESTATE-
Heavy exp; Top firm exp.
▬▬ agency ▬▬

PARALEGAL CORP
Park Ave Law Firm requires Paralegal with corp law exp & training. Please send resume to: ▬▬ 6 floor, ▬▬ Park Ave.

PARALEGAL to $23,000 f/pd agency
Become Managing Clk w/noted firm.
Thoro litig exp, knowl courts req

[¶202] EXAMINING PARALEGAL INSTITUTIONS

There are two major training options available to an employer which are:

1. Hire a paralegal with some prior outside training (and perhaps previous work experience); or
2. Promote a secretary who must be thoroughly trained within the office.

In order to help you weigh the factors involved in making this decision, we will:

1. Present a thorough discussion of outside training programs (¶202.1, ¶202.2, ¶202.3);
2. Explain how you can evaluate outside schools (¶203 et seq.);
3. Examine and evaluate the process of full "in-the-firm" training (¶204 et seq.; also Chapter 4).

There are a phenomenal number of paralegal institutions throughout the United States, over 300 at last count, and increasing rapidly. They range from approved ABA institutions to part of a community college set-up. The curricula are as varied as the time and fees involved in each respective program.

Programs of short duration, particularly those accepting primarily college graduates, tend to gear their program toward preparing specialists, devoting their entire three- to four-month program to developing expertise in one field of legal practice.

In certificate programs, other than at the community college level, there is generally little opportunity for transferring credits. Most paralegal programs relate to laws of their respective states, and that adds to the difficulty of transferring credits. A regionally organized random sampling of qualified private institute and college training programs follows.

[¶202.1] Some Paralegal Training Programs in the Eastern United States

(A) Institute for Paralegal Training, Philadelphia, Pennsylvania

One of the first schools to train students in the field of paralegal education was the previously mentioned ABA approved Institute for Paralegal

Training. The Institute offers five specialty courses, which are generally the most popular offered by schools in this field:

- ☐ Corporate Law;
- ☐ Employee Benefit Plans;
- ☐ Estates and Trusts;
- ☐ Litigation;
- ☐ Real Estate.

Each course lasts three months and students concentrate in one specialty. At the present time this is the only school that assures the graduate of a job, utilizing the paralegal skills obtained at school, within four months of graduation, or a portion of the student's tuition is refunded.

There is also a General Practice Course that covers the aforementioned courses in a general way. This is especially recommended for applicants who want to work in small cities or suburban areas where most firms may not concentrate exclusively on one of the specialties. Finally, there is a Criminal Law course designed to prepare the applicant to work in both the public and private sectors of the criminal law field.

The partial refund policy does not apply to either the General Practice or the Criminal Law specialty courses. A bachelor's degree is required for admission to the school and this requirement will be waived only for employer sponsored applicants. An admissions test is required for all applicants.

(B) Adelphi University, Garden City, New York

The Adelphi University Lawyer's Assistant program, also ABA approved, was begun in 1973, and its curriculum is almost identical to that of the Institute for Paralegal Training. It does, however, offer a part-time program for the working applicant, but only in the generalist studies area. This is a six-month course given six hours per week and six hours two or three Saturdays per month. A baccalaureate degree is required and a waiver is granted only upon employer sponsorship.

(C) George Washington University, Washington, D.C.

The George Washington Legal Assistant program also has the approval of the ABA and has been in existence since 1972. The student can elect an intensive fifteen-week program or a one-year part-time schedule. A bachelor's degree or its equivalent in education and experience, plus acceptable LSAT scores are required for registration in the certificate program. The program is remarkably similar to that experienced by a first-year law student including courses in:

- ☐ Legal Research and Analysis;
- ☐ Civil Procedure;
- ☐ Virginia Practice;
- ☐ Evidence;
- ☐ Real Property; and
- ☐ the Legislative Process.

(D) New York University Institute of Paralegal Studies, New York, New York

The Institute of Paralegal Studies is part of the Continuing Education in the Law and Taxation Program of New York University School of Continuing Education. Its programs are designed for men and women entering the field, as well as for those already at work as paralegals. Among the distinctive resources it offers students are:

- ☐ A fully integrated curriculum that combines a broad background in the field with practical, technical training in specialized areas;
- ☐ A faculty made up of prominent attorneys from the Metropolitan area;
- ☐ Access to the University's Law School Library, one of the finest in the country;
- ☐ Assistance from the University's Business and Industry Placement office.

A unique feature of the Institute is that it offers two programs that serve the field in different ways. The Diploma Program gives students the comprehensive training they need to become paralegals; the Certificate Program offers practicing paralegals an opportunity to continue their education and acquire new skills. It's much like having an undergraduate and graduate program in the same edifice.

The Paralegal Diploma Program is a one-year (two-semester) program. It requires the completion of the basic concepts in the Paralegal Education Course and one advanced concept course. The student will, upon the satisfactory completion of the basic concepts course, select one of the three advanced concepts courses:

☐ Business Organizations;
☐ Wills, Estates and Trusts;
☐ Litigation.

Upon satisfactory completion of both courses, the student will be granted a diploma in Paralegal Education. Those who wish to continue their studies in this area beyond the diploma requirements are permitted to take one or both of the remaining advanced concepts courses for no credit at one-half the tuition rate.

The minimum requirement for admission to the Diploma Program is an Associate Degree or the equivalent (satisfactory completion of sixty academic credits). Official transcripts must be submitted, if possible, before the interview. In some exceptional cases, substantial law-related work experience and letters of recommendation from employers and members of the bar attesting to the applicant's suitability, may satisfy admission requirements.

Each applicant is given a personal interview to determine his or her suitability for the program.

Because of the nature of the program, transfers with advanced standing are not allowed. Students are required to take the program in its entirety.

Among the many other programs in the East are:[3]

☐ the Manhattanville Paralegal Studies Program;
☐ the University of Bridgeport;
☐ Fairfield University Paralegal Studies Program.

---

[3] See Appendix A for a more complete list.

We are examining *some* schools in depth, so that you may see the variety of criteria you have for evaluating *all* of the available training programs.

[¶202.2] Some Paralegal Training Programs in Middle America

Middle America has many legal assistant programs that lead to the Associate in Business Degree, with a major in Legal Assistant Technology. Many of these schools emphasize courses in the secretarial skills in addition to developing legal concepts necessary in the paralegal field. Also, many midwestern schools feature a worthwhile overall emphasis on an area of growing concern to attorneys—law office administration. It is encouraging to note that many legal assistant programs throughout the United States have been patterned after the model curriculum devised by the American Bar Association's Special Committee on Legal Assistants.

(A) North Hennepin Community College, Minneapolis, Minnesota

An Associate Degree in Applied Science from North Hennepin Community College includes courses not only in substantive law but in paper writing and legal drafting, plus legal internship programs. These may be invaluable to the practicing attorney, corporation, or governmental agency employing the paralegal. Tuition includes a full two-year community college experience.

This program offers students the knowledge necessary to be of value to the lawyer in the areas of research, procedure, legal forms and office management. The program also offers students an understanding of the lawyer's role in society, legal institutions and a general understanding of the many fields of law in which the student may eventually be employed. Those completing this program are eligible for an Associate in Applied Science Degree.

(B) Capital University, Columbus, Ohio

Capital University offers a General Practice course designed to give exposure in the areas of legal research, contracts, torts, civil procedure, criminal procedure and domestic relations, among others.

The program is jointly sponsored by the Law School and the Columbus Bar Association, with the closest attention to the standards suggested by the American Bar Association Committee on Legal Assistant Education.

The primary goal of this program is to provide a foundation upon which the prospective legal assistant will develop an awareness of the *procedural resources* available to the legal profession. The overall objective is to prepare the student to be able to assist the employing attorney by acquiring the skills necessary for the interpretation and use of these resources.

Graduates will be capable of performing paraprofessional services under the immediate supervision of an attorney, including investigating facts, preparing thorough legal research and writing a detailed case synopsis, conducting initial client interviews, and drafting legal documents and forms. These procedural and practical aspects are not restricted to the private law office practice. The program is broad enough to encompass preparation for employment in the public and governmental sectors as well.

(C) St. Louis Community College, St. Louis, Missouri Area

A college level curriculum in "legal assistants" was offered at the St. Louis Community College as early as 1969, probably the first such program offered by a two-year college. An interesting feature of the program was its basis in a survey that preceded it. The college, with the assistance of the Bar Association of Metropolitan St. Louis, mailed a questionnaire to 2,058 members of the Bar Association. Of the 443 questionnaires returned, more than half indicated the need for the specific training program contemplated (and eventually set up) and also indicated that there would be employment opportunities for persons so prepared.

The program offers both a Certificate of Proficiency and an Associate Degree in Applied Science. The latter requires additional courses in business, communications and social science and requires two years of full-time study, while the former is a one-year course offering a similar curriculum but in less depth.

(D) William Woods College, Fulton, Missouri

William Woods College offers a Bachelor of Science with a major in Paralegal Studies. All students in this field have to complete the following courses:

- ☐ Introduction to Law;
- ☐ Introduction to Paralegal Studies;
- ☐ Professional Ethics and Responsibilities;
- ☐ Legal Research;
- ☐ Civil and Criminal Procedure; and
- ☐ Constitutional Law.

The elective courses are equally impressive, including:

- ☐ Estate Planning;
- ☐ Wills, Trusts and Probate Administration;
- ☐ Family Law;
- ☐ Legal Accounting and Management, just to name a few.

Among the other programs in the Midwest are:[4]

- ☐ The University of Minnesota;
- ☐ Avila College in Kansas City;
- ☐ Rockhurst College in Kansas City.

[¶202.3] Some Paralegal Training Programs on the West Coast

The West Coast not only offers a host of ABA approved schools; the State of Oregon offers the first program of paralegal certification. Other state bars, state legislatures, paralegal organizations, and educators, attorneys, and the ABA are all watching this program very carefully to see how well it works.

(A) Portland Community College, Oregon

Portland Community College offers not only nearly all the courses previously mentioned in connection with paralegal schools, but a full panoply of first-year law school courses as well.

---

[4] See Appendix A for a more detailed list.

How to Locate Qualified Paralegals

As required by the Oregon State Department of Education, the student shall take a minimum of 18-credit hours of general education courses as part of his or her Associate of Applied Science Degree Program from three or more of the following course areas:

- ☐ Arts and Humanities;
- ☐ Social Science
- ☐ Communication;
- ☐ Health and Physical Education;
- ☐ Science and Mathematics.

These are in addition to the required courses. Among the required courses are the following:

- ☐ Introduction to Law and Law Ethics;
- ☐ Introduction to Law Office Management;
- ☐ Introduction to Family Law;
- ☐ Introduction to Legal Research and Library Use;
- ☐ Introduction to Probate Practice;
- ☐ Introduction to Estate Planning;
- ☐ Introduction to Litigation;
- ☐ Introduction to Property Law;
- ☐ Introduction to Income Tax Law;
- ☐ Introduction to Bankruptcy Law;
- ☐ Introduction to Insurance Law;
- ☐ Introduction to Corporate Law Practice;
- ☐ Introduction to Legal Terminology;
- ☐ Introduction to Criminal Justice System;

Portland Community College has kindly consented to allow us to reproduce materials through which we can focus in on the precise training their students receive. Appendix C illustrates the complete curriculum required for legal assistants, both course titles and descriptions; also presented is the syllabus for their Introduction to Family Law course—including the "task inventory" of which the student should be capable upon completion of the course.

(B) U.C.L.A. Extension Attorney Assistant Program, Los Angeles, California

A thorough and exciting approach to paralegal education is provided by the UCLA Extension Attorney Assistant Training Program. In addition to a highly selective admissions program that includes a B.A. Degree or its equivalent in experience and education, plus satisfactory performance on its entrance examination, there is a full-time Job Development and Placement Coordinator to assist successful graduates in their search for employment.

The program is offered in cooperation with the UCLA School of Law and offers a certificate program in the corporations/litigation field. Students are taught the specific skills of drafting complaints, preparing motions and performing legal research tasks including shepardizing and citation-checking. Skills in writing, interviewing and investigating are integrated with the substantive law in each practice area.

(C) University of West Los Angeles, Los Angeles, California

The School of Paralegal Studies of the University of West Los Angeles offers programs for college graduates as well as those without college degrees; different certificate programs are offered in each category. This program, together with its adjacent law school program, highlights the growing concept of training within a total legal community.

The Bachelor of Science Degree in Paralegal Studies is particularly interesting. It is designed to meet the needs of the two-year college graduate, who can earn a B.S. while simultaneously preparing for a profession.

Each spring, the school's Paralegal Institute seminar provides a series of lectures, group discussions, and workshops in those areas of the law that have undergone significant change as a result of legislation, judicial decisions, or practice. The seminar is two days in length, and concentrates on updating the paralegal in his or her specialized field.

[¶203] HOW TO EVALUATE PARALEGAL PROGRAMS AND COURSES

At this point, you are nearly ready to consider the logical question: "Is it necessary for a paralegal to have attended one of these schools, or is on-

How to Locate Qualified Paralegals

the-job training as good or better a manner of training your paralegal than the formal education route?"

Actually the precise questions you face are:

Are there aspiring legal secretaries working for me now whom I'd be willing to promote?

Have any of them received any paralegal training outside this office?

If I want to promote a legal secretary who has had no formal training, do I need to pay for that, or can I accomplish the required additional training by myself, here in the office?

To begin to answer these questions, you must first be able to evaluate the particular training a paralegal gets at one of these schools. To help you evaluate training programs, lawyers should explore the following issues:[5]

1. What prior educational background and educational performance record do the students have?
2. What textbooks are used in the course, do the texts provide an overview and technical know-how, and are these texts designed to be used by, and appropriate for, paralegals?
3. How many classroom hours are devoted to the area in which you will be using the paralegal?
4. Who teaches the course, and how much do the teachers know about the use of paralegals?
5. Does the educational program include a large number and variety of practice writing assignments.
6. Are there tests or other techniques to eliminate students who are not performing well?
7. What references can the school provide from lawyers, other than teachers, who hired graduates of prior classes? (A complete list of placements is preferable so that a potential employer can make his own inquiries.)

To help you evaluate the efficacy of paralegal training programs at any highly qualified school, there follows an outline of required paralegal training school course coverage by specialty which can serve as a criterion for

---

[5] David Promislo, "Personnel: Paralegals-Staffing Change," 10 *Trial* 33 (September-October 1974).

comparing a school's brochure or an applicant's resume.[6] Following these lists, which conclude at ¶203.8, you'll find some recommendations for putting them to practical use by referring to them in conjunction with several discussions throughout Chapters 4-11.

[¶203.1] Guidelines for Coverage in Courses for Corporate Paralegals

A *corporate paralegal* should be thoroughly familiar with:

- ☐ Organizing corporations (profit, non-profit and professional); draft and file: charter documents, by-laws, initial minutes or consents, 1244 or similar plan; Subchapter S qualifications; employer IRS number; corporate records.
- ☐ Handling ongoing corporate matters; draft and file: corporate minutes and consents and resolutions; amendments to charter documents; amendments to by-laws; issuance of stock; other regular reporting forms (certificates of condition, change of officers, etc.); annual reports.
- ☐ Maintaining corporate records and review procedures, including questionnaires for each corporate client.
- ☐ Dissolving corporations; draft and file: appropriate corporate resolutions; dissolution agreement; Articles of Dissolution; requests for tax waivers or liens; liability forms; requests for involuntary dissolution.
- ☐ Preparing foreign corporation filings: reserve corporate name in foreign states; review law and procedures for qualification; calculation of fees; contact offices of Secretaries of State regarding filing procedure and status check.

[¶203.2] Guidelines for Coverage in Courses for Probate Paralegals

A *probate paralegal* should be thoroughly familiar with:

- ☐ Preparing and filing estate procedure pleadings;

---

[6] The authors gratefully acknowledge the permission given by Bentley College to reproduce their course outlines on corporate, litigation and legal materials and anticipated capacity levels in these fields (¶¶203.1-203.7).

How to Locate Qualified Paralegals

- ☐ Keeping estate accounting records;
- ☐ Preparing individual income tax, federal estate tax, and state inheritance tax forms.
- ☐ Filing Social Security death claims.
- ☐ Preparing probate inventories and petitions for probate of an estate.
- ☐ Obtaining tax identification numbers.
- ☐ Obtaining pertinent information from clients, referees, newspapers, trust officers, etc.
- ☐ Filing forms with clerk of probate court (familiarity with location of offices).
- ☐ Valuing assets (preparing correspondence with banks, obtaining jewelry appraisals, valuing closely held corporations, figuring commuted values of annuities, etc.).
- ☐ Obtaining tax releases of liens (federal and state).

[¶203.3] Guidelines for Coverage in Courses for Litigation Paralegals

A *litigation paralegal* should be thoroughly familiar with:

- ☐ Preparing a deposition summary.
- ☐ Preparing a document summary.
- ☐ Preparing a case chronology (with deposition testimony, interrogatory answers and documents included).
- ☐ Preparing *first* drafts of all court pleadings (especially interrogatories, stipulations for extensions, and answers to interrogatories).
- ☐ The mechanics of document production.
- ☐ The Court docket and filing system (especially federal court).
- ☐ Court rules dealing with filing dates (i.e., answers to interrogatories are due within ____ days).
- ☐ The mechanics of a *large* court action (preparation of expert witnesses—keying deposition testimony to complaint paragraphs, documents with complaint references).
- ☐ The mechanics of service of process (i.e., filing of summons with sheriff, serving of subpoenas).
- ☐ The court's procedures on trial lists and motion sessions.

- ☐ The physical location of federal court and district courts and the docket or clerk's office in each.

[¶203.4] Guidelines for Coverage in Courses for Real Estate Paralegals

A real estate paralegal should be thoroughly familiar with:

- ☐ Classification of property ownership.
- ☐ Preparing a contract of sale for single- and multi-dwelling residences.
- ☐ Commercial structures.
- ☐ Reading and analyzing title abstracts and surveys.
- ☐ The sale and purchase of cooperative apartments and/or condominiums.
- ☐ Preparation for closings:
    Prepare and proof check deeds and other closing documents;
    Obtain necessary transfer stamps;
    Compute tax, interest, insurance and other adjustments;
    Prepare any purchase money, bond and mortgage documents.
- ☐ Handle all transfer documents, mortgage extension or satisfaction documents;
- ☐ Maintaining closing calendar;
- ☐ Notification to title company, mortgage officers, etc.
- ☐ Drafting closing statement: escrow agreements and other post closing documents.

[¶203.5] Guidelines for Courses for Matrimonial Paralegals

A *matrimonial paralegal* should be thoroughly familiar with:

- ☐ Ability to understand and interpret individual, partnership, and corporate income tax returns;
- ☐ Business financial statements;
- ☐ Insurance policies, life insurance, endowment, annuity, casualty, disability and major medical, homeowners, personal property;

How to Locate Qualified Paralegals

- ☐ An understanding and the ability to prepare the required disclosure affidavits;
- ☐ Ability to understand and prepare the required stipulation pertaining to:
  a. Family counseling.
  b. Probation (concerning custody proceedings).
- ☐ Familiarity with general income and estate tax rules and regulations pertaining to transfer of property and the effect of a divorce;
- ☐ Basic understanding of the essential provisions which must be incorporated in a separation agreement as well as filing requirements;
- ☐ Ability to inventory assets including tangible and intangible property;
- ☐ Understanding of the essential elements necessary to establish the alternative causes of action in a contested matrimonial action to facilitate the preparation of a memorandum of sufficiency to the attorney responsible for the matter;
- ☐ Knowledge and ability to draft for the review of the responsible attorney, findings of fact, conclusions of law, and interlocutory orders;
- ☐ Knowledge and ability to work with various tables such as federal price and wage guidelines; actuarial tables; and cost of living indices.
- ☐ Finally, the ability when necessary to deal directly with clients to provide comfort and emotional support in the absence of the responsible attorney.

Also see Appendix C for Portland Community College Curriculum in this same area of law.

[¶203.6] Guidelines for Coverage for Courses in Pension, Profit Sharing and ERISA

This is a highly technical field requiring special knowledge and skills.

- ☐ *An ERISA paralegal* in this field must acquire a working knowledge of both the federal and state statutes and keep current on the changing regulations.
- ☐ The paralegal should also understand the mechanics of the social security system, the Department of Labor requirements, and the rules promulgated by the Internal Revenue Service.

- ☐ The paralegal will often work directly with personnel supervisors and actuaries.
- ☐ Schedules of employees, ages, dates of employment, and salary levels must be prepared and maintained.
- ☐ A plan coordinator will work with the paralegal concerning the preparation and ultimate implementation of the plan.
- ☐ Additionally, the paralegal will report to the trustee concerning transfer of assets and payment of vested interests.
- ☐ The most important function for the paralegal concerns the annual reports required to be filed with the United States Department of Labor and the Internal Revenue Service. Further information reports are required to be distributed to the plan participant together with a statement showing additional amounts which have become vested in each participant account.
- ☐ Finally, the paralegal may assist both the plan administrator and the trustee in processing retirement and death claims.

[¶203.7] Guidelines for Coverage in Courses on Effective Use of Legal Materials

The effective use of legal materials entails:

A Basic Understanding of:

- ☐ Materials and methods of legal research.
- ☐ Meaning of legal authority and precedent.
- ☐ Legal system as it affects the publication of law books and the organization of law libraries.
- ☐ Function of the paralegal in doing legal research—potential and limitations.

Familiarity With:

- ☐ National Reporter System and Key Numbers (West).
- ☐ American Law Reports (ALR).
- ☐ State, Regional and General Digests.

How to Locate Qualified Paralegals 33

- ☐ Annotated Statutes (State, USCA).
- ☐ Administrative Law Materials.
- ☐ Looseleaf Services and Topical Law Reporters.
- ☐ "Shepardizing" Cases and Statutes.
- ☐ Legal Encyclopedias and Directories.
- ☐ Legal Periodicals and Newspapers.
- ☐ Legal Citations and Abbreviations.
- ☐ State Decisional and Statutory Materials.
- ☐ Computerized Research Facilities and Systems.

[¶203.8] Guidelines for Courses in Administrative Law

This field of study requires a practical knowledge of the workings of the various agencies of Government.

- ☐ An administrative agency paralegal must first acquire a working knowledge of the Federal and applicable State administrative procedure acts.
- ☐ Awareness of specific rules affecting the diverse governmental agencies.
- ☐ Familiarity with completing prescribed government forms.
- ☐ Preparing for hearings. Paralegals are frequently permitted under the rules of the various government agencies to participate without benefit of legal counsel at hearings.
- ☐ Understanding the methods taken on appeals within the administrative system or without, to the Court. Understanding the concept of exhausting all available administrative remedies.

[¶203.9] Put Paralegal Training Curricula to Work for You

The course outlines just illustrated represent the focus of only some training programs. Were you to review catalogs from various schools, you would find many similar core curricula, as well as many other types of programs.

In later chapters we'll be discussing how to compile an office manual, how to develop systems for organizing your workflow with paralegals, and how to evaluate the changes you make. The material in ¶203.1 to ¶203.8 and Appendix C (or in a local paralegal school's catalog) can be one handy base for you to work with.

You may find it prudent to develop a job description manual, to contain broad job descriptions for all employees in the firm. The contents of this will change with your experiences, but in the beginning you may find it easy to characterize paralegal responsibilities if you *start* by learning exactly what training paralegal schools provide. Precise degree of actual training may be a good tie-breaker in a tough hiring decision.

Chapter 5 will present a system for organizing each specific area of law in which you practice. Chapters 6–10 are designed to help you coordinate paralegals and your present operations into those systems. While experience will again become the determining factor, developmental gaps can be filled by relying on school curricula as guidelines for paralegal capabilities.

You probably won't be ready to evaluate your new systems until they've been functioning for awhile. You'll be fairly well-acquainted with the capabilities of your staff by then. At some later point though, you may want to compare the work your paralegals are actually involved in with what various schools are preparing them for in each specialized area. You may find that you can broaden the amount of work they're doing; you'll have extra time for weightier matters and more clients.

Finally—if you are going to promote someone from within your firm to a paralegal position, you can formalize the job shift and training program by developing your own "curriculum" using a paralegal school's model as your core or base.

[¶204] BENEFITS AND PITFALLS OF ON-THE-JOB TRAINING FOR YOU AND THE PARALEGAL

Now that you have an idea of what an outside training program has to offer a paralegal, it will be good to consider how effectively and easily you can match it—and whether or not you should supplement or replace in-house training by sending your new paralegal to school.

In addition, the discussions that follow may shed some light on factors to consider regarding whether or not you even want to promote from within your staff. (There is further discussion on this topic in ¶¶205, 411, 411.1, 411.2, 411.3, and 411.4.)

How to Locate Qualified Paralegals

The trends we've discussed are that, while many paralegals presently employed have had no formal paralegal education, it is becoming increasingly more difficult to enter the field without it. The competition for trainee positions is intense and even within firms candidates with some paralegal training may have a better chance of securing a position than their counterparts (usually legal secretaries) with no prior exposure to the field.

The paralegals we interviewed during the research for this book were both on-the-job trainees and paralegal school graduates. Here is what we learned from talking to them:

[¶204.1] One Benefit of On-the-Job Training— Availability of Simultaneous Training in Substance and Procedure

Many large law firms can easily conduct their own *complete* training program, despite the paralegal's previous experience, so that each new employee is exposed to that firm's particular office procedures. One prestigious San Francisco law firm even has some of its training programs on videotape, so that incoming paralegals (or aspiring legal secretaries) in the fields of labor or litigation, may learn (train) without occupying another employee's time.

After viewing the tapes, a buddy system is employed to be certain that what new paralegals have observed was absorbed. The videotapes are also an excellent method of review for those paralegals who desire refresher courses from time to time, or who change from one field of specialization to another within the same office.

A further advantage of this method of on-the-job training is that each firm can incorporate its own methods and procedures into its videotape training sessions thereby saving the time required to accomplish the orientation phase of training.

KEY IDEA: The potential for simultaneous instruction in substance and procedure (in a firm's unique policies) is one of the major advantages in favor of on-the-job training.

[¶204.2] Higher Based Salaries or Less Experience?

Many of today's most financially successful paralegals did not attend a paralegal school simply because there weren't any in existence at the time they began working in the field. Many were fortunate enough to be trained by the partners of the firms which employed them, much like the old-time apprentice system, but this is indeed, today, an exceptional situation.

This might mean higher salaries among non-paralegal school graduates, since many worked for the firm prior to becoming paralegals. They may already have higher base salaries than a graduate paralegal with no prior law-related experience would command (see Chapter 12 on Compensation and Fringe Benefits), and a promotion would necessitate an increase. Similarly, if you want to hire a paralegal with outside training *and* prior experience you will certainly have to top the salaries of perhaps all but your chief legal secretary (office manager). In most areas, paralegals make more than many legal secretaries, and you more than recoup the difference in billing your paralegal's time. Though the bottom line should depend upon how much your firm values knowledge, skills and experience, keeping peace in the office over salaries sometimes becomes the overriding factor.

[¶204.3]   Familiarity With General Office Procedures

The paralegal school graduate will certainly be familiar with requisite legal terminology and procedures. Though school-trained paralegals might be somewhat less familiar with the substantive law in their areas of specialization than those secretaries in the firm who've had extensive opportunity to absorb it, they will be most familiar with standard procedural aspects. Even without knowing the specifics of your office, a paralegal trained outside should quickly become familiar with all the necessary paperwork.

For example, consider preparing findings of fact and conclusions of law in matrimonial actions or preparing the necessary documents to offer a will for probate. Neither task requires an extensive degree of training in procedures particular to a given office.

On the one hand, success in either of these two endeavors by the outside trained paralegal, performing independently, would no doubt strengthen self-confidence, and might increase the paralegal's willingness to take responsibility with minimum supervision.

On the other hand, your legal secretary, especially if she has been in your employ for some time, will most likely be knowledgeable about these forms and procedures already, *and* know the mechanics of your law office practice as well.

[¶204.4] Ensuring Competence in Your Field of Specialization

A potential advantage of on-the-job training is that it can be tailored to the specific duties required by your law office without the accompanying expense of a formal school curriculum, which is often not directly applicable to the skills required by your office. Regardless of a paralegal's prior experience and training, however, the firm would have to provide additional on-the-job instruction until his or her responsibilities can be performed with confidence on the part of both the paralegal and the employer. You should weigh the material in ¶¶203 to 203.8, and ¶¶202.1 to 202.3, against what your legal secretary currently does, to get an accurate view of how much additional training time you may have to invest.

[¶204.5] One Benefit of Many Outside Training Programs— Legal Research Training

Many paralegals found their legal research courses of great utility after graduation, particularly if their subsequent jobs were in highly specialized areas such as banking or consumer credit transactions. But again, it would be virtually impossible for any program to have prepared them completely for all the tasks expected of them. Though for technical tasks such as this, in-house training is likely to be required for *all* new employees, some previous instruction and practice can be a healthy head start.

[¶204.6] Job Transition

Business corporation majors who found jobs in the corporate field seem to have had an especially easy transition period. Trusts and estates is another field which easily lends itself to the formal structure of a classroom environment. One paralegal we interviewed stated that she still uses her trusts and estates classroom notes, some two years later! Another real estate paralegal, a graduate of a renowned eastern school, related his experience with the school environment: "[O]ne of my first school assignments was to abstract real estate documents which turned out to be my very first task in my law office job!"

For the "promoted" paralegal, and depending on previous involvement with similar work in the firm, "transition" may not even amount to an important concern in terms of the work to be performed. However, you'll see in Chapter 4 how "office politics" considerations may come into play. (Also see ¶206.)

[¶205] DECIDING WHICH ROUTE YOU SHOULD TAKE IN HIRING

Since larger firms do have their own in-house training programs, the smaller firms have perhaps the greatest dilemma—paralegal school graduate vs. in-house promotion. It may be very difficult for a sole practitioner or even a smaller firm to relinquish a top-notch secretary, and oftentimes in the smaller practice, the legal secretary does indeed already perform many paralegal tasks. However, if your practice has grown to the point where there are several attorneys, together with an auxiliary staff of non-legal personnel, the decision is imminent concerning a paralegal vs. secretary-paralegal employee. Many persons interviewed felt that the paralegal was even more essential for the smaller law offices where economics are of paramount importance. It is not possible in a smaller firm to pass on most costs to a large corporate client as is often the case in a large firm. For the small practitioner, there is also more peace of mind in knowing that in his absence the office is being staffed by a competent paralegal who has some expertise in his area of practice, and hence long days away from the office in court, or even on an occasional vacation, do not result in the emergency situations which are so prevalent in offices without paralegal assistance. From the paralegal's viewpoint, the work in a smaller firm may be of greater variety, but certain secretarial skills may be required.

The following chart depicts the various criteria examined above. Although it is quite easy to chart many individual criteria, it will be difficult to reach a proper decision unless you consider how they interconnect, and weight them together in the unified context of your firm's particular characteristics.

Figure 2.1
Summary of Criteria for Choosing Between Promoting From Within or Hiring From Without

	Based Upon the Following Considerations	Promote From Within	Hire a Paralegal Graduate
Training	Capabilities in providing comprehensive overall job training	Simultaneous training in substance and procedure	Greater ability to intellecutalize or conceptualize in a specialty area.
	Orientation period	May be unnecessary	A must for incoming paralegals.
Salaries	No experience	Comparable to or less than legal secretary	Potentially higher salary due to advanced training
	Some prior experience		X
Office Procedures	Knowledge of your office procedure	X	
	Solid knowledge of theory regarding office procedure, legal systems and terminology		X
Legal Specializations	Training with procedures and substantive legal information relevant to *your* firm's practice	May be unnecessary	Likely to be required
Acceptance by Staff	Acceptance of paralegal employee by the clerical staff		X
	Distinction necessary to assure smooth working of your law office		X

Figure 2.1 (Continued)
Summary of Criteria for Choosing Between
Promoting From Within or Hiring From Without

	Based Upon the Following Considerations	Promote From Within	Hire a Paralegal Graduate
Miscellaneous	Solid knowledge of legal research skills		X
	Ease of job transition	If immediately accepted by co-workers in the new role	Experience is a factor
	Flexible in terms of intellectual prowess in "Thinking like a lawyer"		X
	Peace of mind garnered by leaving the office with competent staff personnel		X
	Office harmony resulting from advancement opportunities	X	
	Need to hire and train a competent replacement if you promote a secretary		X

[¶206]   **SUMMARY**

Whether you promote from within your office or decide to hire a paralegal from an approved institution, your transition to a paralegal system will definitely broaden your practice and open up new vistas in your legal career.

    In the experience of one of the writers, whose firm consists of fourteen attorneys and five paralegals, the most rewarding practice has been to hire paralegals who are graduates of approved paralegal schools and subsequently provide closely supervised on-the-job training. Smaller-sized firms appear to have a greater preference for hiring paralegals who have completed outside training. Larger firms tend to treat the growth of their paralegal staff as an upper rung in their ladder of forward mobility among their non-professional (non-lawyers) personnel with the result that highly-qualified secretaries through "in-house" training can achieve higher rank within the structure of the firm.

A possible source of law office friction is the relationship between the paralegal and the secretary. Unless the secretaries have been invited to become paralegals, they will often harbor resentment (envy) toward the paralegals who are senior to them in the "pecking order," even if they have no real desire to assume this new role. Jerome T. Wolf, a Kansas City attorney, wrote in a recent issue of *Law Office Economics and Management* (LOEM),[7] that

> "many law offices are concerned that promoting a few select secretaries to the more prestigious status of lawyer's assistant creates substantial morale problems. Many law offices, therefore, have followed the policy of not promoting secretaries to the position of lawyer's assistant and of hiring lawyer's assistants exclusively from outside the law office."

We would submit, however, that the reverse situation can prove equally troublesome. Many a secretary has felt stifled and bored with her present role and has eagerly sought the chance to change positions which, under the Wolf thesis, would be denied her. Indeed, when one of the writers left a firm, and a new person was hired to replace her, a secretary who had wanted to become a paralegal promptly resigned her position.

In those situations where a secretary can be successfully integrated into your paralegal system, encourage the secretary to obtain paralegal training. If you decide upon a "no promotion" policy concerning legal secretaries, those who desire to remain secretaries will not demonstrate discontent, while those who desire to climb the ladder of career development will leave for greener pastures. In most cases, a secretary possessing unique talents will express an interest in pursuing paralegal training as part of an overall career development.

If performance as a secretary demonstrates the capacity to develop into a first class paralegal, it would certainly be in the firm's best interest to encourage that training and the firm should agree to pay for the paralegal training of that individual.

The process of hiring paralegals is the subject of the succeeding chapter.

---

[7] Spring, 1979.

3

Hiring the Paralegal

[¶301] INTRODUCTION TO A FOUR-STEP PROCEDURE FOR HIRING PARALEGALS

Having made the decision to adopt the paralegal system within the structure of your office, the task of hiring qualified legal personnel must be approached with care and consideration for the specific needs of your practice. The ability to interview and hire effectively will not only result in considerable time saving, but will also enable you to achieve the acquisition of highly qualified and motivated paralegal personnel.

The hiring of your new paralegal denotes the transition of your firm from the nineteenth century "cottage industry" methods of handling your legal workload to the twentieth century world of systems analysis. Pat yourself on the back for deciding to become a *businessman* as well as the legal specialist which has traditionally been your forte.

In Chapter 2 we presented a number of considerations to help you evaluate the relative benefits and pitfalls of promoting someone from within the firm or hiring a new employee.

In actual practice, it is most likely that situations where promotion is a possibility may arise regardless of your "policy" or attitudes. The precise

Hiring the Paralegal

factors of any such situations will no doubt allow you to consider your options and make a worthy decision.

Or, if you make it a consistent policy to encourage such advancement, you will handle the transitions according to the dictates of your (or your manager's) relationship with the clerical staff, and your usual hiring practices.

In this chapter, however, we'd like to introduce a method that will drastically simplify the alternate approach of locating and interviewing a large group of qualified candidates from outside of the firm. This method will enable you to interview successfully and at a minimum expenditure of time. The four important steps we'll show you how to take are:

1. Establish criteria for employment;
2. Assemble job candidates for a group interview;
3. Conduct the group interview;
4. Evaluate the applicants and make your decision.

Try to forget your usual interviewing methodology, and concentrate on the following new techniques.

[¶302] STEP ONE: ESTABLISH CRITERIA FOR EMPLOYMENT

Before beginning to interview candidates for your paralegal job openings, you should establish certain qualifications to be met by any applicant. Perhaps of greatest importance is the educational requirement. Whether you want someone who has earned a B.A. degree, or feel that an associate degree from a junior college is sufficient, the important point is to define the minimum criteria for prospective employees. This need not mean that in exceptional situations persons without college degrees be denied employment, but such an occurrence should be the exception rather than the norm. The following chart outlines criteria found useful by most law firms in hiring their paralegals.

[¶302.1] Sample Criteria Satisfaction Table for Prospective Employees

1. College graduate or associate degree;
2. Previous work experience to complement current job opening;

3. Obtain recent writing sample. Is this done in clear, concise, and grammatical English? Does this sample demonstrate the required analytical and logic skills necessary for a paralegal specializing in your area of practice?
4. Does the applicant present a satisfactory appearance? Is this person someone whom you would be proud to introduce to your clients as an integral member of your staff?
5. Does the applicant demonstrate assertiveness during the interview?
6. Does the prospective employee possess good communicative skills, i.e., good grammar and logical thought processes?
7. Does this person possess maturity as shown in the group interview? (Group interviews will be thoroughly discussed below.)
8. Be certain to speak to the prior employer to learn of any problems concerning absenteeism or inability to get along with fellow employees;
9. Does the applicant possess an understanding of the legal processes and procedures necessary in your area of specialization?

An administrator of a large midwestern firm has as one of her most important criteria that of age.[1] She prefers candidates at least twenty-five years of age, and in most cases over thirty years old. Her reasoning is that the character traits of maturity, dependability, integrity, and an energetic attitude toward work often do not manifest themselves until this time.

IMPORTANT NOTE: You are not guilty of age discrimination if you hire only above a certain age, but you can be deemed in violation of the law for hiring only below a certain age.

PRACTICAL TIP: In a large firm, particularly when hiring clerical staff, these criteria should be somewhat broad. That is, they should be able to provide latitude for meeting certain particular wants and needs of the person or people with whom the new employee will be working directly.

[¶302.2]   Develop a Job Description Manual

You may find it extremely valuable to maintain a manual containing job description checklists for each position in the firm, including paralegals.

---

[1] The authors gratefully acknowledge the permission of Betsy Turner, Administrator of the firm of Turner & Boisseau to quote from her lectures and written material on this subject.

Hiring the Paralegal

In addition to the broad general criteria and requirements outlined above, you might include a list of the principal duties and responsibilities of the employee you'll be hiring.

The extent and specificity of a job description checklist will depend upon its source. Paralegal school curricula may provide a backbone for a job description, but may also prove unrelated to actual practice in some degree. In any case, it would be good practice to update the descriptions occasionally anyway.

You may simply wish to draft the list yourself, based on your personal assessment of and experience with the work in each given area of your practice. Again, occasional updating is recommended.

In Chapter 5 we'll demonstrate how you can systematize each area of practice in which you are involved. Extensive and accurate job descriptions might eventually be culled from these systems.

A great degree of precision is not really essential in the job description manual—though accuracy is. This is a tool for you—or your managing partner—to use in hiring. It rounds out the picture of the needed employee so that the best decision may be made. It is not essential, nor even recommended, that this be used as an element in training the new employee. An office manual (see ¶409 ff.) and office systems (Chapter 5) will better serve this purpose.

If a new employee will be working directly with or for someone with distinct needs or preferences, a well-organized job description manual may be able to simplify eventual decision making.

Though we don't necessarily recommend this, it's certainly possible to include a section that qualifies some of the general criteria (¶302.1) according to important "tastes" of individual partners (as well as associates and senior paralegals or secretaries).

In this way, you may prevent the future supervisor or co-worker from having to take time out from legal matters to participate heavily in hiring. This will be of greater concern to larger firms, where hiring is a more frequent and time consuming process.

[¶303] STEP TWO: ASSEMBLE JOB CANDIDATES FOR THE TIME-SAVING GROUP INTERVIEW

Finding competent, mature individuals requires a plan which, if followed, guarantees you a multiple pay-off, most particularly: more available time, with the residual increase in earning capacity, and freedom from the mental distraction and anguish of protracted interviewing. The most successful hiring technique we know of is the group interview. (Also see ¶306.)

[¶303.1]   Announce the Job Openings

The group interview provides a means of interivewing as many as seventy applicants within a six-hour time span. What are the nuts and bolts of hiring via a group interview?

First, you'll need to place an advertisement in the local newspaper and/or legal publications. Some firms prefer to run a blind ad, i.e., a catchy ad describing the quality of the person desired, but with no indication that a law firm is the employer. The responses must be sent to a box number. The process of sorting the resumes then begins.

PRACTICAL TIP: Remember, as Dun and Bradstreet, Inc.'s *Reference for Better Personnel Selection* advises, "You must take the resume with a grain of salt, since it is a self-serving, biased document prepared to make the applicant look good. There is a fair amount of distortion."

To place into focus the "Blind vs. Traditional" form of advertisement, the following chart should prove helpful.

Chart 3.1

Running a Blind Advertisement	*Running a Traditional Advertisement*
1. Blind ad together with group interview should weed out persons unsuited to your law practice.	1. Obtain persons who have previously practiced in this field or are graduates of schools offering degrees in the paralegal field.
2. Obtain good people who might not otherwise consider themselves qualified for a paralegal position (see example in ¶305.2).	2. Recent paralegal school graduates with little prior experience will also respond to advertisement.
3. Job candidates may prove unqualified for your opening.	3. Qualified paralegals may balk at participation in competitive group interview.
4. May be answered by member of *your* own clerical staff.	

Hiring the Paralegal 47

[¶303.2] How to Process the Resumes You Receive

Now you, your law office administrator, or your attorney in charge of personnel can begin to match some of the qualifications listed in your job manual description to some of the resumes now pouring into your office. You'll probably be able to eliminate around 50 percent of the resumes immediately in this fashion. You'll need two form letters for use at this point, each of which may be stored on your word processing equipment, or appear prominently in your forms file.

The first letter is sent to those whom you have eliminated through this screening process, and should thank them for their interest.

The other letter is sent to those who remain likely candidates for the position available. The two letters discussed above might look similar to those which follow:

(A) Sample Form Letter for Saying No Thank You Gracefully[2]

Name and   Date
Applicant's Address
_____

_____

Dear _____:

Thank you for giving us the opportunity to review your resume.

As you can imagine, there were a large number of highly qualified applicants. Screening these applicants was a very difficult task. Unfortunately, your application was not one of those chosen for an interview.

Because of the present growth of our firm, positions are becoming available at an increasing rate. We will keep your application on file for consideration in future openings.

In the meantime, we wish you success in your present endeavors.

                                        Very truly yours,

                                        _____
                                        X, Y, & Z
                                        Attorneys at Law

---

[2] Appendix D contains a few alternate letters of this type, including ones that may be used when resumes arrive unsolicited, or after the interviewing has already taken place.

(B) Sample Form Letter Setting Up the Interview

Name and   Date
Applicant's Address
_____
_____

Dear _____:

Thank you for your response to our recent newspaper advertisement.
We should like the opportunity to interview you together with other candidates for the immediate position available.

Please fill out the enclosed application form and return it, along with your choice of the interviewing time marked on the carbon copy of this letter. A stamped self-addressed envelope is provided for your convenience. The available interviewing times are:

	Date	Location
9:00–11:00 A.M.	_____	_____
1:30–3:30 P.M.	_____	_____
6:30–8:30 P.M.	_____	_____

If you have a recent writing sample, please bring it to the interview. We look forward to meeting with you.

                                                    Very truly yours,

                                                    _____
                                                    X, Y & Z
                                                  Attorneys at Law

Depending on the number of responses, as many as twenty candidates can be interviewed per session. In addition to identifying the law firm as the employer, this letter, as can be seen from the sample above, should offer applicants a choice of times for the interview. A good idea is to schedule one morning, one late afternoon, and one early evening session, either on the same or alternate days. This ensures that all candidates can be easily accommodated. You should plan each interview to last approximately two hours.

[¶304] STEP THREE: THE MECHANICS OF THE GROUP INTERVIEW

Begin by welcoming the four to twenty applicants at the interview and thank them for coming. Explain the dynamics of the group interview and the criteria by which candidates will be judged.

A verbal explanation should be quite sufficient, and even preferable. It will save time, and the applicants are actually more likely to get a crisper understanding of the interview process than if they were required to absorb written instructions.

The dynamics encompass the tests discussed in the following section, as well as the format the interview is to follow—which you will eventually develop to your liking through experience. For example, will candidates responses during the test situations be simultaneous or in a set pattern, clockwise or counterclockwise? Might there be an immediate challenge to a statement made by one of the candidates, or must the challenger await his/her turn?

Once the format is explained, inform the candidates as to the history of the firm, and the areas of practice that comprise the majority of your business. It is also important to walk through the area in which they would actually be working giving them a chance to look you over as well as a chance for you to look them over. The initial explanation of the interview, and the tour through the firm should take about ten minutes or so.

All the applicants should then return to the conference room, receive previously prepared name tags, and be seated around a table with an observer and an interviewer at a separate table five to ten feet away. You should give the applicants another several moments to get acquainted and relax, and to begin to prepare for the interview. In either of the formats we'll outline below, the interview itself should not require much longer than thirty minutes, unless the group is as large as twenty people.

HELPFUL HINT: Though the administrator or his equivalent may eventually conduct these sessions alone quite easily, the presence of a lawyer during the first few group interviews provides an additional viewpoint to be considered as you refine your interviewing methods. You should find it possible to conduct the sessions without a lawyer once this type of interviewing becomes a comfortable aspect of your hiring practice.

[¶304.1] "Testing" the Candidates to Ensure the Hiring of a Top-Notch Paralegal[3]

The "tests" often utilized are sometimes designated the "leaderless type" and the "designated leader type." In the former, candidates jointly discuss an assigned problem. In the latter situation, each candidate in turn acts as chairman of the group for three to five minutes, and after making a statement, answers questions asked by members of the group. The formats may be observed from the chart below.

A. LEADERLESS TYPE TEST FOR USE IN GROUP INTERVIEWS

- ☐ Speak loudly enough for everyone in the room to hear you.
- ☐ Assume that you and the other members of the group are a committee of supervisors who have been assembled to develop recommendations for dealing with the following problem:

In order to represent a new client on a products liability case, it will be necessary to increase the work load by 25 percent. It is anticipated that this increase will be required for about three months.

- ☐ Discuss among yourselves the advantages and disadvantages of the various methods that might be used to meet the situation, such as increasing the staff, lengthening the work day or work week, etc., and try to arrive at a collective recommendation.
- ☐ Decide among yourselves how to handle this question. You are to ask no questions of the observers. You will be rated on your effectiveness in presenting your point of view in this discussion. If you make no contribution, your rating will correspond to that fact.

---

[3] The authors once again express their thank you to Betsy Turner for permitting the use of her two types of interviews to be reprinted from an article in *Legal Economics*, Fall 1978.

Hiring the Paralegal

- ☐ Speak clearly. Start the discussion as soon as soon as everyone has finished reading this statement. Continue the discussion until a signal is given to stop.

B. DESIGNATED LEADER TYPE TEST FOR USE IN GROUP INTERVIEWS

- ☐ Speak loudly enough for everyone in the room to hear you.
- ☐ Your superior has asked each of you to come together to discuss the problems in handling employees, so that all of you can benefit from each others' experience.
- ☐ Each one of you should present a one-minute statement on a problem employee you know about and what you consider to be the best way to handle the situation. After each of you finishes your presentation, the remainder of the group will ask you questions in order to determine whether your method for handling the problem is the best one.

HELPFUL HINT: State a time limit for preparation of the one-minute statement. You might provide a bit of scrap paper for notes. Remember that the apparent advantage of the later speakers to poise themselves and react to earlier comments may be negated by their lack of opportunity to propose any original ideas.

- ☐ This discussion can be started by any member of the group. The group should decide among themselves the order in which the members of the group should speak.
- ☐ The discussion should start after each member of the group has read this statement. The group should decide for itself when each member should finish and the next person start.
- ☐ Speak clearly. You will be rated both on your own presentation and the questions you ask.

Once the interviewer gives the candidates all the necessary instructions, he removes himself from the table and goes off into a corner of the room and allows the group to develop on its own. As the discussion progresses, the applicants are ranked according to their leadership qualities, and other qualifications which your firm deems of paramount importance: consult your own job description manual regarding motivation, attitude, stability, interpersonal skills, maturity, etc. An observer or two will confirm your choices as they will be ranking candidates using the same format as the firm administrator.

[¶304.2] Closing the Interview—Success Formula Completed

At the end of the formal interview, the administrator returns to the table and asks the candidates to fill out a form which includes such vital data as name, address, telephone number, and salary requirements. What a person fills in as his/her salary requirements is often indicative of personality traits. A candidate who responds by requesting a low salary often is found to have a poor self-image which carries through to hamper business relations. On the other hand, a candidate who prices himself/herself out of the job picture shows an unrealistic knowledge of the marketplace and says that his/her expectations in the paralegal field are unrealistic. After they write their own salary expectations the interviewer should reveal the offering salary.

This one step may make the job of sorting the evaluation sheets somewhat easier. Betsy Turner has interestingly observed that candidates with the most education often request the least in the way of a starting salary. By discussing candidates' expectations and revealing the actual salary for the job, you give both yourself and the candidate a basis for judging your respective expectations.

Finally, in addition to revealing the current salary offered, you should indicate what the new employee might expect in the way of a salary six months, and then one year from the present time. The post-interview proceedings need not exceed ten or fifteen minutes.

Before they depart, thank them for their time, and inform them that they will be hearing from you within two or three days. It may astound you that an answer can be given within that short space of time, but you'll often find that you have made your choices before the candidates have left your office.

Sample rejection and hiring letters may also be stored on your word processing equipment, or in your forms file. A sample of each type of letter follows.

(A) Sample Post-Interview Rejection Letter

Name and   Date
Applicant's Address

_____

_____

Hiring the Paralegal

Dear _____:

Thank you for the opportunity of meeting with you.

We have had the opportunity to interview many qualified applicants, and we have selected a candidate whose qualifications most closely match our employment needs.

We will, however, retain your application and contact you if something suitable develops. We wish you every success in your future endeavors.

Sincerely,

_____
A, B, & C
Attorneys at Law

(B) Sample Acceptance Letter

Name and   Date
Applicant's Address

_____

_____

Dear _____:

Thank you for the opportunity of interviewing you on _____.

We are pleased to offer you a position in our _____ department at the salary discussed during our group interview.

We would appreciate hearing from you within one week so that all necessary preparations for integrating you as a member of our office staff can be begun.

Thank you very much.

Sincerely,

_____
A, B, & C
Attorneys at Law

HELPFUL HINT: You may find it a highly enjoyable and rewarding experience to precede or preempt this letter with the courtesy of a phone call. This may also be a quick and precise way to make the initial arrangements for starting employment. We strictly recommend, however, that rejections never be telephoned, no matter how difficult the hiring decision may finally have been.

[¶305] STEP FOUR: HOW YOU MAKE YOUR HIRING DECISIONS

How is it possible to reach an expeditious hiring decision before the group interview has ended? You should match your instinctive reactions with the criteria you've already established in your job description manual. Thus, you will have a quick and ready reference that allows you to search for the specific qualities you've placed at the apex of your "hiring hierarchy."

For example, if there is much client contact in your field of practice, the ability to relate to others may be a most highly prized attribute. Should you practice in the fields of litigation or antitrust where most of the paralegal's time is spent indexing documents or researching esoteric points of law, graduating in the top third of a prestigious university may be the candidate's strongest selling point. In essence, each of you will develop your own system for ranking prospective job applicants—perhaps even building a "personal and professional qualities checklist" tailored to your firm and precisely for use at interviews. Once your system is developed, you'll rarely need to make changes unless you expand the areas in which you practice law.

[¶305.1] Your Staff Can Help You

The beauty of the group interview approach is that attorney's investment of time is at a minimum. If desirable, however, the attorney can schedule separate interviews with the top four candidates or participate in some phase of the group interview as an observer.

Suppose, for a moment, you do encounter some difficulty in making your final choice. You could schedule traditional one-on-one interviews with the top candidates. In doing that, though, you'd lose the time advantage already gained with a group interview. You will also be building up the hopes of one or more candidates unnecessarily.

Hiring the Paralegal

The last few candidates are likely to be so closely matched in technical qualifications that some factor which would normally be extraneous may become decisive, such as a useful foreign language ability, or even simply personality.

You could select certain "tie-breaker" factors to note in your job description, but it's more likely that—where all qualifications are relatively equal—some basically arbitrary factor will emerge to allow you to make your choice.

[¶305.2] Let Your Staff Help You Decide

For the sake of office harmony, we recommend that you involve people on your staff to some degree in the selection process. They can usually spot those persons who would be great assets in their own departments, as the following actual example illustrates.

Betsy Turner, in her recent remarks before the New York State Bar Association sponsored by the Special Committee on Professional Economics and Efficiency Research, and the Committee on Continuing Legal Education, gave this interesting account of the "cloning" of a legal assistant:

Example: One legal assistant, who also had seventeen years experience as a surgical nurse, was hired as a medical records specialist. Her job was to translate all medical records, including all doctors' and nurses' notations on hospital records, and summarize these notes in about two pages of fluent English. This saved the attorneys an inordinate amount of time previously spent pouring over these records.

When the office opened a branch in another city, this one legal assistant/medical records specialist was unable to handle the workload of two offices. She was sent to the branch office to conduct a group interview on her own. She gave all the prospective legal assistants an actual former medical record to analyze, selected her first choice after following the steps previously outlined, and returned to her home office secure in the knowledge that all information needed by the attorneys in the course of litigation would be properly brought to their attention by the new employee. The splendid result: no attorney time was used in hiring this new legal assistant, and the person hired was easily trained consistent with the standard office procedures because of her excellent background in the field.

[¶306] THE BOTTOM LINE OF THE GROUP INTERVIEW: SAVINGS TO THE FIRM IN MONEY AND ATTORNEY'S TIME

The cost savings of using the group interview is perhaps its greatest feature. Multiply the time you would normally invest with a prospective applicant for a position by your usual hourly rate. The cost savings that would evolve from having that chore delegated to another are clearly dramatic. Since there is also no likelihood that as many potential employees could be interviewed using the traditional approach, a potential "dynamo" for your firm could be overlooked.

In summary, the advantages of the group interview are:

1. Savings in terms of time, when up to twenty applicants can be interviewed in the time it might take to interview two applicants on a one-to-one basis, and of course, time savings translate directly into money savings.

2. Group dynamics tend to work to the firm's advantage. Applicants know they are all candidates for the same position, and they therefore tend to assess each other and demonstrate how well they operate under pressures similar to that found in a law firm's daily routine.

3. Finally, when employees can be hired without a great expenditure of attorney time, practicing law becomes less stressful and hence more enjoyable.

4

Training the Paralegal to Function Efficiently in Your Office

[¶401]   **INTRODUCTION:
GETTING YOUR PARALEGAL STARTED**

How do you determine the responsibility of the paralegal in relation to the partners, associates, and legal secretaries within your firm? What is the role of the supervising attorney or paralegal coordinator? How do you define responsibility in a team setting? Will the introduction of the paralegal system cause friction with the current members of your office staff? Should you develop an office manual, and if so, whose responsibility should it be?

    We're going to help you answer these and related questions in this chapter, devoted to the training and integrating of the paralegal within your office infrastructure—so that you may watch your firm's productivity and profits increase.

    Two major concerns requiring careful attention are:

1. Establishing the "pecking order."
2. Avoiding work overlapping. (Parkinson's law—The work will expand in relation to the number of people at work on a given project.)

Both concerns can become major problems if ignored and left unattended. Office morale and productivity will suffer unless careful guidelines are established at the outset and implemented by careful supervision. A proper system for assigning the work load and supervising its progress will assure maximum efficiency within your office. To accomplish this you need a Supervising Attorney (*maybe* yourself) or Legal Assistant Coordinator.

[¶402] WHO SHOULD BE YOUR SUPERVISING ATTORNEY OR LEGAL ASSISTANT COORDINATOR?

For those of you accustomed to the practice of law in small firms where all of the decisions are made by the founding partner(s), the idea of a legal administrator is a novel one.

It is easy, however, to trace many problems faced by law firms to the lack of centralized management. There is, of course, no guarantee that competence in the practice of law is related to competence in managing a business. In fact, the opposite is often the case. Proper law office management translates into big business, and it is our goal to enlighten lawyers in this area so your firms can experience a greater profit margin.

The most important characteristic of the law office administrator is the ability to deal with people at all levels. To help the reader synthesize the desirable qualities of the supervising attorney or legal assistant coordinator, we've developed the following checklist:

[¶402.1] Checklist of Desirable Qualities in a Supervising Attorney or Legal Assistant Coordinator

	Supervising Attorney	*Legal Assistant Coordinator*
(1) Self-assured	X	X
(2) Tact/diplomacy	X	X
(3) Confidence	X	X
(4) Flexibility	X	X
(5) Respect of Partners	X	X
(6) Resident psychologist, i.e., good listener		X
(7) Impartial; no preconceived office loyalty		X
(8) Thoroughness	X	X

From this checklist, it is obvious that the supervising person, be he an attorney or professional administrator must be a person who keeps his finger on the pulse of the firm, ready to expand or contract his staff (permanently, or with the aid of "temporary services") as the firm's needs dictate. Not to be overlooked in your search for a coordinator is a paralegal who now desires an administrative role in law office management. Having risen through the ranks, former paralegals are aware of the difficulties encountered by their colleagues and often serve as a "role model" for others who might be tempted to leave the profession for lack of upward mobility.

PITFALL TO AVOID: If a professional administrator is hired, failure can occur on two levels: 1) the administrator may not understand the nature of the relationships or hierarchies that exist within the firm, *or* 2) the firm refuses to give the administrator the support needed to do the job.

Example: An administrator is placed under the direction of the managing partner who proceeds to "show him how to do his job." The exact reverse situation should occur. The administrator should educate the partner on effective law office management techniques.

To ensure that the administrator will fully understand what is required of him/her, a thorough, detailed job description similar to that below should be utilized.[1]

[¶402.2] Sample Job Description: Law Office Administrator

(A) General Description

The administrator will report exclusively to the administrative partner. He/she shall attend all meetings of both the management committee and the partnership and act as secretary of these meetings.

---

[1] The authors gratefully acknowledge the permission of Bradford W. Hildebrandt and the Practicing Law Institute to utilize the following material originally published in the PLI Handbook (PLI Handbook for Law Office Administration, pp. 86–90, July 25, 1978). Not represented here, but also of potential value to you is the following article: "A Job Description for the Legal Assistant Administrator," John D. Monahan, *Legal Economics*, V. 6, No. 1, January/February 1980.

(B) Administrator's Relationship and Responsibilities with Regard to Personnel

1. Recruit, screen, hire and help train all non-lawyer employees. Where such an employee will be working for a specific individual (i.e., secretary or paralegal), the selection process shall include an interview with the appropriate attorney. The administrator has the authority to admonish and terminate non-lawyer employees, providing such action is taken in consultation with the managing partner.

2. Conduct a regular performance review of all non-lawyer employees, counseling each employee concerning the results of such a review.

3. Prepare initial recommendations for compensation for all non-lawyer employees; implement after approval by the management committee.

When a policy towards a firm budget is established, the administrator should have flexibility to determine compensation to specific employees within the framework of the budget.

4. Supervise work distribution to the secretarial staff and reassign work so as to accomplish effective utilization of all personnel.

5. Evaluate current assignments of each employee and consider reassigning non-secretarial duties to a lower compensated full- or part-time clerk.

6. Develop, review and implement fringe benefit programs for both lawyer and non-lawyer personnel.

(C) Administrator's Responsibilities with Regard to Accounting

1. Supervise the bookkeeping system with respect to all internal accounting functions, including the preparation and analysis of monthly financial statements.

2. Develop management reports for unbilled time, unbilled disbursements and accounts receivable. Assist attorneys in the billing process.

3. Supervise the system for recording attorneys' time and investigate alternative methods available.

4. Prepare an annual budget for presentation to the management committee.

5. Review and recommend improvements in the clients' billing proce-

dures, including the possibility of control billing, and implement a follow-up system for accounts receivable.

6. Sign checks for routine expenditures up to a $500 limit.

(D) Administrator's Relations With Landlord

Handle all contact with landlord of the office premises with respect to maintenance services and any problems that may arise with respect to the firm's lease.

(E) Administrator's Responsibilities Concerning Insurance

Review and maintain the firm's insurance program and make recommendations for improvements as appropriate from time to time.

(F) Administrator's Responsibilities in Supervising/Controlling Systems and Procedures

1. Maintain the docket control and court calendar systems working directly with the litigation attorneys to ensure that all appearance dates are covered.

2. Evaluate the secretarial assignment system, specifically the possibility of utilizing a team approach as opposed to a "one-on-one" arrangement.

3. Study the uses of automated word processing equipment and make appropriate recommendations.

4. Supervise filing systems including procedures for opening, maintaining, closing and distribution of all files. Establish an internal retrieval system for firm memos, opinions, etc.

5. Supervise the upkeep and maintenance of the library and assist a library committee in purchasing additional acquisitions.

6. Review and revise procedures for and supervise office services such as mail room, reproduction, telephone systems, messenger service, etc.

7. Develop an office procedure manual covering all office systems and procedures; review and update at least annually. (See ¶408 through Ch. 5.)

8. Be responsible for purchasing all equipment and supplies. Unbudgeted purchases of furniture and other capital items to be approved by the partnership.

(G) Administrator's Miscellaneous Responsibilities

Meet with other law firm administrators in the area for the purpose of exchanging ideas and seeking solutions of common problems, as well as joining appropriate professional organizations.

The strikes against a law office administrator are many.[2]

1. They are the highest paid non-lawyers in the office with no promotion possibilities.
2. They have no peers and no one with whom to discuss day-to-day problems.
3. Their assignment, simply stated, is "do everything."

Why create this job and pay an administrator if there are so many strikes against him? The answer is a simple one. To practice law as a business is almost an impossibility without a good law firm administrator. There is no "magic moment" at which a firm becomes aware of the need for a law firm administrator. "The real test is not how many lawyers are in the firm but rather how much time is being spent by attorneys on routine office administration. In other words, what is the value of time that is being diverted from productive work to non-billable office administration."[3] If, upon answering this question honestly, you find that almost one-third of your billable time is spent on administrative tasks, it is time to consider the hiring of an office administrator.

[¶402.3]   Where Do You Find a Qualified Legal Assistant Coordinator or Law Firm Administrator?

As previously mentioned in ¶402.1, an experienced paralegal is often an excellent choice as the legal assistant coordinator, especially in larger firms. In any case, someone who has been with your firm a while, and is

---

[2] Bruce D. Heintz, "The Administrator in the Larger Firm," *Legal Economics* (Summer 1978) at 31.
[3] Bradford W. Hildebrandt, "Some Observations on the Hiring of an Office Manager," *New York Law Journal*, June 10, 1980 at 4.

familiar with your office routine is to be preferred over an outside candidate. However, if your firm is new in the hiring of paralegals, it might be wisest to look elsewhere for experienced candidates.

Schools offering courses in law office administration are likely sources, and their placement offices may keep tabs on all alumni. Personnel from other firms, who may be desirous of leaving for a myriad of reasons, can give your firm the experienced hand so necessary in this field.

However, an individual with a strong financial background who has worked in a service environment should not be overlooked. One author's suggestion is that this person should have been required to work with conflicting priorities from various "customers" simultaneously.[4]

Administrators can also be found in commercial businesses of relatively equal size to your own firm. The candidate should have previously managed a department or group of similar size to that in your office.

[¶403]   EDUCATING AND TRAINING PARALEGALS

The best paralegal will perform poorly if not properly motivated by the supervising attorney. The latter will have the responsibility for educating and training each legal assistant in the firm's standard operating procedures. The coordinator must take the responsibility for encouraging other lawyers to delegate work to the paralegal, and if an attorney, must bear the responsibility for the quality of the legal assistant's work product. The coordinator or supervisor (manager) should be a mature person with demonstrated ability to work tactfully with people.

In many larger firms, as has been previously mentioned, the supervisor is not an attorney at all, but an office manager or legal assistant coordinator who is responsible for delegating the work load evenly, with the work product then supervised by an attorney department chief. The legal assistant coordinator acts as the middleman between the professional staff and the clerical personnel to assure continued profitability of the paralegals by monitoring their billable hours and work load. This person should have the respect of the most senior partners in the firm as well as the paralegal staff.

---

[4] Bruce D. Heintz, "The Administrator in the Larger Firm," *Legal Economics* (Summer 1978) at 32.

Each paralegal must be made to feel that he or she is an important member of the legal team. There can be several coaches to give direction but there must be only one manager.

If a paralegal is given too much direction the result will be a loss in productivity. Too much time will be spent in trying to organize the work load without a proper understanding of priorities. The manager, who must be made aware of the office priorities in general, can schedule the work load in relation to its importance to the office. He or she can delegate further as the need exists and insure the avoidance of duplicate effort. With proper skill and a diplomatic manner including the ability to extend praise, the manager can make the difference in the quality of your paralegal system.

[¶403.1] Your Best Approach—Defined Responsibility in a Team Setting

The most successful approach features a team setting in which the office is divided into teams of attorneys, paralegals, and secretaries. The coordinator educates attorneys on proper utilization of the paralegal system, and acts to assure that paralegals are given tasks commensurate with their capabilities.

Here are some proven ways to do this:

- ☐ Make each area of specialization into a department. Involve the paralegal in all departmental meetings and discussions.
- ☐ Have the paralegal coordinator assume responsibility for paralegal administration, i.e., days and time off, vacations, obtaining materials, etc.
- ☐ Have the paralegal coordinator schedule clerical and secretarial needs of the paralegal staff.
- ☐ Instruct the attorneys to avoid disrupting the paralegals' schedule of assignments. If an emergency develops, communicate needs through the paralegal coordinator.
- ☐ Avoid creating the feeling of competition among the paralegals. Praise and criticize privately.

Training the Paralegal

☐ Encourage with financial support and, if necessary, continuing education.
☐ At all times maintain a professional but friendly atmosphere in the office.

Problem and Solution

The larger firm, by not employing a team approach, runs the risk of creating a form of feudal empire.

Example I: A legal assistant is assigned to one attorney full time. Even when that attorney experiences a slow period in his work load, he or she may nevertheless be reluctant to share "his" or "her" paralegal with a colleague. This in turn results in lower billable hours to the firm as well as a frustrating sense of dependence by the paralegal on the productivity of one lawyer.

The answer to this dilemma is the team approach. With this system, the office is divided into units comprised of several attorneys, secretaries, and paralegals. In large firms, an often used ratio is eight attorneys, five secretaries and two paralegals, i.e., 8:5:2. Therefore, if one of the attorneys is experiencing a temporary slack, the billable hours of the other members of the team remain unaffected.

Example II: In one West Coast firm, the coordinator reports to a legal assistant committee that is comprised of both attorneys and legal assistants, although the latter are non-voting members of the committee. The coordinator works with a department chief in each area of specialization to coordinate the work of all legal assistants in each department. The coordinator in this firm also screens all prospective employees via the group interview as discussed in the previous chapter, and if the attorney should be unable to observe the applicants during the group interview, the top three candidates are given short subsequent interviews with the attorney in charge of the department.

To summarize and illustrate the discussion above, the following chart demonstrates the supervisory relationship and all relative relationships of staff members in one typical law office setting:

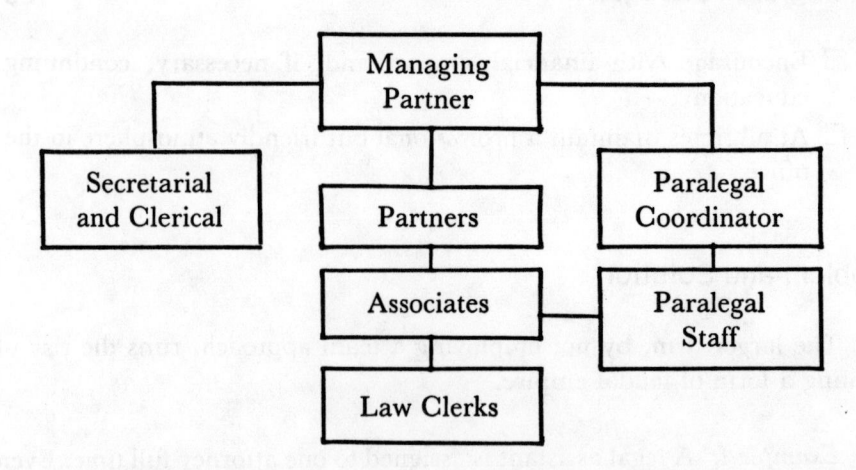

```
            Managing
            Partner
    ┌──────────┼──────────┐
Secretarial              Paralegal
and Clerical   Partners  Coordinator
               Associates ─ Paralegal
                           Staff
               Law Clerks
```

In a specialized team setting the paralegal(s) working in a specialty would generally work under the supervision of an associate although administratively they would report to the paralegal coordinator.

As an illustration, the Estate and Trust Department would be headed by a partner who may have one or more associates assigned to his department. Although the paralegal(s) assigned to this department may participate in conference sessions, with the partner, supervision of their work would be done by the associate(s). However, administrative matters such as salaries, sick leave, vacations, utilizing and hiring clerical staff, etc., would be channeled through the paralegal coordinator. The following chart depicts a specialty team setting:

Estate Department

```
      Partner
         │               Paralegal
      Associate          Coordinator
      Staff
         └──── Paralegal
               Staff
```

[¶404] COORDINATING AND BLENDING THE PARALEGAL WITH YOUR STAFF

Though our heading may seem redundant, you will find that establishing a workable system doesn't absolutely assure smooth operations. Whether your firm is a large or small one, a certain amount of adjustment is going to be required in terms of:

- A. Lawyer acceptance of paralegals;
- B. Restructuring of work assignments;
- C. Defining lawyer responsibilities.

[¶404.1] How to Achieve Lawyer Acceptance of Paralegals

What is meant is essentially recognition of the paralegal as a professional person. Paralegals should not be regarded as clerical personnel. In recognition of his or her professional standing within your firm structure, restraint must be employed to overcome any temptation by force of habit or otherwise to delegate clerical or secretarial tasks to the paralegal. An unintentional display of less than professional treatment to paralegals in the presence of clerical or secretarial personnel will lower their self-esteem and have a negative effect on their productivity. For example, as professionals, paralegals should be reminded to be result-oriented without regard to the time schedules that of course govern a secretary or clerical person's daily routine. In other words, if you want your paralegals to avoid becoming clock watchers, treat them as you would a professional colleague. (Also see ¶405 et seq., ¶411 et seq.)

Example: In one San Francisco firm, new associates are not permitted to delegate tasks to paralegals for at least one year. When they are finally accorded this privilege, they consider it just that and they do not abuse it. This gives the paralegal special status that remains an integral part of their relationship for as long as the association lasts.

The problem of lawyer acceptance can be overcome in another fashion. A different large West Coast firm offers the following solution. Here, the senior litigation paralegal *trains all the new associates* in litigation procedures, and the senior paralegals in other specialized departments perform similar functions.

Example: In local probate law, the paralegal who has been working in the probate area for several years reviews the new associate's procedural work much as would be done for a new paralegal joining the firm. The associates are pleased to receive immediate answers regarding the practical steps of daily practice which they never learned in law school. They also appreciate not having to bother a partner with practical questions which may be presumed to be within their knowledge. This initial contact once again is a favorable experience for both the new associate and the paralegal and adds to their rapport.

[¶404.2] How to Restructure Work Assignments for Maximum Effectiveness

What is meant here is essentially the need to refine methods and procedures for work performance by your paralegal staff. Many firms have standard operating procedures for attorneys, but fail to adopt them in regard to work assignments given to their paralegal staff. Here's an example of a problem this oversight caused: one very promising paralegal was constantly sought after by the majority of partners in a particular firm. Not knowing how to schedule the priorities of her many assignments, she suffered criticism from the partners whose work assignments were delayed in completion. The creation of unnecessary time pressures became unbearable with the result that she left the firm. A top-notch paralegal was lost to the firm. The system failed.

Similarly, conveying the impression that the work being performed by the paralegal is minimal and of no importance can also destroy initiative. Positive motivation is the key for achieving quality performance. Paralegals have a great need to feel a part of the office infrastructure, and not consider themselves the dumping ground for assignments which no one else wants to do. Rather than expect a paralegal to digest depositions continually, vary the assignments so that many phases of the same case can be done by the same person. Your investment in time and money in developing a first-class paralegal staff will pay off with an additional potent dosage of attention given to them. Do not assume that they can function with absolute independence. Remember, they are not licensed to practice law. Their function is one of support. Your accessibility to them and your close supervision are essential for them to achieve maximum performance. They must be made to feel that they are directly involved in the team effort.

Training the Paralegal 69

Example: Some firms do delegate total responsibility in certain instances to a paralegal. Real estate closings, both for private homes, cooperatives and condominiums are prime examples. Regardless of the experience of the paralegal, responsibility for making legal decisions, no matter how minor, is not the function of the paralegal and conflicts with the ethics of the legal profession. If, however, an attorney is accessible at all times certain duties may be delegated consistent with recently published ethical guidelines discussed in greater detail in Chapter 13.

Paralegals should also be invited to the professional work luncheons which are a characteristic feature of many law firms. This adds to the development of a strong team spirit, and promotes self-pride and confidence among the paralegal staff. Here's an example of how you can benefit: Many of the larger firms place their cases on word processing systems. A paralegal who has participated in a work-luncheon where a similar case was discussed, might have a familiarity that could facilitate access through the word processing retrieval system to the file on a relevant case precedent. And, *without* sophisticated word processing equipment, it becomes even more valuable to involve the paralegals in such work luncheons.

Example: A new case comes into the office: it has many similarities to a previous case handled by an attorney, who has since left the firm's employ. A paralegal who has been privy to the research on the earlier case via a work-luncheon, can easily consult the forms file, retrieve the legal memorandum and Shepardize the previous cases used. Time spent on the present case may be considerably less than would have been expended had he or she not known about the earlier legal memorandum.

[¶404.3] Assuring Lawyer Responsibility for Paralegals' Work Product

Throughout the entire delegation process, the attorney remains fully responsible for the work product of his paralegal. Final legal decisions can only be made by an attorney, presumably the lawyer chiefly responsible for the case that has been assigned in part to a paralegal.

Example: While a paralegal may gather all information necessary in the preparation of the Federal Estate Tax Return, when the attorney places his/her signature on the first page, he or she and not the legal assistant is responsible for its contents.

This responsibility should not be a problem source, but rather a recognition of the boundaries placed upon non-lawyers' practice by the American Bar Association and the state Bar Associations.

[¶405] BASIC INTERNAL EDUCATION AND COMMUNICATION (FEEDBACK) HELP PARALEGALS IMPROVE OFFICE PROCEDURES

It has been said that lawyers are people who continuously reinvent the wheel —they do a job once, and then forget where it has been put and must begin from square one. A paralegal who helps systematize an office (systematization will be thoroughly discussed in Chapter 5) will prevent the need to "reinvent the wheel" by establishing an efficient forms file in your office. However, no legal assistant can develop any effective type of systems analysis to the office routine unless truly apprised of the workings of each office.

Tips on Good Communication

Information concerning office routines can be furnished at informal get-togethers and will serve to instill the details necessary for the legal assistant to begin to perform efficiently. As one successful Wall Street paralegal expressed it:

> "As a result of these monthly meetings, I began to get many phone calls from partners and associates to participate in many new kinds of projects. I began to feel increasingly important and I felt really professional about myself and my job."

How you communicate your decisions is important in insuring that a rejection is not treated as a personal rejection. Recognition of the fact that a paralegal is not a trained attorney is frequently ignored. Taking the time to explain patiently why a case may not be on point or why a draft agreement or Will misses the mark will go a long way to ensure that a similar mistake will not be repeated.

Communication is the key to training. Trial-and-error methods are more practical in a busy office than formal training. Learning by doing is the common training procedure in most firms. How you, as the lawyer react to your paralegal's performance is fundamental to the practical training method. *Good students reflect a good teacher.*

Training the Paralegal

[¶405.1] Acknowledge the Paralegal's Work

The same Wall Street paralegal quoted above went on to relate the story of a young associate in her firm who went through a partner's waste basket to learn how his legal memoranda were being treated. Since he had never received any of his work back, he wanted to see if the partner was marking it up or accepting it as submitted. The paralegal is often in the same quandary, which if not corrected will build up great resentment and result either in the departure of the legal assistant or in diminished effort.

What to Do: Paralegals should not only have immediate feedback on the major cases they are fully involved with, but on all cases where they may only have digested a deposition, interviewed a witness, or otherwise prepared a segment of the total case.

Since people tend to perform at the level of others' expectations of them, a low perception of what a paralegal is capable of doing will probably lead the paralegal to function at a low level. To achieve the optimum, interesting assignments coupled with supervision will result in a satisfied employee as well as an excellent result.

PRACTICAL TIP: For the new and relatively inexperienced paralegal, early tasks should:[5]

- ☐ Be short-term assignments where the end product can be seen within a day or two.
- ☐ Relate primarily to fact gathering with a primary ingredient to successful completion being common sense.
- ☐ Have relatively uncomplicated and brief instructions.

[¶405.2] Reinforce Your Appreciation and Increase the Challenge

Once the legal assistant has experienced the first thrill of accomplishment, it becomes easier to reinforce this initial positive perception via the assigning of increasingly more difficult tasks.

Keep the following points in mind:

---

[5] William P. Statsky, "Techniques for Supervising Paralegals," *The Practical Lawyer* (Vol. 22, No. 4), June 1, 1976 at 85-86.

ESTABLISHING A PARALEGAL SYSTEM

- ☐ Carefully communicate easily understandable instructions.
- ☐ Specify time requirements.
- ☐ Involve the paralegal in intra-office discussions involving the assigned matter.
- ☐ Help make the paralegal feel professional.
- ☐ Promptly review the paralegal's work product.
- ☐ Communicate your attitude concerning the work product.
- ☐ Place confidence in your paralegal.
- ☐ Involve paralegal in your final decision.

[¶405.3] The Whole Staff Benefits From Communication

Paralegals benefit because they become aware of the exact relevance of what they are doing in relation to the case as a whole, and can draw both satisfaction and further motivation from positive results. Attorneys benefit from heightened staff morale, which usually translates into higher productivity. *Recognition is the key to a satisfied employee.* Consider the feelings of the paralegal when an attorney, who alone signs a court document or whose name appears thereon, takes official credit for a substantial result gained largely through work performed by the paralegal. One Philadelphia firm has achieved much success in its attorney/paralegal relationships by giving credit to the paralegal on the front cover of any brief in which the legal assistant has made a substantial contribution.

[¶406] HOW TO TRAIN THE PARALEGAL FULLY IN YOUR OFFICE

The individual selected to coordinate the paralegal system need not be the most senior attorney, if indeed an attorney is chosen, but he/she should be someone the seniors respect and can easily communicate with.

As was discussed in Chapter 2 on formal training institutions, every new legal assistant, despite the intensity of prior training must be subjected to an in-house training program. Ms. Mary Guinan, a New York legal assistant (now a law office administrator) writing in the *New York Law Journal* of July 26, 1977, suggested that a training program could be structured as follows:

Training the Paralegal

1. Paralegals working within the firm should complete a skills list prepared by the legal assistant coordinator.
2. Paralegals should then list the types of jobs they have been currently asked to do.
3. A separate list could be compiled of jobs the paralegal would like to do, but which he/she is currently not performing.
4. Informal meetings should then be scheduled between groups of paralegals and attorneys. Paralegals, at this time, should educate the attorneys concerning their skills, training, etc., and provide the written description of their skills and talents for future reference.
5. Follow-up evaluative meetings should be held at set intervals so progress can be analyzed.

These steps provide another method for an effective attorney/paralegal communication network. Thus, it is accurate to state that while it is the responsibility of the attorney to supervise the paralegal, it is also the responsibility of the paralegal to educate the attorney.

After you've developed many of the materials recommended in this discussion, you may store them, as appropriate, in your job description manual (¶302.2), office manual of general procedures (¶409 ff.), or systems binders for specialties of law (¶412; Chapter 5).

Once you have training outlines, progress charts, glossaries, etc., and can use them in conjunction with the elements referred to just above, your personal involvement in training will be streamlined into its most efficient form. You will be able to run through an overview of all your office procedures, quickly, but with enough time for you and your new employee to get on a comfortable footing. Then, given enough time to absorb the office systems on his or her own, the new paralegal may largely be self-trained.

[¶406.1] Training Should Be Thoroughly-Planned and Evenly-Paced

Whether your firm is large or small, or if you are a part of a corporate law department, start your training program at the earliest possible time. Procrastination can only result in the acquisition of bad habits which will become more difficult to break.

Set the tone of your training by outlining (in writing) what will ultimately be expected of each paralegal. Follow this up by detailing your training objectives on a daily basis.

Visual progress charts are handy devices used by some larger firms.

Each area of specialization should be covered but with sufficient time to avoid cramming too much detail into any one session.

Since "definitions" are the working tools of the profession, start out by introducing the key words and terms that will be put to common use in each department. For example, in the real estate department introduce and define words such as "fee," "deed," "covenant," "quit claim," "lease," "mortgage," etc. Similarly, in the estate department the words "will," "codicil," "executor," etc.

[¶406.2] Introduce Paralegals to Your Forms and Start Them Solving Problems

The next step would be to introduce the various legal forms used in each department. For example, in the real estate field/department, show the paralegal your standard lease, mortgage, extension agreement, deed, etc.

Gradually, start to work with hypothetical problems. By employing the problem-solving method you can project a visual understanding of both the substantive and procedural rules applicable to each area of legal specialization. Rote memory exercises are not as effective as the problem solving method. Most law schools today use the case method of instruction because of the greater retention effect.

Practical exercise in the form of a moot office conference is an excellent follow-up technique. For example, simulate a real estate closing complete with the preparation of a closing statement. If your office videotapes attorneys preparing for trial, utilize this mechanism to train paralegals effectively.

[¶406.3] Give Paralegals Complete Assignments— and Always Offer Feedback

At this point the paralegal is ready to work on an actual case, under the close supervision of an attorney. Preparation and filing of a probate petition or participation at a real estate closing are some examples.

During the training period, a critique at the end of each assignment is essential. The critiques should provide constructive criticism where neces-

Training the Paralegal

sary and compliments when justified. The compliment is the sought-after reward that builds self-confidence. The building of self-confidence coupled with experience will produce a valuable adjunct to your practice or staff—a trained quality paralegal.

Figure 4.1
Summary of Steps to Training

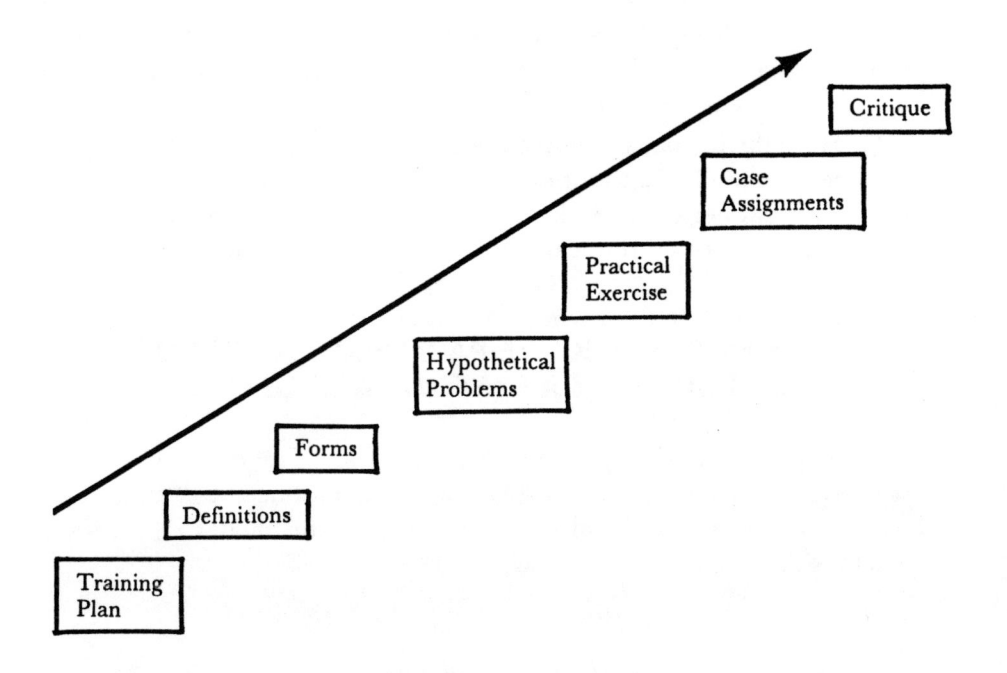

[¶407] **THE SIX DO'S FOR EFFECTIVE PARALEGAL TRAINING**

To recapitulate our discussion on paralegal training, the following "do's" are essential to ensure the success of your paralegal program:

1. Paralegals must be informed as to their role in the entire case, even if asked to do some small task.
2. If the paralegal is treading on new territory, suggest source materials which would deepen knowledge in that area of the law.

3. Utilize forms and checklists (from office manual and systems binders—see ¶408 ff. and Chapter 5) to help the paralegal view the prospective task as manageable. Discuss ways to adapt the form to the task at hand.
4. Do not put a new paralegal into a pool of paralegals on call to several attorneys, as there should be a consistency and uniformity of instructions which is only possible when responsible to one attorney. This "breaking in" process should last for no more than three months when the team approach should be allowed to take over.
5. Provide paralegal feedback via the monthly meeting to ensure that all problems are aired and resolved.
6. Have the paralegal prepare a skills inventory that will reveal aspirations as well as current duties. You may be surprised to learn that your paralegals have skills of which you were unaware, and their utilization could result in happier and more productive employees.

[¶408] THE MOST EFFECTIVE PARALEGAL TRAINING CAN OCCUR IN A SYSTEMATIZED OFFICE

In order to put the paralegal training function of an office manual in correct perspective (¶408.1), we must diverge briefly to outline the complete law office organization "mechanism" presented in this and the following chapters.

It's a unified mechanism with three primary elements.

☐ First is the *job description manual*, which we discussed in detail at ¶302.2. Essentially this is a collection of checklist style outlines that delineate criteria to be sought when hiring people for each position in the firm. It may also outline specific duties and responsibilities of any or all members of the law office staff. Additional elements to aid hiring decisions may be added according to your experience.

This item is for use only by the person or persons responsible for hiring. Because it may contain material that's inappropriate for other employees to see, and because there will not *necessarily* be lists of all duties and responsibilities of an employee, it does not function as any sort of training tool.

Training the Paralegal 77

☐ The second element is the Office Manual. This should be oriented primarily to detailing all aspects of *general* office procedure. It need *not* define any employees responsibilities in your specialized areas of practice.

The office manual should be a single volume with two sections:
1. Brief general descriptions of responsibilities relevant to general office procedures. This serves as a sort of combination outline/overview/index to the second section.
2. *Carefully detailed descriptions* of duties and responsibilities with regard to *all aspects of general office procedures*. This should include samples of all appropriate forms.

☐ The final element is actually a small system in itself. For each area of practice in which your firm is involved you develop a separate binder. The contents of each binder can monitor the overall process of completing every task that might be required in the given area of practice.

Each binder's contents will sequentially define the complete involvement and responsibility of each staff member in completing a case (or other segment of work).

The components of each single binder should be:
1. Master Information List;
2. Procedural Outline and Checklist;
3. Forms (may be integrated).

[¶408.1] Law Office Systemization Provides Multiple Function and Benefits

As you have seen (¶302.2), the job description manual functions primarily as a tool to aid effective hiring, and really merits no extensive discussion in this chapter on training.

The third element in the office organization mechanism above—the systems binders for specialized areas of practice—is the cornerstone of effective management of the office and your entire practice. This deserves the complete and thorough coverage we give it in Chapter 5. (There the individual elements we have just outlined are fully discussed and attributed to their originators.)

These systems binders do serve as a training tool, though, and we will take a closer look at that function in ¶412.

In the next several paragraphs, however, we will be discussing the development and use of the office manual. Though an effective office manual can be most significant as a training tool for any new employee, it is also a key element in maintaining continually smooth functioning by all employees where general office procedures are concerned.

[¶409] BENEFITS AND METHODS OF DEVELOPING AN EFFECTIVE OFFICE MANUAL

Among the duties we've already outlined, the legal assistant coordinator should also be involved in preparing an office manual, that will detail the requisite skills and precise duties of the legal assistant, as well as other members of the office staff.

PRACTICAL TIP: One of the coordinators we interviewed conducted a skills inventory while drafting his office manual. To his amazement, he learned that 10 percent of the legal assistants employed by his firm were bilingual and many enjoyed a strong background in economics with skills in statistics. This information helped the firm channel its legal assistants into areas of mutual interest, which ultimately led to longer retention of its employees than it had previously experienced.

PRACTICAL TIP: An office manual is one way that the coordinator can ensure that legal assistants are not asked to do clerical tasks. One coordinator expressed the reason for this as follows:

> "(W)e shouldn't be billing our clients at paralegal rates for clerical services, and paralegal skills are being wasted with the consequent effect that they will become bored and leave quickly.

Many firms and corporate legal departments have devised office manuals for the guidance and direction of their professional and non-professional staffs. A great variety of successful formats is available for your consideration. You will find that the actual writing of the manual will bring to light many of the current inefficiencies in your law practice. "It's the way we've always done it" philosophy will slowly give way to "we ought to do it this way, because it is obviously the most cost efficient in terms of time expended."

[¶409.1] Materials Necessary to Set Up an Office Manual

You should begin by acquiring 1½ " thick three-ring looseleaf binders that hold letter size (8½ " × 11") paper. This size binder permits flexibility of insertions, expansion, and convenience of storage and handling.

You should also be certain to have an adequate supply of dividers on hand.

[¶409.2] Actual Steps in Setting Up Your Manual

1. For any documents concerned with general intra-office procedures, transfer the appropriate contents from your forms file into the three-ring binder. Place a number in the upper right-hand corner of each document. List each document contained in it and index the list in front of the binder.

2. An annotation sheet should be placed opposite the form so that any instructions as to the use of the form can be given, as well as any practical suggestions, local court rules, etc.[6]

3. Regarding general office procedures, you should enlist the aid of your office manager and your entire staff. Have the office manager write a description of every common task, falling within the category of general office procedures, that he or she performs. As the manual is being written, all the staff members should not only be involved, but should feel that their involvement is a necessary part of the manual's development. Each staff member should also draft a description of his or her involvement in such tasks, which the office manager may then compile in a uniform manner.

4. The materials collected in steps (1) through (3) above should then be assembled into two sections within the binder.
    A. Brief general descriptions of responsibilities relevant to general office procedures. This serves as a sort of combination outline/overview/index to the second section.
    B. *Carefully detailed descriptions* of duties and responsibilities with regard to *all aspects of general office procedures*. This should include the samples of all appropriate forms.

---

[6] J.N. DeMeo, "How to Develop Manuals of Forms and Procedures," 18 *The Practical Lawyer* 37 (December 1972).

5. Forms should go through a constant refinement process and the result should be a distillation of the experience of all its users.

IMPORTANT: One consulting firm reported that secretarial productivity increased by 30 percent in the first year after the firm adopted a system as standardized in its manual which unified procedures, style and paper used in the office.[7]

[¶409.3] Training Benefits Provided by Office Manuals

A law office manual can greatly smooth transition in the turnover of employees, and also helps ease problems often associated with overloads that require the hiring of temporary help. Manuals are as useful for matters that occur frequently as for those that occur only occasionally by operating to prevent any important facet from being inadvertently omitted.

Without this valuable tool, changes in personnel will necessitate someone in the office spending valuable time explaining rather simple, but perhaps detailed, procedures. In matters that occur with great frequency, there can be a tendency toward carelessness when similar forms must be filled in or drafted, or detailed procedures followed.

By having employees receive instructions in basic office procedures via the precise written instructions and samples in an office manual, you may be confident that such procedures will be learned quickly (if not immediately) and thoroughly—and without disturbing anyone else's time, other than for an occasional clarification.

[¶410] BASIC CONTENTS OF A SAMPLE OFFICE MANUAL OFFICE PROCEDURES SECTION THAT CAN BE TAILORED TO YOUR REQUIREMENTS

The larger the firm, the more detailed the manual. However, the essential features of most manuals follow a similar pattern and can be outlined as follows:

    I. General Information (Office Policy)
        A. Attendance—office hours, days off, etc.

---

[7] *Administrative Management*, November 1975 at 22.

- B. Letters—signing letters, etc.
- C. Expense Charges
- D. Interoffice Communications
- E. Work Slips (in connection with copy work sent to the steno room)
- F. Working With a Senior

II. Filing
- A. Methods
- B. Use of File Room
- C. How to File
- D. How to Retrieve Files

III. New Accounts
- A. Opening New Files
- B. Docketing Cases
- C. New File Memoranda
- D. Bookkeeping Instructions

IV. Financial
- A. Reimbursement Slips
- B. Posting Charges:
    - (i) telephone
    - (ii) photocopy
    - (iii) travel and messenger
    - (iv) filing fees
    - (v) special mail
    - (vi) process service

V. Maintaining Work Flow—Time Sheets
- A. Daily Time Records
- B. Desk Calendars
- C. Conference and General Memos
- D. Weekly Reports
- E. Monthly Agenda
- F. Completed Cases

VI. Billing
- A. Procedures
- B. Form of Bill

VII. A. Managing Partner
- 1. Coordinator's Function
- 2. Purchasing and Supplies
- 3. Auxiliary Services

B. Practicing Partners and Associates
C. Paralegals
D. Clerical Staff

HELPFUL HINT: Job descriptions are optional in the office manual. Whether you use them or not, or the degree to which they are detailed if you do use them, will depend upon a number of factors. You may want a complete (or partial) list of the duties and responsibilities of each position, as a basis for occasional performance reviews. You may already have included these in your job description manual, however. If such a comprehensive overview is not required for this or any other reason, the systems binders for specialized areas of practice (Chapter 5) will list everyone's duties and responsibilities, only in the sequential order required for completion of a specific task (or tasks) in an individual area of practice.

VIII. Mail Department
    A. Collections
    B. Information
    C. Messengers

IX. Library

X. Stenographic Department
    A. General
        (i) procedure
        (ii) overtime
        (iii) dictation
        (iv) word processor/vydec/mag card use
    B. Photocopies
    C. Use of Forms:
        (i) form of letters (several)
        (ii) legal forms (several)
        (iii) sample masters of selected office forms
            (a) wills
            (b) contracts
            (c) prospectus
            (d) briefs
            (e) etc.

XI. Miscellaneous
    A. Assignments and Responsibilities
        (i) telephone-switchboard relief
        (ii) condition of room and desk

(iii) current files
(iv) calendaring
(v) use of conference room
(vi) keeping in touch with office
(vii) working with a senior
(viii) neatness and dress
B. Salary and Vacation Policy
(i) firm policy
(ii) fringe benefits
(a) medical and insurance plans
(b) pension plan

[¶411] HOW TO AVOID FRICTION IN ADDING PARALEGALS TO YOUR STAFF

If you bring in outside paralegals, try to assign them at first to projects that require little in the way of support staff. By the time the first few projects are completed, the support staff will be used to the paralegals' presence and accept their role more gracefully.

Where resentment is allowed to grow, the paralegal may find the secretary an extremely reluctant assistant. The paralegal will be slowed down, and the firm's productivity will suffer.

[¶411.1] Know How Your Whole Staff Feels

There is no simple solution to this potential problem, but the following suggestions may prove helpful.

First, when an opening does occur and if your office is a fairly small one, you might call a short meeting at a time convenient for most secretarial personnel. Ask at that time if there are any secretaries desirous of becoming legal assistants.

Example: At 5 p.m., a meeting is called, and the legal assistant coordinator learns that two secretaries have successfully completed paralegal courses, and have in fact been sending resumes to competing firms. Retain the better secretary immediately as a legal assistant. Offer the other additional duties as a paralegal, and the promise that if another opening occurs or business improves to justify expanding the paralegal department, he/she will be retained full-time as a paralegal.

Thus, a sure loss of two excellent employees is avoided through a short meeting.

[¶411.2] Have Well-Defined Promotion Standards

A second approach is to establish extremely high standards for your legal assistants and make these requirements known throughout the office. This may include a B.A. degree and/or graduation from an accredited paralegal institute. If requirements are set high enough, you will obtain, in many cases, high quality personnel without creating resentment from the secretarial staff. However, this may backfire if many of your secretarial staff have the same credentials you are seeking in a paralegal employee. Couple this approach with the previous suggestion to ensure office harmony.

[¶411.3] Always Anticipate the Consequences of Your Decisions

Finally, you should be careful not to pit the paralegal against the secretary inadvertently.

Example: A highly successful attorney recently changed law firms, and his new firm sponsored a cocktail party for his many clients. The paralegals were invited, but the secretaries were not. After the miffed secretaries expressed their displeasure, they were told that it was a mistake to have invited the paralegals. Then it was the paralegals' turn to express their displeasure and what began as a welcoming gesture by his new partners, became a nightmare of friction between the paralegals and secretaries. This type of situation must be avoided at all costs by careful consideration of, or even polling the feelings of your staff beforehand.

Although there are no known statistics, several authors have suggested that many secretaries are happy in their respective jobs and really have no desire to become legal assistants. However, to avoid any potential problem in this area, you should establish a policy to offer secretaries the opportunity to move up the ladder if they desire, so that any possible resentment may be avoided.

As long as you are aware of the possibility of resentment of the secretary toward the paralegal, you can usually avoid it. Where there is a total unawareness of possible problems, they seem to manifest themselves at unexpected moments. Recognition of the problem goes a long way toward finding a solution or avoiding its occurring.

[¶411.4]   Don't Forget Space and Supply Considerations

If the new paralegal will be an additional employee, you may need to "create" some space in the office. In Chapter 12, within the salary surveys, you'll find some statistics on types of office arrangements that have been made for paralegals. Naturally your own specific situation will dictate whether you can afford to give a paralegal his or her own office, have two or more paralegals share an office, or put paralegals together with clerical staff—their own, or yours.

Finally, remember to obtain any necessary office supplies, and be otherwise prepared to budget any temporary overhead costs of adding an additional employee to the staff.

You should bear in mind that a good deal of the work paralegals perform will require the opportunity to work in relative privacy (e.g., client interviews) and/or quiet (e.g., legal research, tax form drafting, etc.). In this context, remember that paralegals are career professionals who value the opportunity to work in the most effective environment you can provide.

An adjunct to the team approach, and to systemization is complementary office organization. Try to keep together the partners, associates, paralegals and clerical staff who concentrate in a specialty of law. By keeping those people who perform the same or related functions together, you add another element of efficiency to your operation.

[¶412]   TRAINING THE PARALEGAL FOR WORK IN YOUR SPECIALIZED AREAS OF PRACTICE

Since we haven't yet devoted exclusive attention to the many ways that you may employ paralegals in specialties of law, a discussion of training may seem premature.

In fact, before we do discuss utilizing paralegals in specialties of law, we are going to detail the methods and benefits of systematizing those areas of your practice (Chapter 5).

And, as luck would have it, or rather logical design, these systems serve as excellent training devices, in addition to keeping work on time, organized and under control. We can examine their benefits as training tools in a general way here.

The detailed systems binders are designed to ensure that any individual working with a case can do so without constantly interrupting other employees for clarification.

By having legal assistants in specialized areas who absorb their instructions via the sequential written instructions and sample forms in these systems, you offer them the opportunity to pay much more attention to detail than would be possible with verbal instructions or by sifting through memos, etc. Without systems, an untrained paralegal would have to spend much more time acquiring the skills needed to function professionally in any particular area of the law.

As you will see in Chapter 5, the systems binders provide a precise means of telling all your office personnel what to do, when to do it, and how to do it in each of your specialized areas of practice. They also standardize and codify the preparation of documents; discuss and prescribe types and sizes of paper as well as the form and arrangement of the contents of documents.[8] This enables you to preserve the results of past work in a manner that will permit instant retrieval for a current task confronting the law office staff. This is essentially the same advantage offered by the office manual for general procedures. Systems can smooth changes in personnel by eliminating needless hours of verbal recapitulation, memo searching, or re-researching a case previously handled by your firm.

The training benefits for new employees—particularly for paralegals who will be involved with more technical matters than the clerical staff—are obvious. They represent the clearest and most time-efficient way of communicating responsibilities to new staff members. They will not only help paralegals (and all your staff) reach full development and potential, they will increase efficiency, productivity and profits in the firm. There are a number of other benefits, though more tangential to training, that offer some more insight concerning the broad value of using systems for practice in the specialties of law.

---

[8] Leo Eisenstatt, "Create a System for the Law Office Style Manual," American Bar Association Section of Economics of Law Practice, Monograph Series (1978).

- ☐ Systems manuals expedite the preparation of legal documents by setting up a "bank" of standardized clauses that are subject to much repetition.[9]
- ☐ Going even further, the systems binders can be keyed into source books, where applicable, and thus become central repositories of all accumulated knowledge on the subject involved.[10]
- ☐ Systems manuals prevent the important facets of any task from being inadvertently omitted. This results in a better work product, with a minimum of effort expended on your part.
- ☐ Finally, the sequential arrangement of "job descriptions" in the office procedure section of each binder delineates the duties and responsibilities of each staff member in a coordinated system. This eliminates duplication, and greatly helps reduce confusion among new employees.

Your viewpoint on the benefits of systemization should have already begun to crystallize. In Chapter 5, we'll demonstrate how you can develop and implement these systems efficiently, and with ease, in your firm.

---

[9] J.N. DeMeo, "How to Develop Manuals of Forms and Procedures," 18 *The Practical Lawyer* 33 (December 1972).
[10] Id. at 34.

Part 2

Effective Utilization of Legal Assistants in the Major Specialized Areas of Practice

5

How to Increase Your Law Office Profits

"A man can do half a dozen jobs at once if he has proper control of time."

ARTHUR T. VANDERBILT

[¶501] WHY YOU SHOULD DEVELOP AND IMPLEMENT A SMOOTHLY FUNCTIONING SYSTEM IN YOUR OFFICE

In the midst of post-industrial society, the legal profession still operates under eighteenth century piecework methods in many ways. This means that for those of you who practice in the probate field, every probate petition is treated as an original work of art, or every letter that emanates from your office is dictated to your secretary, when you could simply give her the number of a letter in your forms file that would just require some appropriate filling in of blanks.

A general example of the ways in which office expenses mount up unnoticed is illustrated in the following cost estimate, made by a Dartnell Corporation Survey in 1967, for creating a letter:[1]

Dictator's Time—7 minutes per letter	$ .42
Stenographic cost = 20 letters per day	.94
Non-productive time	.20
Fixed charges	.61
Materials	.07
Mailing costs	.15
Filing costs	.10
Total Cost	$2.49

Since both attorneys and secretaries enjoy considerably greater income than was the case in 1967, you might expect that this estimate could be revised upward to perhaps $4.00 to $4.75 per letter. You'd be wrong, though. A nationwide cross-industry survey covering every aspect of producing and delivering a letter—including the cost of everyone's time—recently put the figure at a staggering $12.00 per letter!

With these types of hidden costs prowling around your office, you simply can no longer afford to ignore the opportunities that do exist for reducing them. There is quite a lot of work in every law practice that is repetitive, and this chapter proposes to help you gain insight into the benefits of systematizing many aspects of your practice. To break the barrier between eighteenth-century piecework methods and twentieth-century systems management you'll need to take your standard approaches and codify them into established procedures.[2] Utilizing a systems analysis approach also eliminates or greatly reduces the need for much verbal communication between staff members, as well as the repeating of instructions when members of your staff leave for vacation—or permanently.

It is not an overstatement to conclude that a legal assistant cannot operate at full efficiency without the use of legal systems. It is as true of a service profession as it is of any other business: to effect economies of time a task must be routinized. It must be broken down into steps or mini-systems

---

[1] Fred Gleason, "A Yardstick for Legal Records and Information Retrieval," ABA Committee on Economics of Law Practice, Pamphlet 11, 1969.

[2] Lee Turner, "The Employment of Modern Techniques and Technology in Trial Preparation," 11 *Forum* 799 (1976).

and then reorganized systematically so that each procedure is efficiently completed by the least expensive person competent to handle the procedure.

[¶501.1]   Defining Systems Management

In a nutshell, systems management is the ability to organize in written form, and then to delegate in an orderly fashion the tasks to be done. The procedure for developing a systems analysis approach involves the same mechanism regardless of the type of business you're involved in. It has been perceptively stated that systems analysis is nothing more than a systematic approach to problem-solving with a generous application of common sense, planning and organizing.[3]

Systemization reduces repetitive work to a routine and minimizes the involvement of management in handling that work. A system is the gathering together in *one* convenient place of all the information, forms, written descriptions and instructions for completing each task or related group of tasks: these materials are structured in such a way that any law office employee can complete the forms and do the job with a minimum of instruction and supervision.[4] To be effective, the system should have a description of each staff member's role in the system, together with a description of the equipment used to do the work.

The systems approach allows you to delegate while retaining control and brings out the best in support personnel.

[¶501.2]   How Paralegals and Systems Interface to Benefit the Firm

As we mentioned at the close of Chapter 4, this type of systemization facilitates training by centralizing and standardizing procedural information.

As paralegals begin to function more independently with your casework, you'll see benefits begin to accrue; you can turn them into a continuing cycle by broadening your practice.

---

[3] Kline D. Strong & William N. Henderson, "Legal Assistants—The Systems Approach," 15 *Law Office Economics Management* 344 (1974).

[4] Fran Shellenberger, "What is a System?" *Legal Economics* , Spring 1977, p. 19.

Figure 5.1
Benefits From Combining Use of Systems and Paralegals

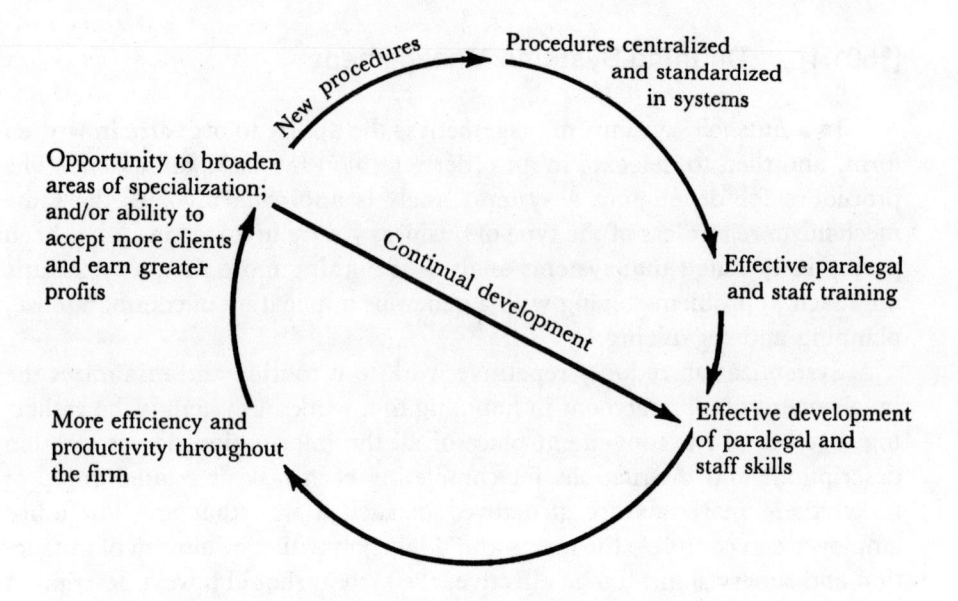

New procedures → Procedures centralized and standardized in systems → Effective paralegal and staff training → Effective development of paralegal and staff skills → More efficiency and productivity throughout the firm → Opportunity to broaden areas of specialization; and/or ability to accept more clients and earn greater profits → (Continual development)

In the next several discussions, we will show you how to create the systems which, along with the addition of paralegals to your staff, will help you achieve maximum productivity and profits from your practice.

[¶502] THREE ESSENTIAL STEPS TO BUILDING YOUR SYSTEM

The next three paragraphs offer a brief overview of the three most important steps required in developing a system, which are:

1. Identify the major areas capable of being systematized.
2. Assemble all the general facts, procedural information, and the full variety of documents you require for each specific job.
3. Organize and sequence all the above information for systematized use (according to the instructions in this chapter).

[¶502.1] Identify Areas of Law for Systemization

To develop an adequate systems analysis approach to the practice of law, it is essential first to analyze the fields of law in which you practice. You will realize the most cost savings by systematizing the areas from which most of your revenue is derived, so you should identify them first. You should prepare a brief financial analysis of each area, carefully examining the areas of real estate, matrimonial matters, estates and trusts, in particular. You might begin your analysis with a chart similar to that below:

Gross Revenue	Real Estate	Matrimonial	Estate and Trusts
Net Profits			
% of Total Profits			

You may wish to plan on organizing your first system in one of those areas. While it is true that a firm which lacks a great volume of work in any specific areas may have greater difficulty identifying tasks that can be standardized and delegated to a paralegal, there are very few of us who do not specialize in one or two areas of the law primarily.

[¶502.2] Assemble Pertinent Information

After you have identified the areas of law needing systemization, you must begin to assemble all the materials you normally encounter when handling work in that area, and begin to prepare these to be systematized.

You should begin preparing all work in that area in duplicate, one for the client and one for the system. To speed development and implementation of your system, you'll also want to examine some of your closed and nearly-closed files in that area of law, and make copies of all relevant data. Assemble more than one copy of each item involved, so that you have a good cross-section of everything that could become involved. Pay particular attention to all documents: letters—in-coming and out-going; standard blank forms; forms and other documents that you either create or receive and process, etc.

Have your staff members prepare brief summaries of how they actually perform each and every task in this area of law. A major component of your system will eventually be the written instructions, directions and procedures you develop for those who will be working with the system. They should be written in a clear, concise fashion, and should bear some indication of staff title, or job level, of the person who normally does this work.

Another view of a system is as a method or procedure for reducing tasks into their smallest components, so that effective delegation can take place. The instructions you assemble initially will eventually be developed into a formal Procedural Outline and Checklist—a complete sequential list of instructions for all work in this area of law. As a blueprint for work, it will indicate not only what must be done, but who must do it. When you finally put this item together—it is the last step in system development—you may happily discover a number of tasks that could be delegated to employees at lower salaries than those who had previously done the work. This affords the opportunity to bill clients less, and frees the professional staff for more strictly professional work.

[¶502.3] Organize and Sequence All Information and Documents for System Utilization

There will ultimately be three principal elements working in the system for each specific area of practice:

1. Letters/Standard Forms/Documents
2. Master Information List
3. Procedural Outline and Checklist

PRACTICAL TIP: These three elements will eventually be stored in a single three-ring binder (large size) as a master copy of the system. You may as well purchase a couple or few such binders right away, since they will be

How to Increase Your Law Office Profits

handy in the preliminary stages for temporarily storing all the assembled materials you'll gradually organize into the system.

Although it is preferable to have only one master copy of the system once it's completed, this may not always be possible. Paragraph 508.1 addresses the matter of effective control of the system's contents in the face of changes and updating that will occasionally be required. The following discussions should provide you with a better understanding of what the three principal system components are and do.

A. *Forms:* By assembling whatever documents, letters, etc., you use repeatedly in one location, in one standard version, you'll enable every task to be completed with a minimum of original thought. Unless the Court changes a form or additional requirements are imposed by statutes, form letters as well as Court forms placed in the system need few changes.
HELPFUL HINT: When you begin reviewing your current case load, every time you ask your secretary or legal assistant to prepare a letter or document, ask them also to type out your instructions. Collect the forms and the instructions in separate binders, and you are on your way to developing your first system. It is essential that all instructions and forms be prepared so that once a system is fully operational, a temporary loss of certain personnel will not result in a reduction of productivity.

B. *Master Information List:* This might be envisioned initially as a yellow legal pad filled with lists of questions that would permit you—the lawyer, paralegal, or other staff member—to complete the work necessary to obtain the stated goal, i.e., effectively administer the estate, procure the divorce, transfer the real property, etc.[5] It is a systematized means of recording data. Each system will have a blank "MIL," which must eventually be duplicated, completed, and filed for every different case you handle; the data contained therein will constitute everything you'd normally need to know in order to bring any specific case to completion.

C. *Procedural Outline and Checklist:* This can be compared to the assignment medium. It simply states: "Please do this task in the following manner." The overall job is broken down into specific, short-term, staccato movements. For example, in probating a Will, the probate petition must be filled in together with numerous other documents in varying quantities. The

---

[5] Adapted from Donald C. Rikli, "The Proficient-Efficient Law Office," *Illinois Bar Journal* (November 1979) at 128.

procedural outline provides the means and medium by which any appropriate employee can do the specific job with a minimum of assistance. This also will be a blank master copy in the system binder, that must be duplicated, and used as a task completion checklist in bringing each specific file from opening to closing.

[¶502.4]   Maintaining Control of System Development

There should be *one* person in charge of developing your new system. We recommend the attorney in charge of the law specialty you're working on. This attorney has likely been weathered by experience, and possesses a useful overview of this field of law. A legal assistant, even if a formidable administrator, may not grasp the full legal significance of each form or other item utilized within the system.

Be certain to hold a meeting with the entire staff prior to putting the system together; that includes secretaries, paralegals and attorneys who will be working with the system. Use their input at each stage of the system to insure its success.

Lee Turner relates an anecdote concerning Napoleon, who apparently asked one of his orderlies to read all orders that were meant for his commanders. If the orderly, who was supposedly of below average intelligence, could understand the order, it was permitted to be sent; if it was not understood, or was misunderstood, it was rewritten, and the process begun over again.[6] There is a good lesson to be garnered from this tale. Attorneys are often so inculcated in the language of "legalese" that they tend to write for everyone in this mode.

When it is necessary to train new employees, attorneys often become frustrated at the time required, especially if they've been through the same procedure a short time before. It has been noted that the best law office system is often devised by a key employee about to embark on a long vacation.[7] Although legal assistants may in fact draft large amounts of your new system in a style designed to be readily understood by all staff members, the attorney should provide constant input, for indeed it is the lawyer who is responsible for all work emanating from the office.

---

[6] Lee Turner, "The Employment of Modern Techniques and Technology in Trial Preparation," 11 *Forum* 800 (1976).

[7] Speech given by J. Harris Morgan, Esq. before the New York State Bar Association, Committee on Continuing Legal Education, August 1978.

Utilization of a systems approach to the practice of law requires the analysis and classification of large jobs according to steps that must be completed. To put such steps into written form requires clear thought. Thus, when instructions must be written, classification and clarification should be the happy result.

Should you wish to see a finished system in operation, the authors can suggest the Texas Probate System, as well as systems devised by various state bars throughout the United States. Many of these systems can be tailored to your own practice with a minimal adjustment. However, the difference between purchasing a system "ready-made" and devising your own may be analogized to having your clothes "made to order" or buying them "off the racks." For most of us, tailor-made clothes are an indulgence not permitted in our daily lives. However, if your practice permits you this luxury, and if the fit is right, you may save a lot of time and trouble by purchasing a pre-prepared system.

Now you're ready to get down to the nitty-gritty of putting the system together. There's a fair amount of assembling and organizing to accomplish before the system will be operable, but if you proceed carefully and patiently, the organizational, productivity and economic rewards will usher themselves in quickly once the system is working.

[¶503] STEP ONE: IDENTIFY AREAS OF LAW FOR SYSTEMIZATION

The first phase is a basic, organizational one, and the material you'll find at ¶502.1 really covers all the necessary steps you must take in order to complete it. You will not be surprised at the results of these analyses; in fact, you probably already know instinctively which area of law will be the first you'll systematize.

[¶504] STEP TWO: ASSEMBLE ALL THE PROCEDURAL INFORMATION, GENERAL FACTS AND THE FULL VARIETY OF DOCUMENTS YOU REQUIRE FOR EACH SPECIFIC JOB

Before we proceed into some more complex steps, we should clarify that it is not within the scope of this book to provide an *absolutely detailed* explanation of all the necessary steps involved in assembling and perfecting your system.

Our presentation here represents a synthesis of our experience and analysis of a variety of published materials. We feel it provides enough of a framework so that you'll be able to succeed—with the opportunity to inject a good deal of your own personal/professional style into the works.

If you'd feel more comfortable with a precise road map to organizational prowess, you can obtain a prepared system—even if it's not your own state's to use as a guide. Or you may go to the most complete source we know of: Roberta Cooper Ramo's "How to Create a System for the Law Office," American Bar Association, 1975.

Now let us forge ahead. Step Two encompasses the majority of the work involved in developing a system. For the sake of organization (and sanity) it's best to break this information-and-document-gathering stage down into a number of small, distinct projects. These projects, however, while remaining independent from each other, can and should be undertaken simultaneously.

[¶504.1] Prepare a Preliminary List of Every Step and Task Involved in Completing All the Work in the Area You've Chosen to Systematize

As was suggested in ¶502.2., begin by analyzing several closed files in the areas you now wish to systematize. Copy all letters, forms, inter-office instructions to your secretary or paralegal for completing a task in the file, etc., and begin to organize all these according to the time sequence usually followed. For example, if you have a client interview questionnaire for new estates, place that first in the system and develop later steps as offshoots of that questionnaire. Thus, your probate petition can be completed based on information garnered from the client interview questionnaire. (See ¶601.2 for a sample client interview questionnaire form.)

Some of the things you'll want to begin to keep track of are:

- ☐ Steps in each task;
- ☐ Who's (job position) involved in each task;
- ☐ What's involved in completing each task (instructions);
- ☐ Standard, blank, pre-prepared forms used;
- ☐ Letters received or generated;

- ☐ Documents created in the office;
- ☐ Documents received;
- ☐ Normal communications of any sort: written or verbal, instructions or responses, memos;
- ☐ Complex tasks that may require special instructions.

After you have analyzed the steps involved from opening to closing a file as well as the many intricacies involved throughout the handling of a case in a specific field, you'll probably find you've already got a better notion of the repetitiveness of much of your practice, and the ease with which you'll be able to delegate to others a great deal of this work.

When a case has been placed in chronological order, discuss the "guts" of your new system with those who will be working with it. Perhaps you have always placed your death certificates in the Probate file believing that all official forms should be kept together, but after discussing this with another attorney or paralegal, you realize that it would be better off in the Funeral and Administration file. It is likely that before this juncture, the placing of a death certificate in a client's file never occupied much thought, and you placed it in the Probate file because your predecessor did likewise.

Systemizing involves a questioning of "why" things are done in a certain fashion. Be certain that you can cost-justify the continuing of your law practice without using the modern system analysis approach before deciding that systemization is too difficult or time consuming for you.

[¶504.2] Organizing, Assembling and Redrafting "Universal" Versions of Documents

Among the items, assembled in your review of case work in the systematized area, there are a great number of documents: letters, previously prepared forms, and created documents.

Most such items can be reduced to one fairly standard format, and that is what you must now do with each document. For instance, you may have a batch of similar letters, all to the Secretary of State requesting availability of corporate name.

Create one standard letter for this purpose, and have it prepared so that there is a blank space wherever any piece of information may vary from case to case. Type a rule in each blank space, and underneath the rule, identify the type of information that must be included by a staff member to produce a functional letter for a given client. (See Figures 5.2, 5.3, 5.4.)

You now have a "universal" document that can easily be used over and over again for each of your clients. You'll need to *create "universal" versions of every document, letter and form in the area of work you're systematizing.* You must be able to identify every variable piece of information. Letters and documents you create obviously involve a bit more work than "universalizing" standard pre-prepared forms, since the latter are by and large universal already. (See Figures 5.5 and 5.6.)

Sometimes a document will require a number of known variations in order to be useful. You may as well "universalize" each alternative you may reasonably expect to need. (See Figure 5.7.)

If preparation of a document will be more complex than simply filling in the blanks with a particular client's information, you should develop a brief set of special instructions that clarify the work required—for whomever must perform it. These instructions should always be attached to or included on the document, following its actual contents.

Once you feel you have all your documents universalized, you should take a run-through the whole batch to review the job you've done. Get a critique from your staff; and revise anything that seems to need fixing. Although the usefulness of such "universal" documents must already be apparent to you, they will eventually be refined even further.

In another few paragraphs you will learn how to streamline document preparation even further by employing a Master Information List (MIL). But that's jumping ahead a bit; Step Two has one more phase before it is complete.

[¶504.3]   Prepare a List of Important Dates

Part of work in any area of law involves meeting stipulated deadlines, and this you accomplish via your tickler system. As you are reviewing your case files, be sure to assemble a list of all tasks that must meet some deadline. Prepare a brief description of how the deadline is determined, e.g., from receipt of notice x, item y must be handled not more than 60 days later; tickle file at 40, 50 and 55 days.

Eventually such work instructions will be included in the overall and sequential list of instructions—the Procedural Outline and Checklist. However, we are jumping ahead again, since you won't be preparing this sequential set of instructions until virtually all other work is done. For now just concentrate on tracking down every piece of work that is governed by some specific time limitation. Keep your notes on these in one place.

[¶505] STEP THREE: ORGANIZE AND SEQUENCE THE PROCEDURES, FACTS, AND DOCUMENTS FOR SYSTEMATIZED USE

As stated in ¶502.3, the working system ultimately contains three principal elements—that interface with particular client files:

- A. All the forms, letters and documents you've collected and drafted with blanks for pertinent information.
- B. A Master Information List. A blank master copy stays in the binder containing the system. For each file you open, a MIL must be completed at a prescribed point in the case.
- C. A Procedural Outline and Checklist serves as the complete sequential roster of tasks that must be completed from opening to closing a file. As with the MIL, a blank master remains in the systems binder, while a working copy is kept with each case file and used to keep track of work in progress.

[¶505.1] Drafting a Master Information List

The Master Information List (MIL) constitutes an Index of all information—analogous to a book's index—needed to complete all work in the systematized area of law. You develop it out of all the information you have assembled in Step Two. Each item is a specific type or piece of information for which some client's particular data must eventually be obtained and processed to complete a task, or number of tasks.

For instance, a Probate System MIL would contain, among other items, everything from:

- ☐ Address of client; to
- ☐ List of assets, and how they're held (each a separate item); to
- ☐ Beneficiaries' names (each a separate item); to

- ☐ Client's vital statistics (again, each a separate item); to
- ☐ Executor's name; to
- ☐ Fiduciaries' names; to
- ☐ Known future powers (each noted separately);
- ☐ Etc.

This list *must be comprehensive*. It must include every item of information —categorically—that will be required to produce or respond to any sort of document; produce any other work-product; complete any task involved in the area to be systematized.

It's best to assemble and list this information sequentially as far as possible, as opposed to alphabetically or any other way. Begin by organizing the information that the staff will require in the earliest phases of case work, and continue to build the MIL by adding additional information items as they would be required by your staff.

Once you have all of this information listed more or less in sequential order, you must prepare a numerical cross-reference system between the information items and the documents where this information must appear.

[¶505.2] Creating Reference Numbers for MIL Information

Now you will have to go through the MIL information you've organized and give each item a reference number to identify it. Don't use the same number for two different pieces of information, nor should the same piece of information be given two different numbers simply because it must be included in more than one work-product.

Some systems are more complex than others, but in most cases you'll find that certain items of information are always subsets of other information. You can make your MIL reference numbers conform to this fact. For example, in an estate planning system, two of many assets may be a client's stock portfolio and his or her real estate holdings. A good deal of particular information could be required, so that your MIL reference might look like this:

    Stocks—7.0
    Description—7.01
    Ownership—7.02
    # of Shares—7.03
    Cost—7.04

Annual Yield—7.05
Current Value—7.06
Real Estate—9.0
Description—9.01
Location—9.02
If Residential—9.03
If Income Producing—9.04
If Unimproved—9.05
etc. . . . to:
Mortgagees—9.13
Leinors—9.14
9.15 to 9.19 might be open for future use, then:
Encumbrances—9.20
Amount—9.21
Monthly Payments—9.22
Annual Income (Gross)—9.23
Average Annual Interest—9.24

Figures 5.8 and 5.9 illustrate MIL formats. In order to avoid any confusion in developing this essential element of the system, you might wish to obtain a ready-made system from one of the state bars that produces them. The following states have published substantive systems in the subjects indicated:

State	System
Oregon	Probate
South Carolina	Probate
Texas	Probate
Maine	Probate
Wisconsin	Probate
Oklahoma	Corporations
Nebraska	Corporations
Washington	Probate
Michigan	Domestic Relations
Utah	Corporations, Divorce, Estate Planning

Even if not directly usable, or adaptable to your office, any of these might be a valuable guide for you in developing your own system.

HELPFUL HINT: It is important to remember that this is a system for *your* office. The sequence of information should reflect your style and methods. A final point deserving emphasis is: do not be concerned about the length of the MIL. It is meant to be fully comprehensive, and it will be faulty if it is not.

[¶505.3] Converting Your "Universal" Documents for Use With the MIL Information

In ¶504.2 we discussed the development of "universal" documents. Now that you have a numerically referenced MIL, those documents (see Figures 5.2–5.7) can be further refined.

Your universal documents have blank spaces, with the missing information identified by a word or phrase. You should go through all these documents and place the MIL reference number that corresponds to that particular item of information *in the blank space.*

This process will allow you to make any adjustments that may be required in either the MIL or the documents, and therefore this is a very valuable trouble-shooting phase in systems development. If you have overlooked anything, you'll probably discover it now.

Once all the MIL reference numbers are added to the universal documents, have them re-typed so that only the MIL number (and not the word or phrase describing the required information) appears wherever your staff must include some particular client's data. Figures 5.10 to 5.15 illustrate what these documents look like when completed.

An important point to realize is that each *document* must also have a MIL reference number that corresponds to *it.* Any of these documents may need to be referred to in correspondence, later documents, memos, etc. They therefore constitute information-items in themselves and must be given MIL reference numbers. This is illustrated in Figures 5.10 to 5.14.

You might, for instance, use 11.0 to designate all letters in a particular system. A letter to the Secretary of State regarding availability of corporate name might be 11.02. Standard blank forms might be designated 12.00, with appropriate sub-numbers for each one.

If documents-created were designated 13.0, Articles of Incorporation might be denoted as 13.02.

[¶505.4] Maintaining Integrity of Documents in the System

Statutory and judicial changes occasionally alter the required content of documents you must prepare. Once you have your documents numbered as part of the MIL, you can create a supplementary item that will ensure easy alteration when their content must change.

You'll need to construct a simple grid. List your MIL document reference numbers across the top. List statutes or rulings that may affect any part of any document down the left side. Place a mark at the intersections where any ruling affects *any* document. When something changes you'll quickly be able to see all of the documents affected.

[¶505.5] Eventual Use of the MIL

The MIL ultimately serves two purposes. As a master list of all information required to complete work in a given area of law, a blank copy should remain in the one binder that stores all material in the system. (See ¶502.3.) Copies of the MIL, however, will also have to be duplicated and used as actual questionnaires in each client file that is opened for processing in the systematized area.

Your final version of the MIL, then, would best be constructed so that it may be functional as a questionnaire. (See Figures 5.8 and 5.9.) When and how the MIL—as questionnaire—is to be completed for each client is governed by the instructions provided in the Procedural Outline and Checklist. This is the crowning jewel in your system, and you should now be prepared to construct it.

[¶505.6] Preparing the Procedural Outline and Checklist

Once again, you must turn to all of the materials you assembled in Step Two, and here is where their sequential organization will pay off. You should arrange all task descriptions, sets of instructions, important dates, etc., into the most complete and precise sequence of occurrences required by case work in this area. Interviews, communications, document production, timely dates to be met, responses to incoming material or extra-office events —every single event that may be expected to occur in the course of a normal case must be considered.

To develop the actual Procedural Outline and Checklist, determine the complete sequence of events first. Describe each step as briefly as possible— in terms of a direction or instruction, where appropriate. Always refer to MIL reference numbers where possible in framing these descriptions. Keep these descriptions condensed in the left one-third of a regular 8½" × 11" page.

Next to each step, in a middle column, indicate—by job title—who is responsible for completion of that particular step. The far right column will be used as a progress chart—to show each step that has been completed, and therefore what must be done next as well.

It's obvious from this last direction that the Procedural Outline and Checklist also serves a dual purpose. As a comprehensive blueprint for completing all work in a given area, a blank master copy must be permanently stored in the binder containing the entire system. (See ¶502.3.)

Like the MIL, however, a copy of the Procedural Outline and Checklist is included with each individual case file, to serve as both progress report and director of all work to be done. See Figure 5.11 for a sample portion of a Procedural Outline and Checklist.

[¶506] PUTTING IT ALL TOGETHER

You've now completed your assembly and drafting of the entire system. You have:

A. Documents that are Universalized *and* Referenced to your MIL.
B. Master Information List (master copy).
C. Procedural Information List (master copy).

There may be a few additional items you'll find you'd like to maintain as well, such as the grid for maintaining statutory integrity of the documents. (See ¶505.4.)

All that remains is simply to organize this material in a single three-ring binder, according to the manner you find easiest to employ. If the documents are so extensive that more than one binder is required, well, you can't argue with necessity.

[¶507] SUMMARY OF STEPS IN DEVELOPING A SYSTEM

As we said earlier, it's not within the scope of this book to provide the absolutely detailed type of instructions that would most simplify the systems development process for you. Development of a system will take some time, but is fundamentally not a complex activity.

How to Increase Your Law Office Profits 109

Below, you'll find an outline of the major steps, and its brevity may offer some relief if you have previewed the chapter thus far before beginning actual development of a system.

- ☐ Select one area of the law to systematize at a time.
- ☐ Have all pertinent instructions and documents prepared in duplicate for several weeks, and sift through a number of nearly closed case files.
- ☐ Analyze inter-office instructions and communications.
- ☐ Analyze documents; sort into letters, ready-made forms, documents you create.
- ☐ Draft "universal" versions of letters and documents (with blanks for particular case data).
- ☐ Construct a list of important timely deadlines.
- ☐ Draft the basic Master Information List, for collecting *all* data pertinent to given cases. Add reference numbers to identify each piece of data.
- ☐ Denote each document (of any sort) by means of a reference number.
- ☐ Create the Procedural Outline and Checklist as a complete roster of duties to complete the case work in the systematized area.
- ☐ Assemble the elements in a loose-leaf ring binder according to your most comfortable manner of use.
- ☐ Put the system into use, and modify it as a necessary according to your practice and experience.
- ☐ Continue to develop and refine the system as you become more and more comfortable with it.[8]

If you are still concerned about the complexity of this project, then we recommend again that you obtain Roberta Cooper Ramo's "How to Create a Law Office System," which *will* give you the simplest, most complete and easy-to-follow directions we know of in this regard.

And, if you're tempted to conclude that this work—no matter how easy —couldn't possibly be worth it, we hope you'll finish reading this chapter before you commit yourself to that viewpoint.

---

[8] Some of this synopsis was discussed in the fine article written by Bernard Sternin entitled "Programmed Approaches to Office Paperwork" contained in 21 *The Practical Lawyer* #4, p. 55 (June 1975).

[¶508] BENEFITS OF USING THE SYSTEMS APPROACH

Use of a systems approach will give your firm the following capabilities:

1. Centralized control over work;
2. Flexibility to expand, contract and adapt the system to new and challenging conditions;
3. Continuity of style and procedures—and personnel;
4. Ability to accumulate knowledge and develop new methods.[9]

Let us examine each of these points in detail.

[¶508.1] Systems Give You Centralized Control Over Work

Since all of the system (for each specialized area) is contained in the binder storing the forms, the Master Information List, and the Procedural Outline and Checklist, respectively, all cases that come into your office come within the scope of the system.

Eventually, a binder should be used by your support staff, but only *one* person should be in charge of altering the system. Then, if a new law is passed, or a more efficient manner of doing a specific task is discovered, one person *must* after general consultation be in charge of changing the master copy and all other copies in your office.

[¶508.2] You'll Gain the Flexibility to Adapt to Changes Readily

A system will also allow you to expand, contract or adapt the practice to changing conditions. Attorneys who are well versed in the use of systems analysis have stated that their output has more than tripled when utilizing systems.[10] For a busy trial attorney such as Lee Turner, who tries approximately thirty cases a year and must travel throughout his state of Kansas to

---

[9] Adapted from Hal Cornelius, "Organization of the Modern Paralegal Department," *New York Law Journal*, June 5, 1979 at p. 4.
[10] Lee Turner and Roberta Ramo during a Conference sponsored by the New York State Bar Association, Committee for Continuing Legal Education, August 1978.

do so, this feat would be impossible without the concerted efforts of his legal specialist teams.

Conversely, during a sudden downturn in the need for legal services, one paralegal can work in many areas of the law with systems in each area to back her up. Hence, one day might be spent doing probate work while the next might be spent preparing for a real estate closing. Indeed, the attorney would not have the time to explain the mechanics of the system each time a new paralegal appears on the scene, but with a good system, the instructions should be self-explanatory for whoever is involved with the case. The system is also amenable to changing conditions. When a new law is passed in the tax field, for example, and the rates undergo a sudden change, it is much easier to plug the new rates into an existing system than to revamp completely in an ad hoc manner.

[¶508.3] You Gain Continuity of Style and Procedures

The use of a systems analysis approach leads to continuity of style, procedures, and performance of personnel. Most new employees are surprised to learn that in any one office, the way documents are prepared varies from lawyer to lawyer, paralegal to paralegal and secretary to secretary. The lack of uniformity is astounding, and this individualistic, free-enterprise approach is prone to produce ulcers and errors. One benefit of a systems approach is that the quality of the work emanating from your office is subject to continually high standards and far less contingent on the mood of an employee. Work on a case can continue despite the absence of a specific attorney or paralegal. Errors are less frequent where the procedures have been written down for easy reference. If a mistake occurs, analyze the reasons why, and rewrite that part of the procedure section to avoid repetition.

[¶508.4] You'll Always Be Able to Accumulate Knowledge and Develop New Methods

Systems permit the accumulation of knowledge and the development of new methods for dealing with changing laws, changing technology, or any sort of change that may affect your practice and procedures. Systems get you away from crisis-oriented response, and permit the practice of law in a less stress-laden atmosphere. An attorney need no longer awaken in the middle of the night to wonder if the answer to a motion is due tomorrow or yesterday. Sleep is difficult when there is a possibility of missed deadlines. This becomes an unnecessary worry when the minute a set of papers is delivered to your office, a calendar specialist places it on your tickler and sends out the necessary memo to other members of the firm informing them of the crucial dates. A systems approach works as one of checks and balances, so that even if one member of the firm is caught napping, the slack is immediately noticed by another member without the client's getting wind of it.

[¶509] THREE PITFALLS THE SYSTEMS APPROACH AVOIDS

Spiraling costs are curbed because systems reduce overhead. When a job can be reduced to its most basic components, the time necessary to complete it can all be billed directly to a client. Furthermore, by billing for these services at both paralegal and attorney rates, the client gets the same legal product delivered more efficiently for less money and, the attorney is freed for more work (and more clients).

Secondly, as a result of controlling costs, loss of business to other professions will be stopped. Instead of asking their insurance broker or accountant to draft their estate plan, clients will have you do it all instead. Your firm is selling a service, and if a paralegal can conduct the initial interview and follow-through for the client, the ultimate costs to the client can be kept to a minimum.

Finally, any problems with inadequate client contact can easily be overcome via the use of systems. Monthly billings can include a status update on each open case in your office, and should a client object to all this "paralegal contact" remind him that on his last visit to his medical doctor, all of the preliminary medical procedures were performed by a nurse, and only after all the vital information was obtained did the doctor come upon the scene.

[¶509.1] You Can Reduce Spiraling Legal Costs (While Improving Your Firm's Income)

Perhaps the greatest tragedy befalling the American public, when systems fail to take hold in law firms, is the ever-increasing cost of legal services. To counteract rising costs, the attorney does *not* have to freeze hourly rates. Why not bill clients with an appropriate percentage at paralegal rates?

If you have many of the less complex tasks currently being done by attorneys performed by these fully-qualified non-professionals you'll be freer to work in the complex areas you are trained for—and for a greater number of clients as well. Paralegals and efficient systems allow you to get the maximum output from your practice.

[¶509.2] You Can Cut Down on Loss of Legal Business to Other Professions

Another result of the failure to use paralegal systems will quite possibly be the public's increasing use of "lawyer substitutes." This category includes accountants, life insurance salesmen, real estate brokers, and trust officers. How much easier to ask an accountant about the estate tax implications of a contemplated business enterprise than to engage an attorney—when the accountant is already preparing your annual tax return! How much easier to ask a life insurance salesman to do a study demonstrating the amount of insurance necessary to give your spouse an income of X dollars upon your death than to consult an attorney who may be able to provide viable alternatives for your desires. Real estate brokers will oftentimes discuss the latest tax laws, such as the current ability of senior citizens to sell their residence under certain conditions and not pay a capital gains tax on the first $100,000 of capital gains realized. If attorneys insist on raising their legal fees to meet the mounting inflationary spiral, the continued increase in the use of "lawyer substitutes" will loom constantly brighter on the horizon.

[¶509.3] You Can Eliminate Problems Stemming From Inadequate Client Contact

Finally, without the utilization of systems and paralegals you may lose control of a crucial requirement: effective client contact. You should have a reminder built right into your system, so that once a month clients are sent a status report on their cases. It is important that clients feel the attorney is really going to bat for him.

In a study done in 1964 by the Missouri Bar and Prentice-Hall entitled "Motivational Study of Public Attitude and Law Office Management," clients were asked why they selected law firms, and attorneys were asked why they felt clients had selected them. It is interesting to note that attorneys named "results" as the first factor, while the laymen did not list this within even the top five qualities that motivated them to select a particular lawyer or his firm. The laymen selected friendliness, promptness, courtesy, a non-condescending attitude, and keeping-client-informed as the five prime reasons for selecting a law firm. Results are obviously more important to lawyers than to their clients. With this in mind, it is far easier to cater to your clients' desires through the use of systems and paralegals than to attempt to fulfill this role model singlehandedly.

The Word Processors of America conducted a study in the 1960's in which factory productivity was compared to that of lawyer productivity.[11] The astounding results were that factory productivity increased 7,000 percent since the Industrial Revolution while lawyers' productivity during the same period increased 7 percent!

[¶510] CONCLUSION—A SYSTEM IS THE OBVIOUS CHOICE FOR LONG-TERM EFFICIENCY

Systems analysis has both engineering and management aspects, it's true. But you should simply think of it as a means of organizing work effectively. Systems management means first you organize, then you delegate.

If you decide that writing your own system is too complicated, purchase a ready-made system and then adapt it to your particular office. Kline Strong, a giant in the field of systematizing law offices, has also developed systems that can be purchased directly from the Utah Law Research Institute in Salt Lake City. And as we have indicated earlier, the Texas and North Carolina Bar Associations have developed systems which can be purchased by the practitioner and adapted to his office with minimal changes. Donald C. Rikli is the author of the *Illinois Probate System* which can be obtained by writing to the Illinois Institute for Continuing Legal Education, 2395 West Jefferson, Springfield, Illinois 62702. The *Illinois Residential Paralegal System*, by David Abell, is available from the Illinois Institute for Continuing Legal Education at the above address. Lastly, the *Illinois Corporate System*, by Linscott R. Hanson and Barbara H. Manan, can be purchased from the same source.

Once you have your system, the work for each of its component parts is then delegated to the lowest-paid employee capable of performing the task.

---

[11] J. Harris Morgan, supra note 7.

If an attorney, rather than a legal assistant, writes much of the system, he will have the satisfaction of knowing that not only is he developing a system, but he will be preparing a training manual for present as well as future legal assistants in his firm. Once written, it serves to provide *the* most effective "on-the-job" training for your employees with a minimal incursion upon the attorney's own time.

Technology is not waiting to be developed—it's here—it's just the effective use of it that has yet to be learned. The ball is in your court, your future may very well be determined by how well you institute a systems analysis approach to your law practice today.

[¶511] SELECTION OF SAMPLES FOR REFERENCE AS YOU BUILD YOUR LAW OFFICE SYSTEM

Figure 5.2
Sample "Universal" Letter

(Today's Date)

(Name and address of client)

RE: Estate Planning

Dear (Name of client):

Pursuant to our telephone conversation today, I mentioned that it is the policy of our firm to request clients to complete an estate planning form in preparation for our forthcoming meeting.

You will find our form entitled "Financial Profile" enclosed herewith. Please note that our form also contains plans for inserting the names and addresses of your distributees (relatives required by law to receive note that your will has been submitted to court to be probated) as well as your desires concerning how your estate should be distributed (dispositive objectives).

The information contained in your "Profile" will be kept confidential. Unless you indicate to the contrary, your Profile will be reviewed initially by a trained paralegal in our estate planning department who will thereafter call you should questions arise requiring clarification. As soon as you complete and return this form and we complete our review of same, my secretary will call you to arrange an appointment.

This procedure is intended to save time so that I will be fully informed about your finances as well as your objectives when we meet to discuss the specifics of your plan.

We encourage the presence of your wife/husband at our meeting should that be your desire. (Optional)

Our professional charges are based upon time spent on your matter at the rate of $150 per hour for my time, $100 per hour for an associate's time and $65 per hour for time spent by a paralegal. A portion of our fee may qualify as an allowable income tax deduction in which case we shall advise you accordingly.

It will be our pleasure to provide this very important legal service to you and I look forward to our meeting.

We appreciate your confidence in permitting us to be of service to you and your family.

Very truly yours,

(Name of lawyer)

Lawyer's initials/Secretary's initials
Enclosures

NOTE TO SUPPORT STAFF: Enclosure is Confidential Estate Planning Questionnaire, found in Form File 75-0032. Please attach to this letter.

Figure 5.3
Sample "Universal" Letter

State of Arkansas
Department of Finance
  and Administration
Franchise Tax
Post Office Box 1272 FT
Little Rock, Arkansas 72203

      Re: <u>(Name of Corporation)</u>

Gentlemen:

    Enclosed is the completed Corporation Franchise Tax Report and payment of the tax for the above corporation.

    Please mail the receipt to this office in the enclosed self-addressed envelope.

                                Yours truly,

                                FOR THE FIRM

Figure 5.4
Sample "Universal" Letter

Secretary of State's Office
Corporation Division
State Capitol Building
Little Rock, Arkansas 72201

Re: Availability of corporation name

Gentlemen:

Would you please advise us whether the following corporate name is available for use: _____ or, alternatively,
(Name of corporation)
should this name not be available, the name: _____.
(Alternate corporate name)

The corporation is being formed to engage in the business of _____.

(Primary purpose of business)

The corporation's principal place of business will be _____

_____

(Address of principal place of business)

Thank you in advance for your prompt attention and cooperation in this matter.

Very truly yours,

FOR THE FIRM

How to Increase Your Law Office Profits

Figure 5.5
Sample "Universal" Pre-prepared Standard Form

Form **5300** (Rev. August 1979) Department of the Treasury Internal Revenue Service	**Application for Determination for Defined Benefit Plan** For Pension Plans Other Than Money Purchase Plans (Under sections 401(a), 414(j) and 501(a) of the Internal Revenue Code)	For IRS Use Only File folder number ▶

▶ Church and Governmental Plans.—All items need not be completed. See instruction B. "What to File."

▶ Please complete every item on this form. If an item does not apply, enter N/A. (Get information from file)

1 (a) Name, address and ZIP code of employer   (Name and address of Client)   **2** Employer's identification number

3 Business code number

Telephone number ▶ (   )

(b) Name, address and ZIP code of plan administrator, if other than employer   **4** Date incorporated or business began

5 Employer's tax year ends

(c) Administrator's identification number ▶ .... Telephone number ▶ (   )
(d) Name, address and phone number of person to be contacted if more information is needed:
Name ▶ .... Telephone number ▶ (   )
Address ▶

6 Determination requested for:
(a) *(i)* ☐ Initial qualification—date plan adopted ▶ ....   *(ii)* ☐ Amendment—date adopted ▶
(iii) If *(ii)* is checked, enter file folder number ▶
(b) Were employees who are interested parties given the required notification of the filing of this application? ☐ Yes ☐ No
(c) If this application involves a merger or consolidation with another plan, enter the employer identification number(s) and the plan number(s) of such other plan(s) ▶

7 Type of entity:
(a) ☐ Corporation   **(b)** ☐ Subchapter S corporation   **(c)** ☐ Sole proprietor   **(d)** ☐ Partnership
(e) ☐ Tax exempt organization   **(f)** ☐ Church   **(g)** ☐ Governmental organization
(h) ☐ Other (specify) ▶

8 (a) Name of Plan   **(b)** Plan number ▶
(c) Plan year ends ▶
(d) Is this a Keogh (H.R. 10) plan? . . . . ☐ Yes ☐ No
(e) If "Yes," is an owner-employee in the plan? ☐ Yes ☐ No

9 (a) If this is an adoption of a district approved pattern plan, enter name of such plan   **(b)** Notification letter number

10 (a) Type of plan: *(i)* ☐ Fixed benefit   **(b)** Does plan provide for variable benefits? ☐ Yes ☐ No
(ii) ☐ Unit benefit   *(iii)* ☐ Flat benefit   If "Yes," check appropriate box to indicate type.
(iv) ☐ Other (specify) ▶ ....   *(i)* ☐ Cost of living   *(ii)* ☐ Asset fluctuation
(iii) ☐ Other (specify) ▶

(c) Is this a defined benefit plan covered under the Pension Benefit Guaranty Corporation termination insurance program? . . . . ☐ Yes ☐ No ☐ Not determined

11 Effective date of plan | **12** Effective date of amendment | **13** Date plan was communicated to employees ▶
How communicated ▶

14 (a) Indicate the general eligibility requirements for participation under the plan and indicate the section and page number of plan or trust where each provision is contained: Section and page number *   FOR IRS USE ONLY
(i) ☐ All employees   *(v)* Length of service (number of years) ▶
(ii) ☐ Hourly rate employee only   *(vi)* Minimum age (specify) ▶
(iii) ☐ Salaried employee only   *(vii)* Maximum age (specify) ▶
(iv) ☐ Other job class (specify) ▶ ....   *(viii)* Minimum pay (specify) ▶
(b) Are the eligibility requirements the same for future employees? . . . . ☐ Yes ☐ No
If "No," explain ▶
(c) Does the plan recognize service only with this employer? . . . . . ☐ Yes ☐ No
If "No," explain ▶

* Of plan or trust or other document constituting the plan.

Under penalties of perjury, I declare that I have examined this application, including accompanying statements, and to the best of my knowledge and belief it is true, correct and complete.

Signature ▶   Title ▶   Date ▶

283-478-1 Form **5300** (Rev. 8)

Figure 5.6
Sample "Universal" Pre-prepared Standard Form

X 74—Certificate of Conducting Business as Partners.
    Individual — Corporation.

COPYRIGHT 1973 BY JULIUS BLUMBERG, INC., LAW BLANK PUBLISHERS

Business Certificate for Partners

The undersigned do hereby certify that they are conducting or transacting business as members of a partnership under the name or designation of _____
(Name of Corporation/Partnership)

at _____
(Address of principal place of business)

in the County of _____, State of New York, and do further certify that the full names of all the persons conducting or transacting such partnership including the full names of all the partners with the residence address of each such person, and the age of any who may be infants, are as follows:

NAME Specify which are infants and state ages.   **RESIDENCE**

_____   _____

_____   _____

_____   _____

_____   _____

(Names of client)   (Addresses of clients)

WE DO FURTHER CERTIFY that we are the successors in interest to _____
_____
(Previous members of partnership)

the person or persons heretofore using such name or names to carry on or conduct or transact business.

In Witness Whereof, We have this _____ day of _____ 19____ made and signed this certificate.

_____
_____
_____
_____
_____

State of New York, County of _____ ss.:   INDIVIDUAL ACKNOWLEDGMENT

On this _____ day of _____ 19____, before me personally appeared _____
(Name of client)

to me known and known to me to be the individual described in, and who executed the foregoing certificate, and he thereupon duly acknowledged to me that he executed the same.

Figure 5.7
Samples of Common Variations in a Document
"Universal Version"

Lawyer should choose A, B, or C.

A. Married with Children.

$$\frac{(1)}{\text{(name of testator)}}$$

I, $\underline{\qquad \text{(2)} \qquad}$ residing and being domiciled
(same as 1)
in _____ County, New York, declare this to be my Will, and I revoke all other Wills and Codicils.

I am married to $\underline{\quad \text{(3)} \quad}$ and we have $\underline{\quad \text{(4)} \quad}$
(name of spouse)   (number of children)
children $\underline{\quad \text{(5)} \quad}$
(names of children)

B. Widow with Children.

$$\frac{(1)}{\text{(name of testator)}}$$

I, $\underline{\qquad \text{(2)} \qquad}$ residing and being domiciled
(same as 1)
in _____ County, New York, declare this to be my Will, and I revoke all other Wills and Codicils.

I am a widow and I have $\underline{\qquad \text{(3)} \qquad}$ children
(number of children)

$\underline{\qquad \text{(4)} \qquad}$
(names of children)

C. Divorced with Children.

$$\frac{(1)}{\text{(name of testator)}}$$

I, $\underline{\qquad \text{(2)} \qquad}$ residing and being domiciled
(same as 1)
in _____ County, New York, declare this to be my Will, and I revoke all other Wills and Codicils.

I am divorced and I have $\underline{\qquad \text{(3)} \qquad}$ children
(number of children)

$\underline{\qquad \text{(4)} \qquad}$
(names of children)

122 EFFECTIVE UTILIZATION OF LEGAL ASSISTANTS

Figure 5.8
Sample Master Information
List (MIL) Questionnaire

1.01 Decedent's name as shown on Will _____
1.02 Decedent's full name _____
1.03 Other names by which known _____
_____
1.04 Date of Decedent's death _____
1.05 Place of death:
    A. Address _____
    B. City _____ C. County _____ D. State _____
1.06 Decedent's age at death _____
1.07 Date of Decedent's birth _____
1.08 Place of birth:
    A. City _____ B. County _____ C. State _____ D. Zip _____
1.09 Decedent's residence domicile at death:
    A. Street _____ B. City _____
    C. County _____ D. State _____ E. Zip _____
1.10 Date on which above domicile was established _____
1.11 Date on which current New York domicile was established _____
1.12 Cause of Decedent's death _____
1.13 Length of Decedent's last illness _____
1.14 Decedent's Physicians:

	(A)	B	C
Name	_____	_____	_____
Address	_____	_____	_____
City, State, Zip	_____	_____	_____
Dates/Service	_____	_____	_____

1.15 Decedent's hospital confinements during last 3 years:

	(A)	(B)	(C)
A. Name of Hospital	_____	_____	_____
B. Address	_____	_____	_____
C. City, State, Zip	_____	_____	_____
D. Dates/Service	_____	_____	_____

Figure 5.9
Sample Master Information List (MIL) Questionnaire

3.2 Articles

MIL 101 Name of corporation _____

MIL 102 Alternate corporate name _____

MIL 103 Address of principal place of business

    (include Zip Code) _____

    _____ County: _____

MIL 104 Primary purposes (Article 2(a)) To engage in the business of

_____

_____

_____

MIL 105 Special restrictions in purposes, if any _____

_____

_____

MIL 106 Corporate powers

    Use standard powers provision _____ Yes _____ No

    If no, what limitations _____

_____

MIL 107 Street address of initial registered office

    _____
    (Street Address)

(City)　　　　　　(County)　　　　　　(Zip Code)

Figure 5.10
Sample Letter With MIL Reference Numbers

MIL Letter 10.01

(Today's Date)

MIL 1.02; MIL 1.05

RE: Estate Planning

Dear MIL 1.02

Pursuant to our telephone conversation today, I mentioned that it is the policy of our firm to request clients to complete an estate planning form in preparation for our forthcoming meeting.

You will find our form entitled "Financial Profile" enclosed herewith. Please note that our form also contains plans for inserting the names and addresses of your distributees (relatives required by law to receive notice that your will has been submitted to court to be probated) as well as your desires as to how your estate should be distributed (dispositive objectives).

The information contained in your "Profile" will be kept confidential. Unless you indicate to the contrary, your Profile will be reviewed initially by a trained paralegal in our estate planning department who will thereafter call you should questions arise requiring clarification. As soon as you complete and return this form and we complete our review of same, my secretary will call you to arrange an appointment.

This procedure is intended to save time so that I will be fully informed about your finances as well as your objectives when we meet to discuss the specifics of your plan.

We encourage the presence of your wife/husband at our meeting should that be your desire. (Optional)

Our professional charges are based upon time spent on your matter at the rate of $150 per hour for my time, $100 per hour for an associate's time and $65 per hour for time spent by a paralegal. A portion of our fee may qualify as an allowable income tax deduction in which case we shall advise you accordingly.

It will be our pleasure to provide this very important legal service to you and I look forward to our meeting.

We appreciate your confidence in permitting us to be of service to you and your family.

Very truly yours,

(Name of lawyer)
Lawyer's initials/Secretary's initials)
Enclosures

NOTE TO SUPPORT STAFF: Enclosure is Confidential Estate Planning Questionnaire, found in Form File 75-0032. Please attach to this letter.

Figure 5.11
Sample Letter With MIL Reference Numbers

MIL Letter 10.05

State of Arkansas
Department of Finance
  and Administration
Franchise Tax
Post Office Box 1272 FT
Little Rock, Arkansas 72203

       Re: MIL 101

Gentlemen:

    Enclosed is the completed Corporation Franchise Tax Report and payment of the tax for the above corporation.

    Please mail the receipt to this office in the enclosed self-addressed envelope.

                                     Yours truly,

                                     FOR THE FIRM

Figure 5.12
Sample Letter With MIL Reference Numbers

MIL Letter 10.01

Secretary of State's Office
Corporation Division
State Capitol Building
Little Rock, Arkansas 72201

     Re: Availability of corporation name

Gentlemen:

  Would you please advise us whether the following corporate name is available for use: _____ MIL 101 _____ or, alternatively, should this name note be available, the name: _____ MIL 102 _____.

  The corporation is being formed to engage in the business of _____ MIL 104 _____.

  The corporation's principal place of business will be MIL 103 _____

_____

  Thank you in advance for your prompt attention and cooperation in this matter.

              Very truly yours,

              FOR THE FIRM

How to Increase Your Law Office Profits 127

Figure 5.13
Sample Pre-prepared Standard Form
With MIL Reference Numbers

Form **5300** (Rev. August 1979) Department of the Treasury Internal Revenue Service	**Application for** **Determination for Defined Benefit Plan** For Pension Plans Other Than Money Purchase Plans (Under sections 401(a), 414(j) and 501(a) of the Internal Revenue Code)	For IRS Use Only File folder number ▶ **MIL Form 20.08**

▶ **Church and Governmental Plans.**—All items need not be completed. See instruction B. "What to File."

▶ Please complete every item on this form. If an item does not apply, enter N/A. (Get information from file)

1 (a) Name, address and ZIP code of employer
    MIL 1.02
    MIL 1.05
    Telephone number ▶ ( )

(b) Name, address and ZIP code of plan administrator, if other than employer

2 Employer's identification number

3 Business code number

4 Date incorporated or business began

5 Employer's tax year ends

(c) Administrator's identification number ▶   Telephone number ▶ ( )
(d) Name, address and phone number of person to be contacted if more information is needed:
    Name ▶   Telephone number ▶ ( )
    Address ▶

6 Determination requested for:
(a) (i) ☐ Initial qualification—date plan adopted ▶ .... (ii) ☐ Amendment—date adopted ▶ ....
    (iii) If (ii) is checked, enter file folder number ▶
(b) Were employees who are interested parties given the required notification of the filing of this application? . ☐ Yes ☐ No
(c) If this application involves a merger or consolidation with another plan, enter the employer identification number(s) and the plan number(s) of such other plan(s) ▶

7 Type of entity:
(a) ☐ Corporation   (b) ☐ Subchapter S corporation   (c) ☐ Sole proprietor   (d) ☐ Partnership
(e) ☐ Tax exempt organization   (f) ☐ Church   (g) ☐ Governmental organization
(h) ☐ Other (specify) ▶

8 (a) Name of Plan
(b) Plan number ▶
(c) Plan year ends ▶
(d) Is this a Keogh (H.R. 10) plan? . . . . ☐ Yes ☐ No
(e) If "Yes," is an owner employee in the plan? ☐ Yes ☐ No

9 (a) If this is an adoption of a district approved pattern plan, enter name of such plan   (b) Notification letter number

10 (a) Type of plan: (i) ☐ Fixed benefit
(ii) ☐ Unit benefit   (iii) ☐ Flat benefit
(iv) ☐ Other (specify) ▶
(b) Does plan provide for variable benefits? ☐ Yes ☐ No
If "Yes," check appropriate box to indicate type.
(i) ☐ Cost of living   (ii) ☐ Asset fluctuation
(iii) ☐ Other (specify) ▶
(c) Is this a defined benefit plan covered under the Pension Benefit Guaranty Corporation termination insurance program? . . . . ☐ Yes ☐ No ☐ Not determined

11 Effective date of plan   **12** Effective date of amendment   **13** Date plan was communicated to employees ▶
How communicated ▶

14 (a) Indicate the general eligibility requirements for participation under the plan and indicate the section and page number of plan or trust where each provision is contained:
(i) ☐ All employees   (v) Length of service (number of years) ▶
(ii) ☐ Hourly rate employee only   (vi) Minimum age (specify) ▶
(iii) ☐ Salaried employee only   (vii) Maximum age (specify) ▶
(iv) ☐ Other job class (specify) ▶   (viii) Minimum pay (specify) ▶
    Section and page number *   FOR IRS USE ONLY
(b) Are the eligibility requirements the same for future employees? . . . . ☐ Yes ☐ No
If "No," explain ▶
(c) Does the plan recognize service only with this employer? . . . . . ☐ Yes ☐ No
If "No," explain ▶

* Of plan or trust or other document constituting the plan.

Under penalties of perjury, I declare that I have examined this application, including accompanying statements, and to the best of my knowledge and belief it is true, correct and complete.

Signature ▶   Title ▶   Date ▶

203-478-1   Form **5300** (Rev. 8)

Figure 5.14
Sample Pre-prepared Standard Form
With MIL Reference Numbers

X 74—Certificate of Conducting Business as Partners. Individual — Corporation.   COPYRIGHT 1973 BY JULIUS BLUMBERG, INC., LAW BLANK PUBLISHERS

MIL Form 24.01

Business Certificate for Partners

The undersigned do hereby certify that they are conducting or transacting business as members of a partnership under the name or designation of   MIL 101

at   MIL 105
in the County of   MIL 105   , State of New York, and do further certify that the full names of all the persons conducting or transacting such partnership including the full names of all the partners with the residence address of each such person, and the age of any who may be infants, are as follows:

NAME Specify which are infants and state ages.   RESIDENCE

MIL 200   MIL 201
MIL 300   MIL 301

WE DO FURTHER CERTIFY that we are the successors in interest to   MIL 400

the person or persons heretofore using such name or names to carry on or conduct or transact business.

In Witness Whereof, We have this   day of   19   made and signed this certificate.

State of New York, County of   ss.:   INDIVIDUAL ACKNOWLEDGMENT

On this   day of   19   , before me personally appeared
MIL 200; MIL 300
to me known and known to me to be the individual   described in, and who executed the foregoing certificate, and   he   thereupon   duly acknowledged to me that   he   executed the same.

Figure 5.15
Samples of Common Variations in a Document
"MIL Version"

Lawyer should choose A, B, or C.

A. Married with Children.

                      __MIL 1.01__

I, _____MIL 1.01_____ residing and being domiciled in __MIL 1.09__ County, New York, declare this to be my Will, and I revoke all other Wills and Codicils.

I am married to _____MIL 2.01_____ and we have __MIL 3.01__ children _____MIL 3.11; 3.12; 3.13_____

B. Widow with Children.

                      __MIL 1.01__

I, _____MIL 1.09_____ residing and being domiciled in __MIL 1.09__ County, New York, declare this to be my Will, and I revoke all other Wills and Codicils.

I am a widow and I have _____MIL 3.01_____ children _____MIL 3.11; 3.12_____

C. Divorced with Children.

                      __MIL 1.01__

I, _____MIL 1.09_____ residing and being domiciled in __MIL 1.09__ County, New York, declare this to be my Will, and I revoke all other Wills and Codicils.

I am divorced and I have _____MIL 3.01_____ children _____MIL 3.11; 3.12_____

Figure 5.16
Sample Procedural Outline and Checklist

Name of Corporation (MIL 101): _____

Attorney: _____ Date: _____

Legend: CC = Corporation Clerk, M II = Typist, BC = Billing Clerk, SS = Secretary of State

4.2 Articles and Other Initial Steps.

	Yes/No	Procedure	Person	Date Due	Date Done
1.	YES	Open File	CC		
2.	___Yes ___No	Check name (MIL 101) with SS (5.12)	CC		
3.	___Yes ___No	Reserve name with SS (5.13, 5.14)	CC, M II		
4.	___Yes ___No	Prepare Pre-Incorporation Agreement (5.32)	M II		
5.	YES	Prepare Articles of Incorporation (See MIL 3.2) and Affidavit (5.28)	M II		
6.	YES	Have Articles signed	CC	MIL 114	
7.	YES	File Articles w/ SS and County Clerk (if not Pulaski) ___Regular (5.24, 5.25) ___To be qualified in another state (5.26)	CC	MIL 115	
8.	___Yes ___No	Prepare letter to CT System re: reg'd agent (5.27)	CC, M II	MIL 115	
9.	___Yes ___No	Order minute book (See 5.31)	CC	MIL 115	
10.	___Yes ___No	Prepare and file Sub-S elections (9.12–9.15)	CC	NLT MIL 115 + 30 days	
11.	___Yes ___No	Prepare and file request for IRS EIN (10.11)	CC		

[¶512] USING SYSTEMS AND PARALEGALS PROFITABLY IN YOUR FIRM

With the job descriptions, office manual of general procedures, and individualized systems binders for practice in specialized areas of law, you have the basic framework that will permit you to utilize paralegals most effectively, and make your practice more efficient and profitable.

Bringing life to this framework—in *your* practice—involves determining who can do what tasks. In Chapters 6-10 we will be reviewing the skills and capabilities that paralegals have successfully demonstrated.

Each office is different, in the work that it must produce and in the individual capabilities of staff members. With new employees, and new systems of operation, it naturally takes a bit of time before everything settles into place.

The systems pretty much guarantee that procedures *will* settle into place eventually. In order to set up the system in the first place you need some idea of who should do what jobs. Chapters 6-10 will focus in on the tremendous contributions you may expect from paralegals.

6

Utilizing the Estates and Trusts Paralegal

**[¶601]   BENEFITS OF USING PARALEGALS
         IN ESTATE PLANNING AND ADMINISTRATION**

Lawyers practicing in the estate area have used legal assistants for many years. Paralegals seem especially well-suited to this branch of the law due to the myriad of forms required to be processed in the course of the administration of the estate, and the subsequent ability to systematize the various stages of this process. Premortem estate planning is a newer area for the utilization of legal assistants, and all parties—the attorney, paralegal and client—have greatly profited through the utilization of legal assistants in the estate planning process.

In converting your office procedures over to the systems approach, there is one important and immediate two-faceted goal: assuring greatest ease of conversion, and tailoring your new system to complement the methods you currently find comfortable—as far as efficiency and economy permit.

Utilizing the Estates and Trusts Paralegal

In Chapter 5 you have the method; in your current practice you have the content; in the upcoming chapters you'll find a plethora of material that will help you work paralegals into the plan—so that they may benefit your firm.

[¶601.1] What Kinds of Work are Paralegals Capable of— and Permitted to Do—in Estate Planning and Probate Administration?

Back in Chapter 2 (¶203.2) you had a look at a standard paralegal training curriculum. That is one bank of potential skills and capabilities you might reasonably anticipate from paralegals. The list that follows is a task inventory prepared by Portland Community College.[1] It expresses quite precisely the work which that school expects its graduates to perform.

Following the task inventory below, you'll find discussions, checklists, forms, and other material—all of which taken together, and selectively integrated with your current procedures should put you well on your way to systematizing your estate work.

Figure 6.1
Task Inventory for Estate Planning, Probate, Estate Administration and Conservatorship

Handling Estate Planning—

- ☐ Collect and compile personal data needed to handle estates
- ☐ Evaluate data needed to write legal and correct will(s)
- ☐ Write will(s)
- ☐ Collect and compile information for trust agreement
- ☐ Write legal and correct trust agreement
- ☐ Transfer assets to a Trust
- ☐ Write specific Power of Attorney Document

---

[1] We gratefully acknowledge the permission of Harold C. Hart, Lead Instructor, Legal Assistant Program, to publish the task inventory designed at Portland Community College.

Probating Decedent's Estate—

- ☐ Compile personal data of decedent
- ☐ Determine whether probate necessary from personal data
- ☐ Evaluate data to develop a petition for probate
- ☐ Document legal petition for probate
- ☐ Write affidavit of minutes to the will
- ☐ Document bond for estate executor
- ☐ Write text of court order to admit will to probate
- ☐ Compile information for heirs
- ☐ Write a Note to Interested Persons
- ☐ Arrange required publishing of death notice with newspaper
- ☐ Locate and inform heirs of the death and arrange required actions
- ☐ Locate and establish control of estate assets
- ☐ Appraise value of estate assets
- ☐ Document assets and their value
- ☐ Pay off liens and/or court judgments against the estate
- ☐ Determine necessity of ancillary probate
- ☐ Write documents required for ancillary probate
- ☐ Pay or reject claims against the estate
- ☐ Compile needed data and write out income tax return
- ☐ Write out fiduciary tax returns
- ☐ Prepare Federal estate tax returns
- ☐ Request final audit in writing
- ☐ Apply for release of assets
- ☐ Administer checking account
- ☐ Estimate total cash needed to close the estate
- ☐ Advise heirs and devises of the status of the estate
- ☐ Accomplish a final accounting for the estate
- ☐ Write a Notice of Final Accounting
- ☐ Write court order approving the Final Accounting
- ☐ Arrange transfer of assets to heirs
- ☐ Prepare receipts

Utilizing the Estates and Trusts Paralegal

- ☐ Assemble information for Supplemental Final Accounting
- ☐ Prepare Supplemental Final Accounting
- ☐ Compile and write court order to close estate
- ☐ File Claim against estate
- ☐ File Objection to Final Accounting

Handling Conservatorships—

- ☐ Collect and organize data needed to set up conservatorship
- ☐ Compile petition for appointment of conservator
- ☐ Prepare Order for Citation
- ☐ Prepare Citation
- ☐ Prepare Acceptance of Service of Citation and Waiver
- ☐ Write document needed to place Conservator under jurisdiction of the court
- ☐ Write court order appointing Conservator
- ☐ Document Inventory of assets under Conservatorship
- ☐ Administer conservator checking account
- ☐ Provide annual accounting for conservatorship
- ☐ Compile tax returns affected by conservatorship
- ☐ Write court order approving annual accounting
- ☐ Compile conservatorship final accounting
- ☐ Write court order approving conservatorship final accounting and direct distribution
- ☐ Fill out conservatorship direct distribution receipt
- ☐ Write court order closing conservatorship
- ☐ Prepare conservator's petition for sale of real property
- ☐ Prepare and serve citation for sale
- ☐ Write court order to sell real property under conservatorship
- ☐ Write conservator's petition for sale of personal property
- ☐ Write court order to sell personal property under conservatorship

[¶602] INTEGRATING YOUR PARALEGAL INTO ESTATE PLANNING WORK

After your secretary has set up an appointment with your client, send a fact sheet similar to that below to the client. This alerts him generally to the type of information which your office must have to plan his estate adequately, as well as confirms his appointment for a scheduled meeting. The fact sheet below also serves to divide the estate planner from the Will draftsman. The former seeks to learn all pertinent information for devising an effective estate plan, while the latter inquires into the dispositive wishes of his client. Paralegals can do both, though they will probably not devise the actual estate plan.

Utilizing the Estates and Trusts Paralegal

[¶602.1] Inventory and Fact Sheet
for Efficient Estate Planning

PRELIMINARY INVENTORY QUESTIONNAIRE

FAMILY DATA

1. **Name**   Date of Birth   Health   Insurable
   Husband
   Wife

2. **Residence**
   Home address
   Business address
   Present main residence -- State
   Period of residence in present State
   If less than 10 years, list prior residences:

   Any other residence or place which may be considered a residence or domicile, such as apartment or house maintained elsewhere, including summer house, voting address, church membership, club membership, etc., in other state?

3. **Citizenship**
   Husband: USA ( )   Other ( )
   Wife: USA ( )   Other ( )

4. **Children and grandchildren**
   Name   Date of Birth   Married   Number of Children   Occupation*

   *Source of livelihood of married daughter, occupation of husband.

5. **Other dependents**
   Name   Date of Birth   Relationship

6. **Special family problems**
   Previous marriages and commitments therefrom (copy of decree and settlement papers)

   Prospective inheritances

ASSETS

Estimate the value of each of the following items of property owned by you and your wife (if any) and indicate if jointly owned.

		OWNED BY	
	Husband	Wife	Jointly
A. Cash and accounts	$	$	$
B. Notes, accounts receivable, mortgages			
C. Bonds			
D. Stock			
E. Real estate:			
F. Employee benefits (bring in last statement and descriptive booklets)			
G. Stock options:			
Number of shares			
Option price			
Current value			
H. Insurance (bring policies)			
I. Personal effects			
J. Miscellaneous property (patents, trademarks, copyrights, royalties, etc.)			
K. Business interests (bring in last balance sheet and P & L statement, tax returns, buy-sell agreements, etc.)			

LIABILITIES

A. Real estate mortgages			
B. Notes to banks			
C. Loans on insurance policies			
D. Accounts to others			
E. Pledges to churches and charities			
F. Taxes			

Utilizing the Estates and Trusts Paralegal

CHECKLIST OF DOCUMENTS AND OTHER INFORMATION NEEDED

		Delivered	Returned
1) Birth certificate -- yours, spouse's, children's	1		
2) Social Security No. .... Marriage certificate	2		
3) Deeds to realty	3		
4) Leases on property on which you are the lessor or lessee	4		
5) Partnership agreements	5		
6) Business agreement between yourself and associates	6		
7) Purchase & sale contracts	7		
8) Close corporation charters, by-laws & minute books	8		
9) Balance sheets & profit & loss statements for last 5 years, in all businesses in which you have a proprietary interest	9		
10) Personal balance sheets and income statements for last 5 years, if any were made	10		
11) Divorce decrees	11		
12) Property settlements with spouse antenuptial agreements	12		
13) Trust instruments	13		
14) Your will Spouse's will Will of other members of family, if pertinent	14		
15) Instruments creating power of appointment of which you are donee or donor	15		
16) Life insurance policies & dividend data	16		
17) General insurance policies	17		
18) Copies of employment contracts, pension benefits, etc.	18		
19) Other legal documents evidencing possible or actual rights and/or liabilities	19		
20) Income tax returns, federal & state, for past five years	20		
21) Gift tax returns and copies of revenue agent's reports if any	21		
22) Veterans service records	22		

ADVISORS

	Name	Address	Phone No.
Attorney			
Accountant			
Trust Officer			
Other bank officer			
Life Insurance Underwriter			
Investment Advisor			
Stock Broker utilized by client			
Tax Advisor			
General Insurance Broker			
Others			

COMPREHENSIVE INVENTORY QUESTIONNAIRE

Schedule A
CASH AND BANK BALANCES

	Bank	Average Balance			
		Self	Wife	Joint	Total
Cash		$	$	$	$
Checking Accounts					
Savings Accounts					
Total:		$	$	$	$

Schedule B
NOTES, ACCOUNTS RECEIVABLE, MORTGAGES

Debtor	Nature of Debt	Security	Maturity	Yield	Face Amount	Present Value
1.					$	$
2.						
3.						
Total:					$	$

Schedule C
BOND HOLDINGS

Description of Bonds	Ownership	Number of Units	Face Value	Cost	Annual Yield	Current Value
			$	$		$

Government Bonds	Ownership	Maturity	Annual Yield		Death Beneficiary	Face Value
Total Bond Value:						$

Schedule D
STOCKS HELD

Description	Ownership	Number of Shares	Cost	Annual Yield	Current Value
			$	$	$
Total:			$	$	$

Schedule E

REAL ESTATE

	Property #1	Property #2	Property #3	Property #4
Description				
Location				
Residence?				
Income Producing?				
Owned in Names of:				
Form of Ownership				
% of Cost Contributed by Joint Owners				
Date of Acquisition				
Year Joint Ownership Created				
How Acquired (Gift, Purchase, etc.)				
Cost Basis				
Names & Addresses of mortgagees, lienors, etc.				
Encumbrances: Amount				
Monthly Payments				
Annual Income (gross)				
Average Annual Interest				
Annual Depreciation				
Annual Costs (Maintenance, etc.)				
Annual Taxes				
Annual Net Income				
Present Taxable Value				

Schedule F

EMPLOYEE BENEFITS

Employer's Name and Address ....

Type of Plan (Obtain copies of Plans)	Check if Applicable	Retirement Benefits	Amount Vested	Death Benefits
Pension		$	$	$
Profit-Sharing				
Savings				
Deferred Compensation				
Total:		$	$	$

	Company	Benefits	Beneficiary
Group Insurance			
Accident & Health			
Medical			
Surgical			
Hospital			

Stock Options: Number of shares now (........); later (........) list conditions of additional options becoming exercisable ....
Give: Option price $ .... ; Current Value $ ....
Unrealized Appreciation $ _____

Schedule G

MISCELLANEOUS ASSETS

A. <u>Personal Effects</u>   Current Value
     Home furnishings $ ....
     Automobiles   ....
     Jewels & furs   ....
     Collections (art, etc.)   ....
     Miscellaneous personal effects   ....

B. <u>Intellectual Property</u>   Annual Income   Expiration   Current Value
     Patents $ .... $ ....
     Trade-marks   ....
     Copyrights   ....

C. <u>Other Contract Rights</u>: Give details of prospective profits, liabilities and values involved
....

Total Value of Miscellaneous Assets $ ....

Schedule H

BUSINESS INTERESTS

| Co. Name .... | Address .... |
| Corp. .... Part. .... Sole Prop. .... | State Inc. or Law .... |

Partners or Stockholders Name	Age	Stock P'f'd. Com.	% Partner Int.	Title	Notes

Is There a Business Agreement? (give details or secure copy)
Is Partner Financially Responsible?
Type: Criss Cross ☐
       Partnership Entity ☐
       Stock Retirement ☐
How Is Value Determined?

Date Last Reviewed
How Funded?
Amount of Funding
Any § 303 IRC Stock Redemption Planned?

Corporate Trustee

Is Life Insurance Carried	Insured	Amount	Owner	Beneficiary
Purpose		$		

Capitalization:	Par Value	Div. or Interest Rate	Total Authorized	Total Issued	Callable
Common Stock	$				
Preferred					
Debentures, etc.					

Owner's estimate of value   Liquidation value
Book value as of
Is good will included in book value?
Average net earnings (after taxes), last 3 to 5 years
(Secure balance sheets and earning statements)

Checklist of Business Information

(1) List names, ages, and duties of "key men"

(2) In event of your death, or of any "key man," would there be difficulty in (a) continuing to receive credit? (b) continuing franchise?

(3) In event of your death would it be more desirable to conserve the business or to liquidate the business?
   (a) Does your family have the ability to continue it?

(4) Which associates or employees might like to purchase your interest at your death or retirement (even if they are not in a financial position to do so)?
   (a) Are you grooming replacements for yourself and other key men?

(5) Would you like to dispose of your business during your lifetime -- e.g., near the retirement age?

(6) Do you have any benefit, security, or incentive plans for your employees?
   Have you considered such plans?

(7) Have you a business agreement which governs the disposition of the interest of any associate who dies?

Schedule I

PERSONAL LIABILITIES

Bills and accounts payable	$	Installment contracts	$ ....
Loans and Notes		Joint notes	....
Bank	....	Notes endorsed	....
Insurance	....	Accounts guaranteed	....
Brokers	....	Realty taxes	....
To others	....	Personal property taxes	....
Mortgages	....	Disputed or past due taxes	....
Current income tax-estimates	....	Unsettled damage claims	....
Rent on unexpired leases	....	Miscellaneous	....
Total			$ ....

Schedule J

INCOME DATA

Income sources	Self	Wife	Others
	$	$	$
Salary			
Bonuses			
Commissions			
Dividends			
Interest			
Net Rents			
Royalties			
Business profits			
Annuities			
Trusts			
Other			
Total:	$	$	$

For Last 5 Years	1	2	3	4	5
Total family income	$	$	$	$	$
Total tax					
Living expenses					
Insurance premiums					
Available for other savings					
Top income tax bracket	%	%	%	%	%

Notes: 1. Obtain copy of income tax returns.
2. Identify all items of community property income if you live in a community property state.

WILLS, GIFTS, TRUSTS

WILLS — Get copies of wills of all family members. Review pertinent data on present and future will plans including the following: Specific Bequests; Specific Devised; Disposition of Residuary Estate; Tax Apportionment; Marital Deduction Provisions; Survivorship Presumptions Created; Trusts; Nomination of Executors, Guardians & Successors; Authority of Executor to Continue Business.

GIFTS — Obtain pertinent data on gifts previously made including the following information: Date; Donated Property; Donee; Value of Time of Gift; Present Value; Donor's Cost Basis; Has a Gift Tax Return Been Filed?; Have Tax Authorities Examined Returns?; Circumstances & Reason for Gift; Has Donor Retained Control?; Remaining Unused Lifetime Exemptions Under Federal & State Laws; Are Further Gifts Under Consideration? (Obtain copies of gift tax returns and any Revenue Agent's Reports.)

TRUSTS — For EACH trust, obtain copy and pertinent data including: Trustee; Date Created; Purpose; Revocable or Not (if revocable, how?); Nature of Corpus; Value of Corpus; Corpus Income; Beneficiaries; Gift Over; How are Income & Principal to be Distributed; Term of Trust.

POWER OF APPOINTMENT — If any member of the family group has the right to dispose of property not owned by him or her, be such right during lifetime or by will, details should be given and copies of instruments creating such right should be attached and the approximate value of the property given.

INTEREST IN ESTATE — Obtain copies of any instruments and pertinent data including: Is estate owner beneficiary of outright will? Trust? Does he have a life interest? A contingent interest? Value of interest $........... Estimated income $.......... Disposition if he dies before receipt? Is he a grantee of a power to appoint outside of expected class? Right of withdrawal? Portion of amount? When? Restricted? Value of property subject to right $.......? Year grantor deceased? Trust created before 10/21/42?

OBJECTIVES

I. Death or Disability:
   a) What are your spouse's minimum income requirements?
   b) What income would you want her to have if possible?
   c) What is the minimum income required for your family until all the children are no longer dependent?
   d) Will any child be dependent after attaining maturity? Give details.
   e) To what degree is wife capable of managing financial affairs?
   f) Will wife continue to live in present home?
   g) Should mortgage be paid off?
   h) Social Security status?
   i) Should she be protected against: 1--possible senility,   2--possible second husband,   3--her caprices,   4--anything else?

II. Retirement:
   a) At what age do you wish to retire?
   b) What is the minimum income you need for retirement?
   c) What income would you consider ample during retirement?
   d) Do you want excess of income over your minimum needs to go to your children, or to you?
   e) What are your investment objectives? Growth? Income? Safety?

III. Children:
   a) What are your hopes for your children and what are their capabilities?
   b) Shall your children be permitted to consume capital or only income?
   c) When and how should capital be distributed?
   d) Should any special problems be considered and special allowances made, as for example, for physical defects, personality, ability, etc.?
   e) What educational and business opportunities do you wish them to be provided for, if possible?

Schedule K

EDUCATIONAL FUNDS

Children	Preparatory Date	Preparatory Amount	College Date	College Amount	Professional Date	Professional Amount
		$		$		$
Total:		$		$		$

IV. Gifts:
   1) Do you have any plans for gifts to your relatives or others during your lifetime? If so, give details.

V. Charity:
   1) To which charities do you contribute regularly and how much per annum?
   2) Which charities would you like to provide for, how much, and in what manner?

NOTES ON OBJECTIVES

Schedule M

ASSETS

		CLIENT	Check Box If Jointly Owned		SPOUSE	Check Box If Jointly Owned	
			w/SPS	w/Other		w/Clt.	w/Other
A.	Cash and accounts:						
1.	Cash in banks regular checking	$ _____	☐	☐	$ _____	☐	☐
2.	Deposits in banks savings and others	_____	☐	☐	_____	☐	☐
B.	Stocks:						
1.	Stocks, liquid	_____	☐	☐	_____	☐	☐
2.	Stocks, illiquid	_____	☐	☐	_____	☐	☐
C.	Bonds:						
1.	U.S. Govt. Bonds......	_____	☐	☐	_____	☐	☐
2.	Other bonds..........	_____	☐	☐	_____	☐	☐
D.	Real estate:						
1.	Residential	_____	☐	☐	_____	☐	☐
2.	Unimproved..........	_____	☐	☐	_____	☐	☐
3.	Income producing.....	_____	☐	☐	_____	☐	☐
E.	Receivables:						
1.	Notes...............	_____	☐	☐	_____	☐	☐
2.	Mortgages...........	_____	☐	☐	_____	☐	☐
F.	Personalty:						
1.	Autos, boats, etc.	_____	☐	☐	_____	☐	☐
2.	Jewelry and furs	_____	☐	☐	_____	☐	☐
3.	Objects of art	_____	☐	☐	_____	☐	☐
4.	Furniture and household effects	_____	☐	☐	_____	☐	☐
5.	Apparel and personal effects	_____	☐	☐	_____	☐	☐
G.	Business interests:						
1.	Proprietorships.......	_____	☐	☐	_____	☐	☐
2.	Copartnerships	_____	☐	☐	_____	☐	☐
3.	Close corporations.....	_____	☐	☐	_____	☐	☐
H.	Shares in trust funds:	_____	☐	☐	_____	☐	☐
	<u>Total</u>	$ _____			$ _____		

Utilizing the Estates and Trusts Paralegal

Schedule M (cont'd)

Total Carried Forward:

		CLIENT	SPOUSE
		$ _____ Check Box of Beneficiary — SPS / Est. / Other	$ _____ Check Box of Beneficiary — SPS / Est. / Other
I.	Insurance and annuities:		
	1. Ordinary life	_____ ☐ ☐ ☐	_____ ☐ ☐ ☐
	2. Group life	_____ ☐ ☐ ☐	_____ ☐ ☐ ☐
	3. Endowment	_____ ☐ ☐ ☐	_____ ☐ ☐ ☐
	4. Annuities	_____ ☐ ☐ ☐	_____ ☐ ☐ ☐
J.	Corporate benefits:		
	1. Pension	_____ ☐ ☐ ☐	_____ ☐ ☐ ☐
	2. Profit Sharing	_____ ☐ ☐ ☐	_____ ☐ ☐ ☐
	3. Deferred Comp	_____ ☐ ☐ ☐	_____ ☐ ☐ ☐
	4. Stock Bonus	_____ ☐ ☐ ☐	_____ ☐ ☐ ☐
	TOTAL ASSETS (owned).	$ _____	$ _____

LIABILITIES

		CLIENT — Check Box If Jointly Owned w/SPS / w/Other	SPOUSE — Check Box If Jointly Owned w/Clt. / w/Other
A.	Real Estate Mortgages	$ _____ ☐ ☐	$ _____ ☐ ☐
B.	Notes to Banks	_____ ☐ ☐	_____ ☐ ☐
C.	Loans on Insurance Policies	_____ ☐ ☐	_____ ☐ ☐
D.	Accounts to Others	_____ ☐ ☐	_____ ☐ ☐
E.	Pledges to Churches and Charities	_____ ☐ ☐	_____ ☐ ☐
F.	Taxes	_____ ☐ ☐	_____ ☐ ☐
	TOTAL LIABILITIES (owned).	$ _____	$ _____

SUMMARY

Total Client's Assets .... $ _____
   Less Liabilities............................ _____
      Net Estate............................. $ _____

Total Spouse's Assets........................... $ _____
   Less Liabilities............................ _____
      Net Estate............................. $ _____

Schedule N

ESTATE INVENTORY SUMMARY

Assets & Liabilities of: _____

Item	Present Value	Amount Taxable	Availability for Liquidity	Cost Basis

Bank Accounts:
   Checking
   Saving

Bonds:

Stock:

Unrealized Stock Option Appreciation:

Real Estate:
   Residence
   Other: _____

Profit Sharing Plan:

Life Insurance:
   Permanent
   Group
   Cash value of insur. on: _____

Personal and Household:

Gross Estate Inventory
   Less Debts:

Net Estate Inventory

Schedule O

SUMMARY OF DISTRIBUTION OF PROPERTY

A. <u>Your Property</u>

    (1) <u>Passing by Will</u>

    (2) <u>Passing by Operation of Law</u>

    (3) <u>Passing by Contract</u>

B. <u>Mrs.   Property</u>

    (1) <u>Passing by Will</u>

    (2) <u>Passing by Operation of Law</u>

    (3) <u>Passing by Contract</u>

Schedule P

LIFE INSURANCE SUMMARY

Insurance on: _____   Owned by: _____

Present Age: _____   Health: _____   Present Agent: _____

Policy	#____	#____	#____	#____	Totals
1. Company					
2. Age at Issue					
3. Type of Policy					
4. Face Value					
5. Dividend Additions or Accumulations					
6. Terms Riders					
7. Total Death Value					
8. Net Premium					
9. Cash Value					
10. Policy Loans					
11. Primary Beneficiary					
12. Settlement Option					
13. Remainderman					
14. Secondary Beneficiary					
15. Settlement Option					
16. Remainderman					
17. Amount Qualified for Marital Deduction					
18. Notes					

Schedule R

LIQUIDITY CALCULATION

Assuming that _____ dies _____

Cash Requirements:

    Expenses $

    Debts

    Federal taxes

    State taxes

    Cash bequests

    Exercise stock options

    Capital gain on profit sharing plan

    Other: _____

    $ $

Cash Available:

    Government bonds $

    Bank accounts

    Insurance

    Listed stock

    Stock redemptions

    Other: _____

    $

Shortage $

Schedule S

NET DISTRIBUTION SUMMARY

Assuming that _____ dies _____

Transfers by ▶	Will	Operation of Law	Contract	Less Exps., Debts, Taxes	Total
Outright to:					
_____					
_____					
_____					
_____					
_____					
In Trust #__ for:					
_____					
_____					
In Trust #__ for:					
_____					
_____					
In Trust #__ for:					
_____					
_____					
Other Death Transfers to:					
_____					
_____					
_____					

Schedule T

NET INCOME SUMMARY

For: _____

Income on Invested Capital

    Savings accounts $

    Bonds

    Stock

    Real estate

    Annuities

    Other: _____

    _____

        Total $ $

Pensions

Deferred compensation

Social security

Wages

Other: _____

        Total income $

Less income tax

    Net _____ income $

Schedule W

RECAPITULATION OF ESTATE DATA

Name	Date
Address	Phone

-- ASSETS --

Form of Asset	See Schedule	Owned by Self			Owned by Others in Family		
		Original Cost	Present Value	Annual Income	Original Cost	Present Value	Annual Income
Cash & bank balances	A	$	$	$	$	$	$
Notes, accounts rec., mortgages	B						
Bonds	C						
Stocks	D						
Real estate	E						
Life insurance	P						
Employee benefits (vested)	F						
Business interests	H						
Miscellaneous assets	G						
Total Family Assets		$	$	$	$	$	$

-- LIABILITIES --

	Self	Others in Family
Total -- See Schedule I	$	$

Present Net Worth $............ $............

FUTURE INCREMENTS

	Self	Others in Family
Difference between cash and face value of life insurance	$............	$............
Prospective gifts and legacies	....	....
Death benefits under employee benefit plans	....	....
Total:	$............	$............
Probable Estate	$............	$............
	Self	Others in Family

Utilizing the Estates and Trusts Paralegal

Schedule W (cont'd)

INCOME AND EXPENSE ANALYSIS

	Self	Others in Family
Income:		
Annual earned income	$	$ ....
Annual investment income	....	....
Total Income:	$	$ ....
Expenses:		
Annual living expenses	$	$ ....
Income taxes	....	....
Insurance premiums	....	....
Total Expenses:	$	$ ....
Balance:		
Available for other savings or investments:	$	$

FUTURE INCOME

Annuity and insurance income	$ ....
Other investment income (per year)	....
Social Security (per year)	....
Company pension plan (per year)	....
Other employee benefits (per year)	....
Total Future Income:	$ ....

FUTURE INCOME REQUIREMENTS

At retirement age (per year)	$ ....
For family after death (per year)	....

CAPITAL NEEDED AT DEATH

Clean-up fund (see Schedule Q	$ ....
Education capital (see Schedule K)	....
Capital needed to meet income deficit, if any	....

Figure 6.2
Stock Data Form

Decedent:_____

No._____ B._____ STOCK

_____

B._____ shares of _____
(Name of Corporation)

_____ registered in the name_____ of _____
(Class of Stock) (State *exact* name(s))

_____, as _____, evidenced by the following certificates:
(How held)

No. Shares	Certif. No.	Date Issued	No. Shares	Certif. No.	Date Issued

_____Check if continued on separate sheet

Name and address of transfer agent: _____

_____

_____Value at date decease $_____ (Bid: $_____ Ask: $_____ Closing: $_____

_____Exchange listed on: _____

_____Accrued dividends at $_____ per share to stock of record on_____

Origin: Community:_____ Separate:_____ Other: _____
(Explain)

_____

If joint tenancy: Contribution by survivor _____

_____

PROCESSING GUIDE

Notification letter sent on_____ Transfer instructions received on_____

Documents needed:_____ Certif. copy letters_____ Consent_____ Stock assignment

_____Certif. copy death certif. _____Affidavit of domicile

Original shares received on_____ Documents sent on_____

New shares received on_____ Shares delivered to transferee on_____

NOTES

Utilizing the Estates and Trusts Paralegal

Figure 6.3
Bond Data Form

Decedent: _____

No. B. BOND

B. _____ _____
           (Type of bond and due date)

_____
(Name of corporation, etc.)

registered in the name(s) of _____

_____, evidenced by the following
(How held-exact)

certificates: Certif. No.   Amount   Date issued

                  _____ $ _____ _____

                  _____ $ _____ _____

                  _____ $ _____ _____

                  _____ $ _____ _____

_____ Check if continued on separate sheet

Name and address of transfer agent _____

_____

Value at date decease (per unit) $ _____ Bid $ _____ Ask $ _____

                                                                              Closing $ _____

Exchange listed on: _____

Accrued interest per unit to (Date:) _____ $ _____

Origin: Community: _____ Separate: _____ Other: (explain) _____

_____

If joint tenancy: Contribution by survivor: _____

_____

PROCESSING GUIDE

Notification letter sent on _____ Transfer instructions received on _____

Documents needed: _____ Certif. copy letters _____ Consent _____ Stock Assign.

                            _____ Certif. copy death certif. _____ Affidavit of domicile

Original bond(s) received on _____ Documents sent on _____

New bond(s) received on _____ Bond(s) delivered to transferee on _____

NOTES

Figure 6.4
Securities Valuation Form

Estate of _____

Prepared for _____
Prepared by _____

Date of Valuation _____

Shares or Principal Amount	Security Description	Symbol	Lo/Bid1	Hi/Ask2	Lo/Bid3	Hi/Ask4

Utilizing the Estates and Trusts Paralegal

Figure 6.5
Stock Notification Letter

(LETTERHEAD)

ATTENTION: STOCK TRANSFER AGENT

Gentlemen:

Subject: _____, Deceased.

Company_____

This firm represents _____ as

_____ Surviving joint tenant

_____ Executor of the will of the above named decedent

_____ Administrator of the estate of the above named decedent

Would you kindly furnish the data requested on the enclosed sheet and return it to us in the self-addressed envelope enclosed for your convenience.

All future dividends, notices or communications with respect to the securities, identified above and on the attached data sheet, should be sent to:

(Name and address)   (Soc. Sec. or ID No.)

If you do not maintain shareholder records for the above company, please forward this letter and data sheet to the proper company or transfer agent, with a copy of the transmittal letter to us for our file.

Your co-operation in this matter will be greatly appreciated.

Very truly yours,

Figure 6.6
Stock Inquiry Letter

— Stock Inquiry Letter

PLEASE COMPLETE THIS REQUEST FOR STOCK INFORMATION AND RETURN TO:

(LETTERHEAD)

To: Re:

                                                Date of Death:
                                                Social Security No.:

1. <u>Stock Data.</u> COMPANY:
   Shares registered in the name(s) of

No. of Shares	Certificate No.	Date Issued	Type of Share

2. <u>Verification of Above Information.</u> Is the above information correct as of _____ (date of death)?
   YES:____ NO: ____ If "No", please give details:_____
   _____

3. <u>Recent Stock Splits or Dividends.</u> Were there any that affect the number of shares reported above?
   YES: ____ NO: ____
   If "Yes", please give details _____
   _____

4. <u>Dividends Declared But Unpaid as of:</u>
   Were there any? YES: ____ NO: ____ If "Yes", please provide details_____
   _____ . _____

5. <u>Exchange on Which Listed.</u> (Please state) _____

6. <u>Transfer Requirements.</u> Please advise for transfer to
   _____ Surviving joint tenant
   _____ Heirs of decedent's estate

7. <u>Name and Address of Transfer Agent:</u> (Please state)
   Name:
   Address:

   _____
                                                (Name of Informant)
   Dated:_____   Title: _____

Utilizing the Estates and Trusts Paralegal

[¶602.2] Paralegals Can Compute Model Estate Taxation for Various Potential Occurrences

If this fact sheet is received prior to the initial client conference, and this is preferable, *the legal assistant can compute the federal and state estate taxes which would be currently due* if:

1. The husband died first.
2. The wife died first.
3. Both parties were to die simultaneously.

Armed with this arsenal of information, the attorney is ready for the initial interview with some concrete estate planning suggestions. If the client is unable to complete the fact sheet, the legal assistant can usher the client into the conference room prior to the initial meeting and obtain the missing data. This leaves the attorney with the most creative aspects of his legal training at hand. He is now the specialist. All the facts have been provided for him; the legal advice remains to be given.

[¶602.3] Completing the Estate Plan

After the initial conference, the attorney drafts a memo to the legal assistant entitled "Pending Estate Planning Work for Mr. & Mrs. X." The attorney checks off the information still needed to draft the estate plan that has been discussed with the clients. It's possible to put the chart supplied in ¶602.1 to use in doing this. For example, should a revocable or irrevocable insurance trust be desired, an excerpt from the checklist would appear as follows:

Ins. Policy	Type	Face Amt.	Date of Issue	Insured	Owner	Changes Desired	Date Completed	Initial
(Number and Company)						(For example,) Make the irrevocable trust the owner and beneficiary of the above policy		

This information is relayed to the attorney upon completion of the desired changes and a similar chart can be utilized for other phases of changes desired with respect to other aspects of the estate plan.

Utilization of the paralegal in this manner frees the attorney to do much of the creative analysis necessary in the estate planning field as previously mentioned, but of even greater importance is the fact that it enables him to produce a better product in less time than was previously possible at a lower cost to his client.

[¶603] PARALEGALS CAN PERFORM A GREAT DEAL OF WORK IN ESTATE ADMINISTRATION

While the use of paralegals in the estate planning area is somewhat novel, the use of legal assistants in estate administration is not. Indeed, many legal assistants may be better suited by temperament than the attorney for whom they work. In one case we know of, the daughter of a decedent client came into the office personally each month to deliver the rent monies. Her excuse was that she didn't trust the mails and used this ploy to come into town to do her shopping, etc. The attorneys were always sure to be "in conference" during her monthly visits, and it was the paralegal's "job" to hold her hand for two hours monthly while in the office.

[¶603.1] Liberating the Attorney to Practice Law

When an estate comes into the office, it is usually the attorney who greets the widow or other family members to express condolences. After that, though, the attorney is free to do other work while the legal assistant, who has been properly introduced, ascertains the information necessary to prepare the probate papers. The attorney returns to answer any legal questions the family has and to assure all those present that the office will handle estate affairs as expeditiously as possible. While the attorney is answering any questions, the probate papers are brought in for signature. With the institution of a systems approach as discussed in Chapter 5 the attorney may not see the client again until it becomes necessary to file the Federal Estate Tax Return, some nine months later. All of the client's interim contact will be with the legal assistant, who will have an "Estate Progress File" in her binder similar to that below:

Utilizing the Estates and Trusts Paralegal

[¶603.2] Estate Progress File

ESTATE OF _____
OFFICE FILE NO. _____

Date of Death _____
Domiciled at _____
*Family Members (Spouse, Children, Distributees) _____
_____
_____

Surrogates Court, County of _____
Probate No. _____ Tax I.D. No. _____
Decedent's Social Security No. _____
*Executors _____
_____

Letters Testamentary Issued On _____
*Trustees _____
_____

Letters of Trusteeship Issued On _____
*Accountant _____

*Bank _____

*Stockbroker _____

Item	Responsibility of Attorney	Paralegal	Initial
Probate Will		X	
Letters Testamentary or Administration		X	
Letters of Trusteeship		X	
Waiver of Fiduciary Commissions	X		
Order Certified Copy of Will		X	
Obtain additional Certificates of Letters		X	
Arrange for Safety Deposit Opening		X	
Apply for Tax I.D.#		X	
File Notice of Fiduciary Relationship, i.e., Form 56		X	
Residence (terminate lease, sell house, etc.)	X		
Transfer Cars		X	
Open Estate Checking Account		X	
Obtain Tax Waivers (even for items under $10,000 so that a complete record is available when preparing the 706, Federal Estate Tax Return)		X	
Ancillary Proceedings	X	X	
Foreign Tax Proceedings	X	X	

*Include address and telephone number

EFFECTIVE UTILIZATION OF LEGAL ASSISTANTS

Item	Responsibility of Attorney	Paralegal	Initial
Transfer Securities[2]		X	
Transfer Bank Accounts		X	
Apply for Social Security Death Benefit		X	
Apply for Veterans Benefit		X	
Determine Pension Benefits	X		
Collect all insurance benefits, both disability and medical payments		X	
Value securities as of date of death. Note on tickler to revalue six months from date of death, the alternate valuation date		X	
Life Insurance; File Claims: Obtain 712's and 938's		X	
Obtain decedent's checkbooks, savings accounts, income and gift tax returns, and brokerage statements		X	
Arrange Appraisals		X	
Pay Debts		X	
Close Charge Accounts and write all credit card companies for balance and closing of accounts		X	
Charitable Pledges	X	X	
Pay or deliver legacies to legatees	X	X	
Pay State Estate or Inheritance Tax and Apply for Extension		X	
Revalue on Alternate Valuation Date		X	
Rough out the 706		X	
Prepare the 706 in final form	X		
Prepare to Redeem Treasury Bonds in Payment of Estate Tax	X	X	
Consider election under IRC 6166	X		
Consider Redemption under IRC 303	X		
Consider whether expenses should be deducted on the 706 or 1041	X		
Recompute State Estate or Inheritance Tax Payment		X	
Arrange for Perpetual Care		X	
Choose Fiscal Year:			
Estate	X		
Trust(s)	X		
Pay Executor's Commissions and other administrative expenses		X	
Assemble income tax data for Accountant	X	X	
Check that final 1040 has been filed and gather data for 1041		X	
File 1041 (if it's a customary practice of your office, rather than having Accountant do so)	X	X	
State Tax Proceeding		X	
Final Accounting, Informal or Judicial	X	X	

---

[2] Suggested forms for effecting a transfer of securities is contained in Appendix F. These forms can be tailored to achieve a transfer of bank accounts as well.

[¶603.3]   Teamwork Triumphs

Using the "Estate Progress File" chart (¶603.2), the time an attorney spends on routine estate administration is absolutely minimal. Naturally, there is a direct correlation between the quality of the legal assistant and the amount of time the attorney will spend on administrative details. Nevertheless, the attorney knows that when the legal assistant has completed a specific task, her initials appear in the required column and that the attorney need not be further concerned with the matter. With a binder that holds only current estates, the attorney can pick it up at any moment and know the status of any estate in the office.

[¶604]   SUMMARY

With a totally systematized procedure, little room remains for human error. The subsequent reduction of fears of missed deadlines and dreaded malpractice suits is a luxury you can now afford, in fact it's no longer a luxury. You are free to do what you know best—practice law.

7
Utilizing the Litigation Paralegal

[¶701]   **INTRODUCTION**

Alexander Kerr, an attorney and administrator of the paralegal program at Pepper, Hamilton & Scheetz in Philadelphia, paid a great tribute to the paralegals in his litigation department in his recent remarks:[1]

> With paralegals we've been able to increase our practice and at the same time significantly reduce average billing rates for clients while still giving top flight representation. Paralegal research has significantly augmented our ability to win. With large litigation suits, it is often the side which is the best organized and best able to get the necessary information that wins the case. Our paralegals have helped put us in that position. I think specifically we've defeated many class action motions because of better utilization of paralegals.

---

[1] *National Law Journal*, February 19, 1979 at 39.

Utilizing the Litigation Paralegal

[¶701.1] Get Paralegals Involved Early in Each Case

The paralegal in a litigation case must be brought in at the very early stages of a case, so that when a "game plan" is determined, the legal assistant feels an important and integral part of the team. When the strategy of a case is discussed, which includes the filing of all important documents, many of which will be primarily drafted by the paralegal, the latter under the team approach is there to contribute important input as an integral member of the office staff.

All correspondence on a case should be routed through the paralegal for two reasons:

1. It permits the legal assistant to follow a case from beginning to completion and permits instant knowledge concerning any new developments.
2. The paralegal will see that the correspondence is properly filed and will bring it to the attention of the attorney in charge. Faster retrieval of important documentation is also accomplished.

[¶701.2] How Paralegals Help Make Preparing for Trial a Less-Pressured, More Manageable Endeavor

Although a paralegal's use is often determined by the lawyer's need and the legal assistant's training, certain basic tasks may be effectively prepared by a litigation paralegal. These include:

1. Abstracting witnesses' statements.
2. Document control and exhibits.
3. The searching of the records for conflicting testimony (statements).
4. Digesting of depositions.
5. Assembling cited cases, indexing them as well as indexing all documents involved in the order in which they will be argued at trial.
6. Shepardizing cases.
7. Helping in the preparation of the interrogatories, request for admissions, production of documents, etc.

8. Coaching witnesses who are to appear in a particular case, and conducting a dress rehearsal for the cast of characters appearing in a case.

[¶701.3] Paralegal Capabilities in Litigation Support

We refer you again back to the paralegal training program curriculum in Chapter 2 (¶203.3), for an alternative view of paralegals' litigation support capabilities. You might want to look into the training provided by paralegal schools in your own vicinity.

Additionally, the following task inventory is quite likely one of the most complete checklists of litigation support work appropriate for paralegals.[2]

Figure 7.1
Task Inventory for Paralegals
in Litigation Work

Handling Litigation Matters—

☐ Collect and organize data about a complaint
☐ Analyze complaint data and write a demand letter
☐ Document a legal complaint
☐ Compile a motion for court action regarding complaint
☐ Write legal demurrer objecting to legal basis of opposing party
☐ Collect information needed to answer a demurrer
☐ Analyze data and compile answer to demurrer
☐ Collect and organize data needed to reply to (answer demurrer)
☐ Write legal reply to (answer demurrer)
☐ Collect and organize data needed for motion
☐ Collect and organize data needed for interrogatories
☐ Write draft of Interrogatories for litigation
☐ Arrange for depositions needed in litigation

---

[2] We gratefully acknowledge the permission of Harold C. Hart, Lead Instructor, Legal Assistant Program, to publish the task inventory designed at Portland Community College.

Utilizing the Litigation Paralegal 171

Figure 7.1 (Cont'd)
Task Inventory for Paralegals
in Litigation Work

- ☐ Collect and organize data needed for deposition question
- ☐ Write draft deposition questions for litigation
- ☐ Compile resume of terms of deposition
- ☐ Index Deposition per attorney request
- ☐ Arrange medical examination for litigant
- ☐ Compile and write a legal subpoena
- ☐ Document covenants for litigation
- ☐ Write document for release
- ☐ Compile court order of dismissal
- ☐ Distribute proceeds of settlement
- ☐ Collect and organize information needed for trial
- ☐ Notify witnesses required for trial
- ☐ Collect and organize information for jury instructions
- ☐ Write draft of jury instructions for litigation
- ☐ Collect and compile information for jury verdict
- ☐ Compile legally correct jury verdict
- ☐ Record required notes at trial
- ☐ Collect and organize data needed to write
- ☐ Write draft of judgment
- ☐ Collect and organize data needed for litigation cost bill
- ☐ Write draft of litigation cost bill
- ☐ Prepare Satisfaction of Judgment
- ☐ Compile and write a document to transfer judgment
- ☐ Collect and compile data for Notice of Appeal in litigation
- ☐ Prepare Notice of Appeal
- ☐ Order bond from bonding company
- ☐ Collect and organize information for appellate brief
- ☐ Write legally correct order of Mandate
- ☐ Administer and coordinate control of court docket
- ☐ Investigate scene of a crime
- ☐ Locate witnesses to a crime

Figure 7.1 (Cont'd)
Task Inventory for Paralegals
in Litigation Work

- ☐ Acquire services of a bail bondsman
- ☐ Obtain presentence report from court
- ☐ Request Preliminary hearing by court
- ☐ Write court order allowing psychological examination
- ☐ Write legally correct motion to produce
- ☐ Write formal Document of Election to have trial by jury
- ☐ Prepare subpoenas needed in litigation

[¶702] WHERE PARALEGALS SHOULD SUPPLANT ATTORNEYS IN PRE-TRIAL WORK

The scenario for a litigation assistant working in a firm specializing in personal injury cases may be similar to the following:[3]

1. When a potential personal injury client telephones the office, all calls are monitored to the Investigation Coordinator who makes an appointment for the client with one of the firm's attorneys;
2. If the firm decides to handle the case, it is turned over to the Processing Department, Litigation Coordinator, or whomever is responsible in your office for calendaring.
   - ☐ The legal assistants in this department perform the preliminary work-up and one legal assistant is assigned permanently to the case.
   - ☐ The legal assistant in charge obtains information needed from governmental agencies, necessary medical data, and then turns the file over to the attorney awaiting further instructions.
   - ☐ Before doing this the paralegal must be certain that all pertinent accident and medical reports are available.
   - ☐ If a separate investigator is to be utilized, the legal assistant gives the latter an assessment sheet giving a brief description of how

---

[3] Sally S. Fairbanks, "Assistants in the Personal Injury Case," 10 *Trial* September–October 1974, 38.

Utilizing the Litigation Paralegal

the accident occurred, names of witnesses, defendants involved so that a complete investigation can be done.
- Letters are sent to the defendant's insurance company notifying it of the firm's representation.
3. After thirty days, the file is completely reviewed by the managing partner who assigns the case to a trial attorney for negotiation, settlement, or trial.

Even during the initial thirty days a great deal of attorney time is saved. Most difficulties that arise are managed by the legal assistant handling the file. The attorney is then free for more urgent matters. While the lawyers continue to make all the legal decisions, the actual step-by-step processing of a case from its inception to conclusion is largely handled by legal assistants.

[¶702.1]   Activity Documentation Chart for Litigation Team

The chart on the following page will illustrate how this technique is followed by some firms who rely on the paralegal system in their litigation practice:

[¶702.2]   One Attorney's System for Success

Lee Turner, a trial attorney who tries more than thirty cases per year, has a litigation system that has been developed into a science:

- Immediately upon receipt of a file in his office, it goes through calendar and docket control before being channeled to an attorney.
- How many of you litigators spend an hour or more reviewing mail and calendaring answer dates, trial dates, hearing dates, appointments, etc.? A calendar specialist can do all of these chores successfully and do so before any attorney even sees his or her mail.
- Once an attorney dictates any part of an answer that is not pre-recorded and stored on automatic typing equipment, the trial specialist carries the ball until the actual trial. She/he prepares the interrogatories and submits same to the attorney for review.
- The legal assistant prepares ticklers for the answer dates.

Figure 7.2
Litigation Chart

Date	Attorney in Charge	Assigned Paralegal	Caption of Case	Attorney for Opposing Side	Date of Summons	Date Answer Due	Bill of Particulars	Exhibit	Notice of Trial	Jury Demand	Trial Memo	Witnesses Notified of Subpoena	Memo of Law	Final Disposition

- ☐ If the answers to interrogatories are not forthcoming after requesting same, the legal assistant in consultation with the attorney prepares a motion to compel an answer.
- ☐ The trial assistant has the burden of seeing to it that the case proceeds with dispatch, and exerts pressure not only upon the adverse attorney, but upon the office attorney as well.[4]
- ☐ The appointment specialist maintains a master file of all territories where litigation is pending. As soon as the notice to take deposition is received, the deposition specialist reviews the file to determine what witnesses can be deposed in the same general direction of travel.
- ☐ The calendar specialist arranges the many details involved at deposition, such as contacting the witnesses, issuing mileage and per diem payments, arranging for the court reporter, and the transportation involved.[5]
- ☐ At the trial itself, the trial assistant reviews the jury list and does an analysis of the prospective jurors, as well as assist the trial attorney throughout in the ways previously mentioned.

[¶703] PARALEGALS CAN BE PARTICULARLY USEFUL DURING DISCOVERY

Drawing on the experiences of several national law firms utilizing legal assistants in their litigation practice the following scenario and accompanying checklists have been extracted and will provide useful guidelines.

[¶703.1] Paralegal Activities Upon Receipt of a New Case—Plaintiff

It is first desirable for the lawyer to ascertain the nature of the complaint and determine whether a conflict of interest exists, briefly discuss the essential facts and circumstances of the case to determine whether the firm is

---

[4] Lee Turner, "The Employment of Modern Techniques and Technology in Trial Preparation," 11 *Forum* 797 (1976).

[5] Id. at 805.

interested in representing the client, and discuss and agree upon the fee arrangement.

The client is then taken directly to the trial assistant, where a comprehensive checklist of relevant facts and circumstances will be completed. Each law firm which follows this procedure will doubtless have to develop its own specific checklist, particularly if it conducts litigation in a variety of highly specialized fields.

For a plaintiff's case involving personal injury, the checklist followed by the trial assistant would include at least the following:

- ☐ Past medical history.
- ☐ Past history of accidents.
- ☐ Details of the present accident, including names and addresses of all known witnesses.
- ☐ Pertinent facts and circumstances in detail, such as condition of the highway, weather conditions, visibility and so forth.
- ☐ Present medical history including detailed history of client's present physical complaints.
- ☐ Job history.
- ☐ List of doctors who have treated the client.
- ☐ Medical expenses incurred.
- ☐ Medical authorizations obtained.
- ☐ Employment contracts prepared.

[¶703.2] Personal Data Sheet to be Completed During Interview Between Personal Injury Client and Legal Assistants[6]

This interview and follow-up interviews handled by the trial asssistant may consume many hours, but these hours may be far more profitably spent by an experienced and skilled legal assistant than by an overworked lawyer. As directed by the lawyer, the trial assistant will prepare letters of notification to the adverse party and insurance carrier, if known. The trial assistant may also be instrumental in arranging for interviews with representatives of the adverse party and carrier.

---

[6] The authors gratefully acknowledge the permission of attorney John E. Norton, Norton, Bonifield & Associates, Belleville, Illinois to utilize these forms.

Figure 7.3
Personal Data Sheet

_____
Name
(one for each client)

I. PAST MEDICAL

1. Have you been hospitalized for any reason for a period of fifteen years prior to the date of this accident? Please give information requested below.

   Hospital   Location   Date   Treating Doctor
   _____
   _____
   _____
   _____
   _____

2. If you have been hospitalized for a period of fifteen years prior to the date of this accident, please indicate below what conditions or illnesses you were treated for.

   Date   Condition
   _____
   _____
   _____
   _____
   _____

3. If you have been treated on an out-patient basis by any physician, osteopath, chiropractor, physical therapist or other medical personnel for a period of fifteen years prior to the date of this accident, please indicate the date, name of the physician, etc., and condition you were treated for below. (If exact dates are not known, estimate as nearly as possible.)

   Date   Physician   Condition
   _____
   _____
   _____
   _____
   _____

4. If you have been X-rayed or were given other tests (i.e., EEG, EKG, etc.) regarding any treatment for a period of fifteen years prior to the date of this accident, please indicate so, as to the dates, physician ordering the X-rays or tests, and the place where the X-rays or tests were taken.

    Date   Doctor   Where Taken

_____

_____

_____

_____

II. CURRENT ACCIDENT CONNECTED MEDICAL TREATMENT

1. Have you been hospitalized for any reason connected with the accident since the date of this accident or injury now in question?

    Hospital   Location   Date   Treated By

_____

_____

_____

_____

2. If you have been hospitalized for any reason connected with the accident in question since the date of the accident, please list the dates of your hospitalization and the condition or illnesses you were treated for.

    Date of Treatment   Condition   Hospital

_____

_____

_____

3. If you have been treated for any reason connected with this accident on an out-patient basis by any physician, osteopath, chiropractor, physical therapist, or other medical personnel since the date of this accident, please indicate the date, name of such person, and condition you were treated for below.

_____

_____

_____

_____

4. If any X-rays or other tests have been taken since the date of this accident, please indicate so as to the dates physician ordering the X-rays or tests, and the place where these X-rays or tests were taken.

    Date   Doctor   Where Taken

_____

_____

_____

III. ACCIDENT-CONNECTED MEDICAL EXPENSES

1. If you have had any period of hospitalization since the date of this accident which were connected to the injuries received in the accident, list the dates, the hospital, and the amount of the hospital bill as incidated below. (Please list each period of hospitalization separately.)

Date of Admission	Date of Discharge	Hos.	Location	Treating Dr.	Bill
				Total	

2. If you have had any expenses for treatment by doctors or other medical personnel since the date of the accident for injuries received in this accident, please indicate below the dates of each doctor's visits, the name of the doctor, and the amount of his bill. Please indicate here the total bills, whether they have been paid by your insurance, or not.

Dates of Visits   Doctor   Bill

_____

_____

                                  Total _____

3. If you have had any X-rays or other tests as a result of injuries received in this accident, please indicate below the dates of those X-rays or tests, the doctors who ordered those tests or X-rays, and place where the X-rays or tests were taken, and the bill for those X-rays.

Dates   Doctor   Where Taken   Bill

_____

_____

                                  Total _____

IV. OTHER ACCIDENT-CONNECTED EXPENSES

1. Please list below any specific expenses which you have incurred as a result of your injury, indicating what the cost was, to whom it was paid, and how much the cost was. Include here such things as ambulance expense, help in the home, drugs, medical appliances such as neck braces, rib belts, etc.

   For What   To Whom   Cost
   _____
   _____
   _____
   _____
                              Total _____

2. If any of your personal property was damaged as a result of this accident, please indicate below what was damaged and the amount of damage incurred.

   What   Amount
   _____
   _____
   _____
   _____
                              Total _____

V. EMPLOYMENT DATA

1. List below your employment history for a period of fifteen years prior to the date of the accident, giving the dates, the employment, the employer and the approximate yearly earnings on that Job.

   Date   Employer   Yearly Earnings
   _____
   _____
   _____
   _____
   _____

2. Please indicate what your employment was at the time of the accident, listing the date you began that employment, your employer, exact wages or hourly rate, and the type of work which was performed.

   Date   Employer   Exact Wage or Hourly Rate   Type Work
   _____
   _____
   _____

3. If you have changed employment since the date of the accident, please indicate where you are now employed, the dates of your employment, exact wages, type of work, and the reason for leaving the employment at the time of the accident.

_____

_____

Why did you change jobs? _____

_____

VI. LOSS OF WAGES OR INCOME

1. If you have lost work or income as a result of the injuries in question, please indicate the dates of that lost work, and the amount of dollar loss for the work missed. Please list the dates of work lost regardless of whether you are paid on a sick-leave basis, or have a contract of insurance which would pay in a result of injury. Please indicate gross losses before deduction of income taxes, or other deductions.

Dates	Employer	Dollar Loss
		Total _____

VII. SUBSEQUENT INJURIES

1. If you have been injured in any way since the date of the injury in question, please indicate below what the injury was, how it was received, and the hospitals and treating physicians involved.

_____

_____

_____

VIII. PREVIOUS LITIGATION OR CLAIMS

1. If you have made a prior claim or filed suit in regard to a personal injury, including Workmen's Compensation Claims, please indicate below where that suit or claim was filed, the attorney or adjusting company, and what moneys were received as a result of that claim or law suit. Please describe fully on the lines listed below.

_____

_____

_____

[¶703.3]   Plaintiff Investigation and Preparation Checklist for Use by Paralegal in Personal Injury Case[7]

Figure 7.4
Investigation and Preparation Checklist
(Initial and date when completed or in file)

1. VERIFY FACTS
   (a) Clients interview _____
   (b) Clients insurance report _____
   (c) Copies of statements given by client (Motion) _____
   (d) Police and accident report _____
   (e) Weather report (if necessary) _____
   (f) Diagram scene (lighting—visibility—traffic controls, etc.) _____

2. STATEMENTS
   (a) Client (including "My Day") _____
   (b) Defendants _____
   (c) Witnesses _____
   (d) Witness evaluations _____

3. PHOTOGRAPHS
   (a) Client vehicle _____
   (b) Defendant vehicle _____
   (c) Scene of accident _____
   (d) Other Photos (Products, etc.) _____

   (e) Photos of injuries _____
   (f) Photos of traction, physical therapy, etc. _____

4. BODILY INJURY & LOSS OF EARNINGS
   (a) Hospital records _____
   (b) Physicians reports _____

---

[7] Id., John E. Norton, op. cit.

Figure 7.4 (Cont'd)
Investigation and Preparation Checklist

    (c) Casts and demonstrative evidence on injuries _____
    (d) Medical, hospital bills _____
    (e) Loss of time and wages verified _____

5. PROPERTY DAMAGE & OTHER LOSSES
    (a) Estimates _____
    (b) Final repair bill _____
    (c) Loss of use of vehicle _____
    (d) Receipts of payments _____
    (e) Receipts or estimates of other losses _____

6. REPORTS OF PRIOR HEARINGS
    (a) Transcript of pleas of guilty _____
    (b) Coroners inquest _____
    (c) Defendants previous criminal record _____

7. GENERAL—BEFORE SUIT
    (a) Lien letter sent after defendant contacted _____
    (b) Corporate name and registered agent verified _____
    (c) Liquor licensee verified _____
    (d) Expert consulted (Products, Malpractice, Reconstruction, etc.) __

8. PRE-TRIAL INFORMATION
    (a) Complaint filed _____
    (b) Answer filed _____
    (c) Reply (if necessary) _____
    (d) Interrogatories sent _____
    (e) Answers to interrogatories received _____
    (f) Defendants interrogatories received _____
    (g) Answers to defendants interrogatories sent _____
    (h) Demands for admissions _____
    (i) Motions disposed of _____

Figure 7.4 (Cont'd)
Investigation and Preparation Checklist

    (j) Depositions _____
        1. Defendant _____
        2. Plaintiff _____
        3. Evidence _____

9. FINAL PREPARATION FOR TRIAL
    (a) Notify client for interview and date of trial _____
    (b) Pre-trial medical letters _____
    (c) Special damage list _____
    (d) Demand letter _____
    (e) Subpoena list _____
    (f) Order photos for trial _____
    (g) Supplement answers to interrogatories _____

                                INVESTIGATION COMPLETE ____
                                READY FOR TRIAL _____

[¶703.4]   A Tip on Billing Your Paralegal's Time

    Associated with litigation is the fear of clients that the costs will outweigh the ultimate success of court action. Of equal concern is the attorney's fear that the time and effort put into litigation will not be fully compensated by the client. This dilemma may be beneficial in deterring specious litigation but it proves a real problem when there are no alternatives to litigation. Here is where the economic value of the paralegal really pays off for the benefit of both the lawyer and the client.

    A statistical analysis of the average litigated matter will show that 75–80 percent of the time involved in a case from start to finish consists of fact finding and pleading. The trial lawyer, trained in the art of advocacy, should confine his efforts to his unique skill played out in the courtroom. The paralegal supports the trial lawyer by fulfilling the duties of fact finding and

Utilizing the Litigation Paralegal 185

pleading for which they are trained. With experience and practice, their talents in these duties soon surpass the abilities of the average lawyer.

Since litigation must be billed on a constant basis, the client will be relieved and inclined to pay promptly time charges billed at paralegal rates during the preliminary (pre-trial) stages of the litigation. To defer litigation billing until after the trial creates risks that the results will dictate the client's willingness to accept a rendered bill. The client will not appreciate the fact that pre-trial services may have been billed at a lower rate.

The busy trial lawyer is free to concentrate his time and efforts in matters where he can bill his full hourly rate.

Clients have come to accept the role of the paralegal in the litigation process and appreciate the economic advantages of minimizing pre-trial costs. The paralegal and trial attorney achieve a synergistic balance of skills maximizing efficiency and economy.

[¶703.5] Paralegal Activities Upon Receipt of a New Case—for the Defendant

When a defense case is received, the lawyer first outlines the general procedure to be followed, listing the witnesses to be interrogated or deposed and describing the general area of questions to be covered by interrogatories, depositions and requests for admissions. The trial assistant will then follow up with the following procedures relating to interrogatories and requests for admissions:

- ☐ Prepare interrogatories or requests for approval by the lawyer.
- ☐ Prepare a tickler for the due date of answers.
- ☐ Prepare a follow-up letter if this due date is missed.
- ☐ If the follow-up letter produces no response, prepare a motion to compel answers or dismiss.
- ☐ Follow-up with defense interviews with client and all other witnesses, following a checklist prepared for that purpose, similar to the one described above.

Paralegals can be effective in investigating facts of a case, and many schools train paralegals in legal research.

Figure 7.5
Task Inventory for Paralegals: Inventory Work

Investigation—

☐ Negotiate with client for client's necessary data
☐ Collect document needed to verify reported facts
☐ Obtain police report of event affecting client
☐ Record statements of involved parties and witnesses
☐ Diagram scene of event in which client involved
☐ Canvass neighborhood of event for witnesses and information
☐ Determine value of damage to property
☐ Check index bureau at police department
☐ Determine credit of involved parties
☐ Subpoena records needed for clients case
☐ Set and keep surveillance of person(s) who may reveal facts for case

Legal Research

☐ Collect and compile definition and data on research problem
☐ Locate and analyze citations using U.S. Constitution and pertinent court decisions
☐ Locate and analyze decisions cited in U.S.C.A.
☐ Find and analyze pertinent opinions cited in the Federal Reporter
☐ Find and analyze pertinent judgments cited in the Federal Supplement
☐ Find and analyze pertinent arguments cited by U.S. Agencies
☐ Find and apply pertinent opinions based on Oregon Constitution
☐ Find and analyze pertinent passages in Oregon Revised Statutes
☐ Find/analyze pertinent citations in Advance Sheets
☐ Find/analyze pertinent arguments cited by Oregon Agencies
☐ Find/analyze pertinent administrative regulations
☐ Find/analyze pertinent Attorney General opinions
☐ Find/analyze pertinent city code provisions

Utilizing the Litigation Paralegal

- ☐ Find/analyze pertinent citations in CJS
- ☐ Find/analyze pertinent verdicts cited in jurisprudence American
- ☐ Find/analyze pertinent citations in American Law Reports
- ☐ Find/analyze pertinent opinions cited in Oregon Digest
- ☐ Find/analyze pertinent citations in Pacific Digest
- ☐ Find/analyze pertinent verdicts cited in Federal Digest
- ☐ Find/analyze pertinent arguments cited in U.S. Digest
- ☐ Find/analyze pertinent cases in Shepherd's Citations
- ☐ Find/analyze information and precedents for a case
- ☐ Compile memo of information gathered in research
- ☐ Find/analyze pertinent decisions of the U.S. Tax Court
- ☐ Find/analyze pertinent decisions of the Oregon Tax Court

[¶703.6] Paralegals Can Draft Competent Pleadings

It is usually the case that a lawyer's assistance is needed for pleadings, unless the pleadings are highly stylized as in uncontested divorces and routine probate. Nevertheless, once pleadings have been prepared for a particular kind of case, whether a plaintiff's case or a defendant's case, a legal assistant who is highly trained and thoroughly experienced can usually prepare an acceptable draft, especially if she is sensitive to differences that exist between the facts of a current case and the facts of a previous case, and is perceptive enough to ask for assistance at crucial points.

[¶703.7] Paralegals Should Handle All Incoming Interrogatories

When interrogatories are received, the trial assistant places them in the tickler file and then follows an established procedure. This procedure is substantially as follows:

- ☐ Prepare a motion requesting additional time in which to answer, if this appears necessary.
- ☐ Review the file and prepare tentative answers consisting of information contained in the file.

- ☐ Forward a copy of the tentative answers to the client for his preliminary review.
- ☐ Collate the client's responses with the tentative answers and other file information to be certain that inconsistencies are reconciled or eliminated.
- ☐ After reconciling these proposed answers with assistance from the client, submit the proposed answers to the attorney for his final review and approval.
- ☐ Upon final approval, prepare interrogatory answers in final form, submit the same for execution by the client, and forward these answers to those entitled thereto.

ONE HEADACHE GONE: Any experienced lawyer knows how devastating it is to have interrogatory answers that are not consistent with information a client may be compelled to supply. Having a trained legal assistant carefully review the file and compare all information available therein with interrogatory answers accomplishes an indispensable chore, eliminating an unnecessary burden upon a modern, busy lawyer.

[¶703.8] Paralegals Can Also Reduce Your Time Managing Depositions

Although the actual taking of a deposition is essentially a lawyer's function, all of the mechanical procedures associated with this process may be handled by a deposition assistant. These supporting tasks include the following:

- ☐ Issue notices to take depositions and subpoenas of various kinds.
- ☐ Calculate and prepare mileage and per diem payments, and arrange for all ground and other transportation.
- ☐ Make appointments with clients in advance of the deposition, if necessary.
- ☐ Forward instructions to defense witnesses.
- ☐ Arrange for court reporters and facilities unless the deposition is being taken on the premises.
- ☐ Obtain copies of depositions and furnish same to client for review.

- ☐ Ascertain that depositions have been properly filed, together with all exhibits.
- ☐ Index depositions.
- ☐ Compare statements relative to pertinent facts and circumstances in one deposition with other depositions to determine consistency or inconsistency as an aid to trial preparation.
- ☐ Digest depositions. Prepare index to deposition exhibits.
- ☐ Make sure any corrections to the depositions are forwarded to the court in proper form.
- ☐ Determine if additional information should be requested in supplemental depositions or interrogatories.

[¶704] THE PARALEGAL IS INDISPENSABLE AT TRIAL PREPARATION

In the logical sequence of the litigation process, the next step is trial preparation. This involves a multitude of sub-systems, each of which may be operated by a legal assistant. In a very small firm, a lawyer's secretary may perform all of these tasks, whereas in larger firms, functional specialization among the non-lawyer staff is so pronounced that a single person might do nothing more than index depositions, or prepare financial returns in probate proceedings, or maintain the tickler. Regardless of the form in which a particular firm organizes its work, the following functions should largely be performed by trial assistants.

- ☐ Prepare routine notices in connection with court appearances.
- ☐ Issue subpoenas or otherwise arrange for appearances of witnesses, both expert witnesses and others.
- ☐ Identify, organize and collect documentary evidence and arrange for same to be used as exhibits.
- ☐ Index, summarize and prepare extracts of depositions as directed.
- ☐ Review files to condense pertinent factual information and compare this information with data gathered from depositions and other records assembled for trial, noting all discrepancies and inconsistencies.

- ☐ Procure from the retrieval system, as directed, briefs prepared in previous cases which are germane to issues involved in the instant case.
- ☐ Shepardize cases cited in previous briefs which are intended to be used again, and otherwise perform research functions under the direction of the attorney in charge in connection with the preparation of a trial brief.
- ☐ Prepare trial book.
- ☐ Assist in preparing lay and expert witnesses for trial.
- ☐ Prepare Request for Charge to the Jury.
- ☐ Evaluate prospective jurors.
- ☐ Prepare case summary.
- ☐ Prepare witness files.
- ☐ Where a trial or other hearing is postponed, continued or settled, transmit notices to all involved persons, including the client, witnesses and others, and as follow-up, advise these persons of the rescheduled date and arrange for the appearance of expert and other witnesses.
- ☐ Notify the client of the results of a trial or hearing by preparing the transmittal for signature by the attorney in charge and photocopying necessary documents.

[¶704.1] Paralegals Can Assist in Preparing an Appeal

A well-designed system will permit a trained legal assistant to handle all non-legal functions related to an appeal.

- ☐ Draft post-trial motions and rulings on post-trial motions for review by a lawyer.
- ☐ Prepare all routine papers in connection with appeals.
- ☐ Comply with all time and jurisdictional details such as filing of a notice of appeal.
- ☐ Prepare the initial abstract (or designation) for the record, followed by a final abstract as directed by the lawyer in charge.
- ☐ Prepare and file motions for additional time, if necessary.

Utilizing the Litigation Paralegal 191

- ☐ Procure briefs from the retrieval file that are pertinent to the issues on appeal.
- ☐ In cooperation with the lawyer in charge, perform research functions, including shepardizing of cases.
- ☐ Handle all negotiations with the printer.
- ☐ Monitor, by tickler system or otherwise, final preparation and filing of briefs and other papers.

[¶705] OTHER LITIGATION-RELATED FUNCTIONS

Many firms employ legal assistants (sometimes law clerks, retired policemen or former court clerks) to perform the following functions which relate to the litigation process.

- ☐ Attend court calls.
- ☐ Obtain signatures of court clerks and other court and administrative agency personnel on routine pleadings and papers.
- ☐ Obtain signatures of judges on routine matters or in non-litigation procedures.
- ☐ Investigate pertinent details relative to jury lists.
- ☐ Interview witnesses and obtain signed statements.
- ☐ Serve papers on opposing counsel and file actions and papers with court clerks.
- ☐ Take photographs of the scene of an accident or prepare sketches, graphs or charts.
- ☐ Accumulate and collate accident reports, weather reports and other pertinent information from police records and elsewhere.
- ☐ Conduct factual investigations, including the collation of findings of other investigative agencies such as the sheriff's office, bureaus of financial responsibility and hospitals.
- ☐ Search records, check titles and otherwise perform routine and specialized investigative procedures.

If you wish to provide your staff—particularly paralegals—with a comprehensive working guide to litigation support work, the following book is recommended: *Paralegals Litigation Handbook*, by Carole Bruno (Institute for Business Planning, 1980).

[¶706] BENEFITING BY USE OF PARALEGALS IN DOMESTIC RELATIONS PRACTICE

Since litigation is an extension of the adversary system where unresolved issues must be submitted for resolution to an external authority, *i.e.*, judge or jury, the parties are presumed to have exhausted all efforts to settle their disputes out of court. As the scenario shifts from the law office to the courtroom, an illustration of the role of the paralegal in this milieu is superbly demonstrated in domestic relations practice.

There is no area of the law generating greater emotional interaction than a disputed matrimonial action. Whether the attorney is representing the husband or the wife a great deal of time must be spent in communication. The emotional needs of the clients compel them to seek out his or her attorney at all hours of the day and night. Simple assurance provides a necessary source of comfort that can be as important to the client as any forms of pendente lite relief.

[¶706.1] The Paralegal is an Excellent Source of Contact

Since most matrimonial attorneys are under constant time pressures the paralegal should be brought into the lawyer-client relationship at the earliest stage in the proceeding. A proper introduction with assurances from the lawyer that the paralegal can provide an essential communication link, will quickly substitute the paralegal as the recipient of frequent contact. This should be accomplished before discussions with the lawyer makes the client too dependent on direct contact. The paralegal can listen patiently to (usually) lengthy emotional problems which become many as the drama unfolds. A trained paralegal can synthesize the client's dilemma to the underlying legal issue, which can then be submitted to the attorney. A speedy response should be sent back to the client by the paralegal. The client's confidence in the paralegal will grow as a result of the prompt and efficient system that has been put to use.

Utilizing the Litigation Paralegal

Here again we refer you to the paralegal curriculum outlined in Chapter 2 (¶203.5)—or to the catalogs from local schools so that you may survey the training received by paralegals in your area.

The following are tasks that a paralegal should be able to perform in assisting the domestic relations attorney.[8]

Figure 7.6
Task Inventory for Paralegals: Domestic Relations Work

Handling Domestic Relations—

- ☐ Collect and organize data needed for legal actions on domestic relations
- ☐ Write draft of petition for dissolution of marriage
- ☐ Write draft of petition for separation of bed and board
- ☐ Write petition of annulment
- ☐ Write legally correct summons to appear in court
- ☐ Collect data needed for respondents' answer to a petition
- ☐ Write respondent's answer to a petition
- ☐ Collect data for petition for order to show cause
- ☐ Prepare petition for order to show cause
- ☐ Collect data to write order to show cause
- ☐ Write draft of citation
- ☐ Compile and write court order to show cause
- ☐ Collect data needed to prepare restraining order
- ☐ Write legally correct restraining order
- ☐ Collect data needed for property settlement
- ☐ Write agreement on property settlement
- ☐ Fill out legally correct record of dissolution

---

[8] We gratefully acknowledge the permission of Harold C. Hart, Lead Instructor, Legal Assistant Program, to publish the task inventory designed at Portland Community College.

- ☐ Collect data needed for affadavit of non-military service
- ☐ Fill out legally correct affadavit of non-military service
- ☐ Assemble data needed for order of default
- ☐ Write legally correct court order of default
- ☐ Prepare motion and affadavit for decree
- ☐ Assemble data to prepare decree of dissolution of marriage
- ☐ Prepare decree of dissolution of marriage
- ☐ Assemble data to prepare property settlement agreement
- ☐ Prepare property settlement agreement
- ☐ Compile petition for order to show cause regarding contempt
- ☐ Write court order to show cause regarding contempt
- ☐ Compile petition to modify child support
- ☐ Write petition to modify child support
- ☐ Write court order to modify child support
- ☐ Collect data for petition to change custody
- ☐ Write legally correct petition to change custody
- ☐ Write court order to change custody
- ☐ Collect data needed for consent to adopt
- ☐ Document consent to adopt
- ☐ Collect data for petition to adopt
- ☐ Write petition for adoption
- ☐ File petition on consent to adopt and pay filing fee to court
- ☐ Serve petition on welfare department
- ☐ Request copy of report from welfare department
- ☐ Telephone court clerk to get date of hearing about adoption
- ☐ Collect data needed for decree of adoption
- ☐ Write legally correct decree of adoption
- ☐ Collect data needed to order new birth certificate
- ☐ Order new birth certificate
- ☐ Collect information needed to change name legally
- ☐ Apply for change of name
- ☐ File application and filing fee with court for name change
- ☐ Post public notice of name change

Utilizing the Litigation Paralegal

- ☐ Obtain hearing date to change name
- ☐ Collect data needed for decree to change name
- ☐ Prepare decree to change name
- ☐ Post notice of change of name at courthouse

[¶706.2] Paralegals Should Be Responsible for Preparation of Financial Data

At the root of most matrimonial matters is a division of property and provision for support and maintenance.

Considerable time must be spent in preparing asset inventories:

- ☐ With previously prepared forms or checklists, the paralegal can function independently of the attorney in preparing, with the client, all relevant financial data in appropriate schedules.
- ☐ Paralegals can also compute average annual earnings from income tax returns covering the preceding three years.
- ☐ Finally, the paralegal and the client can prepare and review budgets and cash flow statements necessary to arrive at appropriate levels of required support.

Most jurisdictions require that litigants in matrimonial actions file a detailed financial affidavit similar to the form of affidavit required under New York practice. The New York affidavit is reproduced here because of its thoroughness and requirement for detail; the time required to complete it will become apparent. To assign this task to your secretary may be undesirable because of the confidential nature of the information sought. Moreover to respond properly to the requested data requires a working understanding of the manner in which certain property is held and of the rights pertaining thereto. The paralegal trained in domestic relations will be well suited to handle their preparation.

Figure 7.7
Affidavit of Net Worth—New York Form for Use in Matrimonial Actions

159—Affidavit of net worth, income and assets transferred: matrimonial 9-75

COPYRIGHT 1975 BY JULIUS BLUMBERG INC., LAW BLANK PUBLISHERS
80 EXCHANGE PL. AT BROADWAY, N.Y.C. 10004

COURT

COUNTY OF .... Index No.

.... Plaintiff,

- against -   *AFFIDAVIT*

.... Defendant

STATE OF .... COUNTY OF .... ss.:

the *plaintiff defendant* herein, being duly sworn, deposes and says that the following is an accurate statement of my net worth (assets of whatsoever kind and nature and wherever situated minus liabilities), statement of income from all sources and statement of assets transferred of whatsoever kind and nature and wherever situated:

INSTRUCTIONS:
1. Type or print description of item and amount in the appropriate space.
2. Furnish additional information as indicated.
3. If additional space is required use a separate rider refering to the category, section letter and/or number and incorporate the rider by specific reference within the appropriate section.
4. Under H-W-J column insert H if owned by Husband, W if owned by Wife and J if owned jointly.
5. Under Amount column insert total value of asset.
6. Under Deponent's Share column insert full value if wholly owned by deponent or amount of actual value if jointly owned.

STATEMENT OF NET WORTH AS OF .... 19......

                                                                                           H-W-J   *Amount*   *Deponent's Share*

I. ASSETS
   A. Cash accounts   *financial institution, address, account number*
      1. Cash......................
      2. Checking..............
      3. Savings (individual, joint, totten trusts, etc.)

      4. Security deposits, earnest money, etc.

      5. Short term paper (certificates of deposit, treasury notes, etc.)

   B. Marketable securities (at market value)
      1. Bonds, notes, mortgages
          obligor   *maturity date*   *principal amount*

Figure 7.7 (Cont'd)
Affidavit of Net Worth—New York Form
for Use in Matrimonial Actions

	H-W-J	Amount	Deponent's Share

2. Equity securities, options and commodity contracts (at market value)
   no. of shares *description* *cost*

C. Brokers margin accounts (broker and credit balances)

D. Loans and accounts receivable

E. Value of interest in own business and any business in which your interest exceeds 10% of net assets (describe investment giving name and address of company, if it is a corporation, partnership, sole proprietorship or trust, your capital contribution, net worth of the business, percent of your interest, and any other information bearing upon valuation)

F. Partnership interests (name, address, per cent and amount of interest and partners names)

G. Cash surrender value of life insurance   *carrier and policy*

H. Vehicles (auto, boat, plane, truck, campers, etc.)

I. Real estate (include all types of interests such as leaseholds, life estates, etc., at market value)
   location and description   *cost*

Figure 7.7 (Cont'd)
Affidavit of Net Worth—New York Form
for Use in Matrimonial Actions

		H-W-J	Amount	Deponent's Share

J. Vested interests in trusts (pension, profit sharing, legacies and others, principal amount)

K. Deferred compensation   *date due*

L. Contingent interests (stock options, interests subject to life estates, prospective inheritances, description and basis of valuation)

M. Jewelry — total market value
   describe items which cost more than $1,000   *cost*

N. Household furnishings   *list each residence and market value thereat*

O. Art, antiques, precious objects — total market value
   describe items which cost more than $500   *cost*

P. Gold and other precious metals

Q. Other assets (tax shelter investment, collections, hobbys, judgments, causes of action, patents, trademarks, copyrights, and any other assets not hereinabove itemized, at market value)

TOTAL ASSETS $

II. LIABILITIES
A. Accounts payable
B. Notes payable

C. Installment accounts payable (security agreements, chattel mortgages)   *monthly payment*

D. Brokers margin accounts (debt balance)   *name of broker*

E. Mortgages payable on real estate   *maturity date*

Figure 7.7 (Cont'd)
Affidavit of Net Worth—New York Form for Use in Matrimonial Actions

		H-W-J	Amount	Deponent's Share
F. Interest payable	*date paid up to*			
G. Taxes payable	*date paid up to*			
H. Loans on life insurance policies				
I. Other liabilities				
	TOTAL LIABILITIES		$	

III. NET WORTH (I. ASSETS minus II. LIABILITIES) .... $ _____

IV. INCOME   *state source of income and annual amount*

	Husband	Wife

A. Salary or wages (State whether income from employment of deponent or spouse has changed during the year preceding date of this affidavit.................. If so, set forth name and address of all employers during preceding year and average weekly wage paid by each. For deponent's salary payments, attach pay slip, W-2 Form or letter from employer. For data concerning spouse's income, indicate source of deponent's knowledge.)

B. Bonus, commissions, etc.

C. Partnership and proprietary

D. Dividends and interest (state whether taxable or not)

E. Real estate

Figure 7.7 (Cont'd)
Affidavit of Net Worth—New York Form
for Use in Matrimonial Actions

	Husband	Wife
F. Sale of assets (state whether held more or less than six months)		
G. Royalties		
H. Trust, pension, profit sharing and annuities		
I. Fees (directors, executors, administrators, notary, etc.)		
J. Gambling, awards, prizes		
K. Employment fringes (use of assets, facilities, memberships, etc.)		
L. Bequests and legacies		
M. Legal settlements, insurance recoveries		
N. Other income		

O. Tax preference items
 1. Long term capital gain deduction $_____
 2. Excess depreciation, amortization or depletion   *amount*

 3. Stock options — excess of fair market value over amount paid $_____

P. If any child is employed, state what contribution is made by the child and to which parent the contribution is made...............

V. EXPENSES

	Husband	Wife	Children if Separate
A. Salary and wages (domestics, chauffeurs, etc.)			
B. Interest (list separately amortization due within one year)			
C. Residences (rent, maintenance, R.E. taxes and assessments, insurance, fuel, painting, gardening, water, repairs, etc.)			

Utilizing the Litigation Paralegal

Figure 7.7 (Cont'd)
Affidavit of Net Worth—New York Form
for Use in Matrimonial Actions

	Husband	Wife	Children if Separate
D. Taxes (income and other)	....	....	....
	....	....	....
E. Food	....	....	....
F. Clothing	....	....	....
G. Insurance (life, health, accident, etc.)	....	....	....
	....	....	....
H. Education	....	....	....
	....	....	....
I. Travel	....	....	....
J. Transportation (commutation)	....	....	....
K. Vacations	....	....	....
L. Vehicles (maintenance, insurance and fuel)	....	....	....
	....	....	....
M. Alimony and child support	....	....	....
N. Medical expenses	....	....	....
	....	....	....
O. Entertainment	....	....	....
P. Appliances, furniture and furnishings	....	....	....
Q. Cleaning and maintenance (clothes, furniture, appliances, etc.)	....	....	....
R. Utilities (telephone, electric, gas)	....	....	....
	....	....	....
S. Precious objects and art	....	....	....
T. Membership dues and assessments	....	....	....
U. Books and periodicals	....	....	....
V. Sporting goods and hobbies	....	....	....
W. Other expenses:	....	....	....

Figure 7.7 (Cont'd)
Affidavit of Net Worth—New York Form
for Use in Matrimonial Actions

VI. ASSETS TRANSFERRED

List all assets transferred in any manner during the preceding three years, or length of the marriage, whichever is shorter (transfers in the routine course of business which resulted in an exchange of assets of substantially equivalent value need not be specifically disclosed where such assets are otherwise identified in the statement of net worth).

Asset	Cost	Date of transfer
......	......	......
......	......	......
......	......	......
......	......	......
......	......	......

VII. FAMILY DATA:
  A. Husband's Age .... B. Wife's Age .... C. Date Married .... D. Date Separated ....
  E. No. of Children .... F. Ages of Children .... G. *Husband Wife* has .... minor children of prior marriage.
  H. Custody of children is now with ....
  at ....
  I. Marital residence is now occupied by ☐ Husband ☐ Wife ☐ Both.
  J. Occupation of Husband............... Wife...............

VIII. SUPPORT REQUIREMENTS:
  A. The husband is presently paying the wife $............... per week, and prior to separation gave her $............... per week to cover expenses for...............
  B. The wife requests for support of the child(ren) $............... per week.
  C. The wife requests for temporary alimony $............... per week.
  D. The day of the week on which payment should be made is...............

IX. COUNSEL FEE REQUIREMENTS:
  A. The wife requests for counsel fee and disbursements the sum of $...............
  B. The wife has paid her counsel on account of his fee and disbursements the sum of $............... and has agreed with her counsel concerning his fee as follows:...............

X. Other data concerning the financial circumstances of the parties that should be brought to the attention of the court in connection with the allowances requested are...............
....
....

The foregoing statements *and a rider consisting of* .... page .... *annexed hereto and made part hereof*, have been carefully read by the undersigned who states that they are true and correct under the penalties of perjury.

Sworn to before me on .... _____

[¶706.3] The Paralegal Can Interview Witnesses Skillfully

Every legal action requires thorough preparation. In matrimonial actions in particular, corroboration of claims and counterclaims takes on an even greater importance in providing adequate testimony from witnesses. A trained paralegal should understand the elements of proof necessary to sustain the causes of action that have been pleaded. Although a private investigator will frequently be employed to determine misconduct, proof of the commission of misconduct must be carefully prepared and evaluated in order to withstand the rigors of cross examination. Extracting material and relevant information, even from an experienced private detective, requires the kind of skill that a trained paralegal can share with the attorney. Obviously, the more of this work the paralegal can perform, the more time the attorney will have available for more complex work.

[¶706.4] You Can Entrust the Paralegal With Preparation of Notices to Creditors and Financial Institutions

It goes without saying that prompt attention must be given to the need to protect bank and brokerage accounts in the face of aggravated disputes. Notices to creditors to head off avaricious reactions to the realization that a marital partnership is about to be dissolved requires immediate attention. The contents and legal sufficiency of such notices is within the knowledge of your trained paralegal. Frequently, such communications result in telephone calls seeking clarification or further confirmation from the concern receiving such notice. These calls can be delegated to your paralegal who should keep a chart of each concern to which notice is given, the date of the notice, proof of receipt, acknowledgment or other follow-up required. Such a chart will prove useful, if for example, a dispute should arise with a credit card company as to who is responsible for charges.

[¶706.5] Preparation of Pleadings Can Be Handled by the Paralegal

The nature of matrimonial actions often compels resort to provisional relief different from other civil actions. For example, an order of protection

Figure 7.8
Chart for Recording Notices to Creditors
and Financial Institutions

Notice Mailed Date	Creditor	Address	Acknowledgement Received	Follow-up Required	Compliance
7/1/80	Macy's	Herald Square, New York	7/7/80	Payment of current open balance-surrender of card -per letter 7/7/80	Payment made by client 7/8 card surrendered

Utilizing the Litigation Paralegal

or temporary support may be sought in different forums. In New York, relief may be obtained in the family court notwithstanding the fact that the supreme court will be the ultimate forum to hear a divorce or separation action.

Some other provisional remedies may include: custody of children; temporary child support; temporary alimony; counsel fees pendente lite; exclusive occupancy of the marital premises to mention just a few.

Here is where the skill and knowledge of your trained paralegal can really pay off. Although the final documents must always be reviewed by the attorney, preliminary drafting can and should be performed by a qualified paralegal. Transmittal to the appropriate court can also be performed by your paralegal.

The ultimate pleadings in a separation, annulment or divorce action can also be drafted by your paralegal.

Certain proceedings such as guardianships, adoptions, change of name, filiation, conservatorship and incompetency, particularly lend themselves to preliminary handling by a qualified paralegal. The drafting and filing techniques are suitably performed by paralegals as well. A busy attorney need not devote time and attention to completion of forms. The proper treatment of such forms however is beyond the expertise of even a highly experienced secretary and should never be delegated as a clerical assignment. Care and skill in preparing such documents effectively is a legal function but one that can be accomplished by a paralegal subject to final review by the attorney.

[¶706.6] Checklist of Supplemental Matters Your Paralegal Can Also Handle Well

- ☐ Frequently, separation agreements provide for cost of living adjustments based upon one of several indices. The computations and resulting adjustments are a suitable function for your paralegal.
- ☐ Post closing transfers such as insurance policies, stocks, bonds, deeds and other instruments of assignment can also be effectively performed by a trained paralegal.
- ☐ The paralegal should prepare a schedule of all documents to be assigned and transferred following the execution of a separation agreement or court ordered disposition of property. This schedule should provide a tickler or reminder for follow-up action.

☐ Legal documents and instruments of assignment (stock and bond powers) and other pertinent documents can be prepared by the paralegal who in many instances is qualified to supervise proper execution.

All of these details will enable the busy attorney to maximize his time and attention to settlement negotiations and trials. As can be seen, a team system can be particularly beneficial in domestic relations matters.

8

Utilizing the Real Estate Paralegal

[¶801]   **INTRODUCTION**

The area of law that affords paralegals the opportunity to function (legally) most akin to a lawyer is real estate practice. Here the paralegal may learn to work with great independence, assuming almost total responsibility for a matter from start to finish. For these reasons, real estate paralegals are perceived as extremely valuable to a firm and may receive higher compensation than their counterparts in other departments. It follows, logically, that an experienced real estate paralegal may be expected to be more productive for the benefit of the firm or the single practitioner. In large corporate departments, title companies and banks, their acceptance and use of legal assistants has become quite standard, and their contributions are deemed invaluable. Indeed, qualified legal assistants are often sought in preference to real estate attorneys, whose level of compensation for comparable performance put them at a disadvantage in this job market. Naturally, you can reap the same financial reward as these large offices.

For one overview of paralegals' skills and capabilities in real estate work, you can refer back to the lists in Chapter 2 (¶203.4), or check catalogs from local paralegal training programs.

The following tasks might all be performed by paralegals.[1] *Some* state bars have objected to allowing paralegals to function independently (*e.g.*, for title insurance companies in Virginia) at title closings, and as of this book's printing, the final verdict is not yet in.

Chapter 13 will discuss the ethical employment of paralegals, and offer some suggestions on obtaining clarifications over matters of "unauthorized practice" about which you may be concerned.

Figure 8.1
Task Inventory for Paralegals in Real Estate Work

Handling real estate matters—

☐ Compile data and calculate correct earnest money amount
☐ Assemble valid data and complete earnest money formal documents
☐ Determine type conveyance requested, or which has occurred
☐ Collect data needed to order title report
☐ Order title report
☐ Determine water rights and farm deferment
☐ Draft contract
☐ Document Contract for permanent records
☐ Make certain truth-in-lending requirements are met
☐ Collect valid data and fill out formal deed
☐ Compile satisfaction of Mortgage document
☐ Collect valid data and fill out formal lien clearance
☐ Collect valid data and fill out formal Promissory Note
☐ Collect valid data and write accurate assignment Documents
☐ Pro-rate property taxes to establish owner's equity
☐ Pro-rate fire insurance to establish buyer's cost

---

[1] We gratefully acknowledge the permission of Harold C. Hart, Lead Instructor, Legal Assistant Program, to publish the task inventory designed at Portland Community College.

Utilizing the Real Estate Paralegal

- ☐ Fill out forms needed to state financial terms of transaction
- ☐ Specify actions needed to amplify standard escrow instructions
- ☐ Express terms and conditions of lease in legally binding language
- ☐ Express terms and conditions of Prep lien in legally binding language
- ☐ Express terms and conditions of Mortgage in legally binding language
- ☐ Express terms and conditions of easement
- ☐ Collect and verify accuracy of data for Bill of Sale
- ☐ Express terms and conditions of Bill of Sale in legally binding language
- ☐ Collect and review data needed to subdivide real property
- ☐ Compile and file Preliminary Note of Intention
- ☐ Compile data for transfer form and specimen
- ☐ Fill out subdivision questionnaire
- ☐ Advise as escrow agent of compliance with statutes
- ☐ Ask for qualified agents approval letter
- ☐ Research legislation, regulations, and ordinances for RE transaction
- ☐ Prepare Uniform Commercial Code forms
- ☐ Fill out Bulk Sales and Security Agreement Documents
- ☐ Compile instruction for recording
- ☐ Implement OLCC Regulations in all matters
- ☐ Research data to determine that real estate transaction is legal and correct
- ☐ Compile request and authorization to Foreclose
- ☐ Order Trust Deed Foreclosure Report
- ☐ Set date and place of sale to satisfy both parties
- ☐ Prepare and record Notice of Default and Election to Sell
- ☐ Order Supplemental Title report
- ☐ Mail Note of Sale
- ☐ Arrange personal service of Notice of Sale
- ☐ Publish Note of Sale
- ☐ Determine status of title
- ☐ Determine Federal Tax Lien status
- ☐ Prepare and record Affidavit of Mailing of Notice of Sale
- ☐ Record Return of Service
- ☐ Record Affidavit of Public Notice of Sale

- ☐ Record Trustee's certificate if property not occupied
- ☐ Compile foreign and domestic annual reports
- ☐ Analyze and compile Articles of Dissolution
- ☐ Arrange sale of property and paying to trustee
- ☐ Compile Trustee's Deed
- ☐ Fill out and record certificate of non-military service
- ☐ Arrange distribution of funds and distribute the funds
- ☐ Cancel note and trust deed

[¶802] PARALEGALS CAN EFFECTIVELY DRAFT AND REVIEW RESIDENTIAL AND COMMERCIAL LEASES AND AGREEMENTS OF SALE

Since most leases are now standardized, and many jurisdictions require basic provisions to be drawn in "plain" English, formal legal training is no longer *as* essential to the document drafter. Paralegals can be trained to tailor standard agreements to conform to certain specific provisions, which of course must be left to the attorney to negotiate.

Example: While a final review of a contract of sale should be performed by the attorney, the standardized form, which can adopt pre-designed special clauses (usually pre-stored in memory typewriters or computerized magnetic cards or tape), could be prepared by the paralegal. Details such as describing items of personal property and special considerations are easily dealt with by a trained paralegal.

[¶803] PARALEGALS WILL CAREFULLY REVIEW TITLE REPORTS AND SURVEYS

Here, more experience is required before delegating responsibility for reviewing and seeking remedies to objections and exceptions noted on title reports and surveys. Strictly speaking, however, these duties, which can be time consuming to the attorney, can easily be taught to a competent real estate paralegal.

Examples: Liens and judgments can be verified by simple telephone calls and follow-up correspondence. Inheritance tax waivers are issued by

Utilizing the Real Estate Paralegal

non-lawyer administrators, so obviously the means to obtain such releases can be sought by paralegals.

[¶804] PARALEGALS SHOULD DRAFT AND REVIEW MORTGAGE AND OTHER FINANCING DOCUMENTS

Since almost all financing documents are standardized on familiar printed forms, their preliminary completion is well within the competence of a trained paralegal. Repayment schedules are common reference works. Familiarization with local filing requirements is easily learned. Given the financial details of the transaction, the paralegal should routinely be able to prepare the entire package of legal documents necessary for any type of financing quickly and completely, necessitating only a brief final review by the attorney.

[¶805] PARALEGALS SHOULD DRAFT AND REVIEW DEEDS

The key here is to be able to follow a given description and compare it to the description contained in the title report, and if necessary compare the description as shown on a survey. Most legal secretaries routinely prepare deeds, however, it would be more appropriate to have the paralegal review the description for discrepancies or deficiencies.

The formalities of proper execution require strict compliance with details that vary in relation to facts and circumstances. For example, a post-divorce conveyance or a "qualified interspousal gift" may require clarifying recitations normally excluded within the descriptive body of the deed. Moreover, such factors as "consideration" will determine ultimate tax questions with potential detrimental consequences if such details are ultimately relegated to clerical performance.

Since a deed intends to convey legal title not only must the description match the prescribed metes and bounds that will be insured by reference to a filed survey, but the nature of the title must be described. For example, title may be held jointly with a right of survivorship or as a tenant in common. In the latter, although title remains undivided, it is severable and may be further conveyed or devised by a will. Deeds may be characterized as "quitclaim," "bargain and sale" or "warranty." Surviving warranties, if any, are implied from the characterization of the deed. A title company will insure no greater title than that spelled out in the deed of conveyance.

It is obvious, therefore, that there is a major advantage in having a trained paralegal draw deeds and other title instruments. Additionally, the practice of billing for a secretary's time raises many ethical questions. Such questions are avoided in the case of billing for a paralegal's time.

The paralegal-attorney team approach is as sound professionally as it is economically. The client gets the benefit of prompt, efficient service while the attorney avoids any doubts about fully accounting for his billable time.

[¶806] PARALEGALS CAN BE RESPONSIBLE FOR DEALING WITH TITLE COMPANIES

From the moment a real estate transaction develops, the paralegals should be involved, so that the first steps in dealing with the title company can be instituted by the paralegal with full knowledge of all of the pertinent facts. Placing the call to the title company and ordering a search can be time consuming to the attorney, since there can be considerable detail that must be researched and furnished before a search can be undertaken. Let the paralegal do *all* of this.

Have the paralegal establish the introduction of the search to the title company. That line of communication can then persist, thereby reducing time-consuming telephone contact for the attorney. Upon receipt of the abstract, a cordial dialogue having been established, the paralegal can facilitate an orderly disposition of most preliminary problems before the attorney is called in to prepare the final report.

The most common problems confronted in advance of closing may require the paralegal to undertake the following:

☐ Prepare affidavits satisfying exceptions based upon judgments. Example, similar name but unrelated.
☐ Prepare satisfactions of judgments, liens and mortgages.
☐ Prepare assignments and subordinations of prior mortgages.
☐ Pay all outstanding taxes, assessments and other dischargeable liens.
☐ Prepare for corporate borrower, all appropriate authorizations. Example, enabling resolutions, evidence of corporate standing, secretary's certificate, tax certificates.
☐ Compute and verify tax, insurance, fuel and utility adjustments.

Utilizing the Real Estate Paralegal 213

- ☐ Certify correctness of rent roll. Verify stabilization table, if applicable.
- ☐ Prepare applicable escrow agreements.
- ☐ Obtain and present, where applicable, current dated fiduciary letters of appointment; court order authorizing sale (example, a religious institution); federal and state release of lien; proof of payment of taxes.

All of the above are within the knowledge of the trained paralegal and can be performed with ease and efficiency and of course, billed to the client at a time rate far less than the busy attorney's rate. The attorney is now able to concentrate on other billable matters.

[¶807] PARALEGALS SHOULD PREPARE CLOSING STATEMENTS AND ATTEND CLOSINGS

Many firms engaged in an extensive real estate practice will use paralegals almost exclusively to close cooperative apartments and some condominiums. Real estate concerns which manage co-ops frequently employ paralegals to draft and close documents on behalf of management. Similarly, the sale or purchase of co-op or condo units, unlike complex land deals, are relatively routine with the result that such transactions are well within the competence of a trained paralegal.

In other real estate transactions, as already noted, most of the documents can be prepared by the paralegal for final attorney review in advance of the closing. Pre-closing conferences will establish the existence of deficient or missing documents which the paralegal can easily remedy. In preparing for the closing the adjustments for interest, taxes, fuel, insurance and revenue stamps are well within the capability of the paralegal. Delegating these responsibilities is not only a savings in the attorneys' time, but given the penchant of many attorneys for mathematical weakness, an intelligent paralegal is often better suited for this kind of detailed work.

The preparation of the post-closing statement usually follows a format prescribed by office policy. Some closing statements are prepared in hardcover binders. Some consist of pre-printed single sheets. Most reputable firms prefer to follow a somewhat detailed format similar to the example shown below. It is evident from a consideration of both of these samples that a comparable product can easily be prepared by a paralegal who has followed the transaction from start to finish.

Of course, the lawyer's presence at the closing is essential to insure that the client receives proper legal representation, so that legal questions which develop there can be disposed of correctly. However, most of the extensive preliminary preparation, as well as development of the closing statement itself can be delegated to the experienced paralegal—with the grand result that the lawyer again saves precious time for more complex legal matters.

Utilizing the Real Estate Paralegal

Figure 8.2
Sample Closing Statement Specimen Form
Simple Transaction

CLOSING STATEMENT

Sale of Premises
New City, New York

and   Sellers
    and   Purchasers

Closing held on June 21, 1979
at the offices of

New City, New York

PRESENT: _____

and	Sellers
ESQ., of	Attorney for Sellers
and	Purchasers
ESQ.	Attorney for Purchasers
ESQ.	Attorney for Mortgagee
	Title Closer (Title No.)

FINANCIAL STATEMENT

CREDITS IN FAVOR OF SELLERS:

Purchase Price	$75,000.00
1978/79 School Taxes ($1,488.78 for period September 1, 1978 through August 31, 1979; period of adjustment June 21, 1979 through August 31, 1979)	295.42
1979 Town Taxes ($1,072.50 for period January 1, 1979 through December 31, 1979; period of adjustment June 21, 1979 through December 31, 1979	563.10
TOTAL CREDITS IN FAVOR OF SELLERS	**$75,848.52**

Financial Statement (Cont'd)

<u>CREDITS IN FAVOR OF PURCHASERS:</u>

Contract Deposit	$7,500.00	
TOTAL CREDITS IN FAVOR OF PURCHASERS		$ 7,500.00
BALANCE DUE AT CLOSING		$68,348.52

Said balance due at closing was paid as follows:

Check #501935820 of   , dated June 19, 1979, payable to the order of   and $ 7,500.00

Check of   and   , dated June 21, 1979, payable to the order of   848.52

Check #1326 of   , as Attorneys, drawn on their Trust Account, payable to the order of   and   34,201.12

Check #1324 of   , as Attorneys, dated June 21, 1979, payable to the order of   in satisfaction of first mortgage, payment approved by   and   25,798.88

                                                            $68,348.52

MISCELLANEOUS DISBURSEMENTS

The following are checks drawn on the account of   and   , dated June 21, 1979, in payment of miscellaneous disbursements:

Check #456 to the order of   Title Insurance Company in payment of the following:

(a)	Satisfaction of Mortgage	$ 8.25	
(b)	New York State Transfer Tax	82.50	
			$ 90.75

Check #457 to the order of   in payment of pick-up charge on mortgage   30.00

                                                            $120.75

Respectfully submitted,

By _____

Utilizing the Real Estate Paralegal 217

Figure 8.3
Sample Closing Statement Specimen Form
Complex Transaction

<u>CLOSING STATEMENT</u>

Sale of Premises

Brooklyn, New York

                                    Seller

                                    Purchaser

Closing held on October 19, 1979
at the offices of

New York, New York

PRESENT:

                                    Seller

ESQ., of   Attorney for
                                    Seller

                                    Purchaser

ESQ.   Attorney for
                                    Purchaser

                                    Title Closer
                                    (Title No.
)

<u>THE TRANSACTION</u>

      The transaction involved the sale of an occupied residential apartment building located at   , Brooklyn, New York for a purchase price of $280,000.00, payable $72,720.28 by Purchaser taking title subject to a first mortgage held by   , and the balance, $207,279.72, in cash.

FINANCIAL STATEMENT

All Adjustments made as of October 19, 1979

CREDITS IN FAVOR OF SELLER:

Purchase Price	$280,000,000
1979/80 Second Quarter New York City Real Estate Tax ($1,301.56 for the period October 1, 1979 through December 31, 1979; period of adjustment October 19, 1979 through December 31, 1979)	1,055.70
1979/80 Water and Sewer Rent ($761.25 for the period July 1, 1979 through June 30, 1980; period of adjustment October 19, 1979 through June 30, 1980)	539.24
Adjustment for Fuel Oil (624 gallons at $.819 per gallon)	511.06
Adjustment for Electric Charges	156.80
Premium Adjustment on Brownstone Agency Fire and Multi-Peril Policy	234.00
Escrow Deposit held by First Mortgagee	1,998.52
Fee for New York City Housing Preservation and Development Multiple Dwelling Registration (Although Purchaser's obligation, Seller made payment and received a credit for same)	6.00
Fee Title Insurance (Although Purchaser's obligation, Seller made payment and received a credit for same)	1,004.00
Survey Inspection (Although Purchaser's obligation, Seller made payment and received a credit for same)	28.00
Departmental Searches (Although Purchaser's obligation, Seller made payment and received a credit for same)	41.00
Deed Recording Fee (Although Purchaser's obligation, Seller made payment and received a credit for same)	13.00
TOTAL CREDITS IN FAVOR OF SELLER	**$285,587.32**

FINANCIAL STATEMENT (Cont'd)

CREDITS IN FAVOR OF PURCHASER:

Deposit on Contract	$28,000.00	
Unpaid principal balance due on First Mortgage held by	72,720.28	
Interest due under First Mortgage (period of Adjustment October 19, 1979 through October 31, 1979)	242.97	
Tenants' Security Deposits	692.02	
Interest on Tenants' Security Deposits	50.00	
TOTAL CREDITS IN FAVOR OF PURCHASER		$101,705.27
BALANCE DUE AT CLOSING		$183,822.05

Said balance due at closing was paid as follows:

Cashier's Check of   , dated October 19, 1979, made payable to the order of $183,822.05

MISCELLANEOUS DISBURSEMENTS

The following checks were issued on behalf of Seller from Seller's fund held by   , Esqs., drawn on its Special Account at   ;

Check #250 dated October 19, 1979, payable to the order of the New York City Department of Housing Preservation and Development for Multiple Dwelling Registration Card $ 6.00

Check #251 dated October 19, 1979, payable to the order of   Title Insurance Company in payment of the following:
(a) New York City Real
    Property Transfer Tax $2,072.92
(b) New York State Real
    Property Transfer Tax   228.25
(c) Fee Title Insurance   1,004.00
(d) Survey Inspection   28.00

MISCELLANEOUS DISBURSEMENTS (Cont'd)

(e) Departmental Searches	41.00	
(f) Deed Recording Fee	13.00	
		$ 3,387.04
Check #253, payable to the order of dated October 30, 1979, in payment of legal fee and disbursements		3,825.50
Check #254, payable to the order of dated October 30, 1979, re: balance of escrow funds		20,781.46
		$28,000.00

MEMORANDUM

1. *Contract of Sale.* Seller conveyed title to the Premises pursuant to a contract of sale dated September 5, 1979 between   , as Seller, and   , as Purchaser.

2. *Letter of Agreement.* Purchaser and Seller entered into a letter agreement dated October 19, 1979 regarding the consent of   Bank to the sale. Purchaser agreed, notwithstanding anything to the contrary in the contract of sale, to assume all obligations in respect of obtaining the consent of   Bank, holder of the first mortgage covering the Premises, to the sale of the Premises to the Purchaser or its designee. The parties further agreed that if the Bank failed to grant its consent to such sale or if as a result of such sale, the maturity date of the note and mortgage is accelerated by the Bank, then such failure to consent or acceleration shall not be deemed an objection to title on the part of the Purchaser nor shall Purchaser be entitled to any abatement or reduction in the purchase price.

3. *Tenants.* The property consists of a four (4) story apartment building with eighteen (18) apartments. On the date of closing, Seller's right, as landlord, in and to all leases were assigned to Purchaser together with all security deposits held by Seller, as landlord, under the respective leases, all as indicated below. Purchaser acknowledged receipt of all security deposits and further agreed to hold the security deposits in accordance with law and to indemnify the Seller against any claim that may be made against Seller in connection with the security deposits received by Purchaser.

The following is a list of the accounts and their security deposits:

Tenant	Apt.	Security	Lease Expiration
	3	$ 90.00	Rent Controlled
	4	55.00	Rent Controlled
	10–11	140.00	3/1/80
	B	239.62	month-to-month
	C	167.40	5/31/79

At closing, a credit of $692.02 was given to Purchaser representing the amount of security deposits assigned. Additionally, a credit of $50.00 was given to Purchaser representing the interest accrued on such security deposits.

Respectfully submitted,

By _____

9

Utilizing the Paralegal in Corporate Practice

[¶901] INTRODUCTION

The nature of corporate practice particularly lends itself to the efficient use of paralegals. Adoption of a system for the maintenance and annual update of the records of closely held corporations can be efficiently delegated to a trained legal assistant. In most instances, annual minutes provide for the election of officers and directors together with the ratification of managements actions for the preceding year. Changes in stock ownership are likewise administrative chores. The attorney need only prepare a memorandum of instructions to the legal assistant who can then attend to drafting minutes, canceling and issuing new stock certificates with appropriate entries in the stock transfer ledger. Required stock transfer stamps can be obtained, affixed and canceled routinely.

The time spent by a firm in handling all of these details can be extensive particularly when many corporate outfits (minute book and stock transfer ledger) are retained in the law firm with the result that an implied responsibility to maintain these records emerges annually. Why substantially reduce your own available time for more complex matters, when your firm can still perform these services, and save your clients money by billing at your paralegal's rate? Indeed, you should pursue this annual review and add a source of revenue to your practice.

[¶902] PARALEGALS SHOULD HAVE RESPONSIBILITY FOR PREPARING AND FILING DOCUMENTS RELATING TO INCORPORATION AND DISSOLUTION

Many firms engage the services of outside concerns to prepare and file the initial certificate of incorporation as well as change of name certificate, amendments and dissolutions and mergers. Usually there is a package cost that includes furnishing the corporate outfit, seal and stock certificates. The cost is relatively modest and is disbursed to the client who is additionally charged the firm's going rate for the formation of the corporation. In most instances, the client is unaware that all of the details were performed by the outside service.

The professionalism of such procedures is debatable when you examine some of the more significant considerations involved in the formation of a corporation. For example, adoption of Subchapter S authorization of §1244 relief must be considered and tailored to the client's and its accountant's attitudes. Adoption of a fiscal year should be carefully thought out. Adoption of by-laws, and indeed drafting the purposes of the corporate business, should not be given "boiler plate" treatment. Moreover, "Not for Profit" or "Membership" corporations require special considerations beyond the expertise of outside service companies.

Chapter 2 outlines a typical paralegal training core for corporate work (¶203.1). You can compare this with the type of training that schools and institutes in your own area provide.

The following is a comprehensive list of duties relating to corporate matters that paralegals may be expected to perform.[1]

---

[1] We gratefully acknowledge the permission of Harold C. Hart, Lead Instructor, Legal Assistant Program, to publish the task inventory designed at Portland Community College.

Figure 9.1
Task Inventory for Paralegals in Corporate Work Specimen Form

Handling Corporate Matters—

- ☐ Determine availability of corporate name
- ☐ Reserve corporate name with Secretary of State
- ☐ Collect and organize data needed for Articles of Incorporation
- ☐ Compile Articles of Incorporation
- ☐ File articles and initial fees with State
- ☐ Collect data for minutes of initial corporate meetings
- ☐ Evaluate data for minutes of initial corporate meetings
- ☐ Draft Subscriber agreement
- ☐ Prepare Waiver of Notice of meeting
- ☐ Draft Minutes of initial shareholder meeting
- ☐ Draft minutes of initial Director's meeting
- ☐ Write draft of resignation
- ☐ Collect data needed for corporate by-laws
- ☐ Prepare corporate by-laws
- ☐ Order Corporate seal, minutes and stock certificates
- ☐ Design and compile stock certificate
- ☐ Establish corporate bank account
- ☐ Collect data for minutes regarding sale of stock
- ☐ Compose minutes of stock sale
- ☐ Collect data for increase of capitalization
- ☐ Write Directors minutes regarding increase in capitalization
- ☐ Collect data for stock split
- ☐ Prepare minutes regarding stock split
- ☐ Develop data needed to decide on stock options
- ☐ Write Director-meeting minutes for stock option decision
- ☐ Collect information on profit sharing decision
- ☐ Collect information about pension plan
- ☐ Write Director's policy on profit sharing and pension plan
- ☐ Collect data for Dividend Distribution
- ☐ Write Director's decision about dividend distribution

Utilizing the Paralegal in Corporate Practice

- ☐ Collect data about election of officers
- ☐ Write minutes of Director's meeting about election of officers
- ☐ Collect data for annual director's meeting
- ☐ Write minutes of annual director's meeting
- ☐ Collect data for annual shareholders meeting
- ☐ Write minutes of annual shareholder meeting
- ☐ Collect data for special shareholder meeting
- ☐ Write minutes of special shareholder meeting
- ☐ Collect data for special shareholder meeting
- ☐ Put together and draft a Buy-Sell agreement for review
- ☐ Obtain and assemble data to qualify corporation in foreign jurisdictions
- ☐ Prepare documentation for qualification in foreign jurisdictions
- ☐ Collect data needed to amend articles of incorporation
- ☐ File Articles of Incorporation amendments
- ☐ Collect information needed to amend by-laws
- ☐ Write amendments to by-laws
- ☐ Collect data needed to apply for assumed business income
- ☐ Apply for assumed business name
- ☐ Collect data needed to cancel/withdraw assumed business name
- ☐ Compile foreign and domestic annual reports
- ☐ Analyze and compile Articles of Dissolution
- ☐ Collect and analyze needed data to fill out required tax forms
- ☐ Documents and information required to merge corporation
- ☐ Document registration data for Corporation Commission
- ☐ Compile prospectus for sale of stock
- ☐ Document information needed for Borrowing Resolution
- ☐ Write formal statement supporting desired salary charges
- ☐ Report to IRS as required upon death of a stockholder

You'll benefit by having all pre-incorporation documents drafted in-house by a trained paralegal. And, corrections, additions or deletions can be more easily determined before the certificate is filed.[2] Instances of dissolu-

---

[2] The authors gratefully acknowledge the permission of Kathleen Commins for furnishing some of the forms that appear in this chapter and in the Appendix.

tions, formulated by outside service companies under an erroneous or inappropriate section of the Internal Revenue Code, once filed and effective, have caused considerable embarrassment and even claims of malpractice when the client discovered the mistake. Once an incorporation, merger or dissolution becomes effective by filing, it is not easily set aside, and may result in irreparable damage. Such mistakes have generally been discovered during tax audits at which time the government will not be dissuaded by eloquent disclaimers.

WHAT TO DO: The better practice therefore is to handle the preparation of the incorporation certificate, by-laws, initial minutes, stock subscription agreements, mergers, consolidations, dissolutions and amendments within your office. Your trained paralegal should be qualified to attend to the initial drafting, which should be reviewed by the attorney with the client present, before filing.

[¶903] PARALEGALS SHOULD PREPARE MINUTES, AGENDA, NOTICES AND PROXY MATERIALS FOR CORPORATE MEETINGS

In addition to state law, the certificate of incorporation and the by-laws must be checked for prescribed time requirements concerning notice of regular and special meetings. Some states now permit waiver of notice by telephone, while other jurisdictions permit notice to be waived by execution of consents ratifying corporation actions in lieu of meetings. Whatever procedure is followed, the drafting can be attended to by the legal assistant. Similarly, necessary proxies can be prepared and ultimately the notice of meeting and verification of a quorum are all well within the capabilities of the legal assistant.

Finally, the legal assistant should be invited to attend the meetings. Assuming that detailed minutes are taken by a secretary or reporter, the ultimate transcription from the typed detailed minutes can be abstracted into proper minutes by the legal assistant.

In the next few pages there are a number of forms that the paralegal may draft, or otherwise assist in preparing. In addition, Appendix F contains a great many more forms, documents, etc., that fit into this category. These are of the variety that can be easily incorporated into the systems binder for your corporate work.

Figure 9.2
Waiver of Notice of Organization Meeting
Specimen Form

WAIVER OF NOTICE OF ORGANIZATION MEETING
of

_____

    We, the undersigned, being all the incorporators named in the certificate of incorporation of the above corporation hereby agree and consent that the organization meeting thereof be held on the date and at the time and place stated below and hereby waive all notice of such meeting and of any adjournment thereof.

Place of meeting

Date of meeting

Time of meeting

_____
Incorporator

_____
Incorporator

_____
Incorporator

Dated:

Figure 9.3
Certificate of Election of Directors Specimen Form

CERTIFICATE OF ELECTION OF DIRECTORS

STATE OF   )
COUNTY OF   ) ss.:

WE, THE UNDERSIGNED, having been elected Inspectors of Election of Directors held at a meeting of Shareholders of * * * a corporation, on the * * day of * * 19 * , at the office of said Corporation, in the * * * and State of * * * do hereby certify as follows:

FIRST: That a meeting of the Shareholders of said Corporation was held at the Corporation's office on the * * day of * * , 19 * * , at * * o'clock in the * * noon.

SECOND: That before entering upon the discharge of our duties we were severally and individually sworn to faithfully execute the duties of Inspectors of Election at such meeting with strict impartiality and according to the best of our ability, and the oath was taken and subscribed to by us, and is hereto attached, marked Oath of Inspectors, and is made a part of this certificate.

THIRD: That a canvass of the votes of such election show that votes representing * * * shares had been cast for the following named person, to wit:

NAMES   NUMBER OF VOTES
* *   * *

That thereupon the said Messrs. * * * having received a plurality of all the votes cast at such election, and none of whom being Directors of the Corporation, were by us duly declared elected Inspectors of Election of * * * for the ensuing year.

IN WITNESS WHEREOF, we have hereunto set our hands this * * day of * * 19 * *.

_____
_____
_____
                INSPECTORS

STATE OF   )
) ss:
COUNTY OF   )

On this * * day of * * in the year one thousand nine hundred and * * personally appeared before me * * * * * * * to me known and known to me to be the individuals described in and who executed the foregoing Certificate, and they severally before me acknowledged that they had made, signed and executed the same for the purposes therein set forth.

The President then presented his report.

* * * * * *

On motion duly made and carried, the same was received and ordered on file.

The Secretary then presented his report.

* * * * * *

On motion duly made and carried, the same was received and ordered on file.

The Treasurer presented his report.

* * * * * *

On motion duly made and carried, the same was received and ordered on file.

The Chairman then stated that the election of the Directors of the Corporation was then in order.

The following were nominated as Directors of the Corporation:

* * * * * *

The Chairman then declared that Messrs. * * * * * * had been appointed inspectors of Election for this meeting by the Board and that they subscribed and verified their oath of office as required by law and had entered upon the discharge of their duties and would receive the ballots of the Shareholders.

On motion duly made and carried the oath of office of the inspectors was ordered spread at length upon the minutes.

Each Shareholder was requested to place his vote on the ballot stating the number of shares he votes and sign his name on the ballot.

On motion duly made and carried the minutes of the last meeting of Shareholders were read and approved.

Thereupon the President and Treasurer of the Corporation made their reports. * * * * * *

Thereupon the Chairman declared the polls closed and the Inspectors of Election proceeded to canvass the vote.

On motion duly made and carried the meeting proceeded to consider other business until the Inspectors of Election were ready to report.

The following action was taken by the meeting: * * * * * *

The Inspectors of Election reported the following votes cast for Directors of the Corporation for the ensuing year.

Names　　　　　　　　　　　　　　　　　　　　　*Number of Votes*
* *　　　　　　　　　　　　　　　　　　　　　　　　* *

The Chairman then declared the following persons duly elected Directors of the Corporation: * * * * * *

On motion duly made and carried the Inspectors were directed to file their report in the office of the Clerk of * * County and a copy thereof with the Secretary of the Corporation.

The Chairman then announced that, in accordance with the By-Laws, it would be necessary to elect two Inspectors of Election in the place of present Inspectors to hold office for the ensuing year.

On motion duly made and carried it was decided to proceed with the election and Messrs. * * * were duly nominated as Inspectors of Election.

There being no other nominations the Secretary was requested to cast one ballot for each.

The Secretary cast such ballot and reported to the meeting such action, whereupon the Chairman declared the Messrs. * * * have been duly elected Inspectors of election for the Corporation for the ensuing year.

The said Inspectors of election thereupon severally subscribed and verified a certificate of election.

Upon motion duly made and carried, it was ordered that a copy thereof be attached to the minutes of the Corporation.

Figure 9.4
Waiver of Notice of First Meeting of Board Specimen Form

WAIVER OF NOTICE OF FIRST MEETING OF BOARD

of

_____

We, the undersigned, being all the directors of the above corporation hereby agree and consent that the first meeting of the board be held on the date and at the time and place stated below for the purpose of electing officers and the transaction thereat of all such other business as may lawfully come before said meeting and hereby waive all notice of the meeting and of any adjournment thereof.

Place of meeting

Date of meeting

Time of meeting

                                              _____
                                              Director

                                              _____
                                              Director

                                              _____
                                              Director

Dated:

Figure 9.5
Minutes of First Meeting of Board of Directors
Specimen Form

MINUTES OF FIRST MEETING OF BOARD OF DIRECTORS
of
_____

The first meeting of the board was held at
on the   day of   19   at   o'clock   M.

The following were present:

being a quorum and all of the directors of the corporation.

                                        was nominated and elected temporary chairman and acted as such until relieved by the president.
                                        was nominated and elected temporary secretary, and acted as such until relieved by the permanent secretary.

The secretary then presented and read to the meeting a waiver of notice of meeting, subscribed by all the directors of the corporation, and it was ordered that it be appended to the minutes of this meeting.

The following were duly nominated and, a vote having been taken, were unanimously elected officers of the corporation to serve for one year and until their successors are elected and qualified:

President:

Vice-President:

Secretary:

Treasurer:

The president and secretary thereupon assumed their respective offices in place and stead of the temporary chairman and the temporary secretary.

Upon motion duly made, seconded and carried, it was

RESOLVED that the seal now presented at this meeting, an impression of which is directed to be made in the margin of the minute book, be and the same hereby is adopted as the seal of this corporation and further

RESOLVED that the president and treasurer be and they hereby are authorized to issue certificates for shares in the form as submitted to this meeting and appended to the minutes of this meeting and further

RESOLVED that the share and transfer book now presented at this meeting be and the same hereby is adopted as the share and transfer book of the corporation.

Upon motion duly made, seconded and carried, it was

RESOLVED that the treasurer be and hereby is authorized to open a bank account in behalf of the corporation with

located at
and a resolution for that purpose on the printed form of said bank was adopted and was ordered appended to the minutes of this meeting.

Upon motion duly made, seconded and carried, it was

RESOLVED that the corporation proceed to carry on the business for which it was incorporated.

The secretary then presented to the meeting a written proposal from

to this corporation.

Upon motion duly made, seconded and carried, the said proposal was ordered filed with the secretary, and he was requested to spread the same at length upon the minutes, said proposal being as follows:

The proposal was taken up for consideration and the following resolution was on motion unanimously adopted:

WHEREAS a written proposal has been made to this corporation in the form as set forth above in these minutes, and

WHEREAS in the judgment of this board the assets proposed to be transferred to the corporation are reasonably worth the amount of the consideration demanded therefor, and that it is in the best interests of this corporation to accept the said offer as set forth in said proposal,

NOW THEREFORE, IT IS RESOLVED that said offer, as set forth in said proposal, be and the same hereby is approved and accepted, and that in accordance with the terms thereof, this corporation, shall as full payment for said property issue to said offeror(s) or nominee(s)   fully paid and non-assessable shares of this corporation, and it is

FURTHER RESOLVED, that upon the delivery to this corporation of said assets and the execution and delivery of such proper instruments as may be necessary to transfer and convey the same to this corporation, the officers of this corporation are authorized and directed to execute and deliver the certificate or certificates for such shares as are required to be issued and delivered on acceptance of said offer in accordance with the foregoing.

The chairman presented to the meeting a form of certificate required under Tax Law section 275A to be filed in the office of the tax commission.

Upon motion duly made, seconded and carried, it was

RESOLVED that the proper officers of this corporation are hereby authorized and directed to execute and file such certificate forthwith.

On motion duly made, seconded and carried, it was

RESOLVED that all of the acts taken and decisions made at the organization meeting be and they hereby are ratified and it was

FURTHER RESOLVED, that the signing of these minutes shall constitute full ratification thereof and waiver of notice of the meeting by the signatories.

There being no further business before the meeting, on motion duly made, seconded and carried, the meeting adjourned.

Dated the   day of   19   .

_____   _____
                                                                Secretary

_____

_____   _____
                                                                Chairman

_____

_____

A true copy of each of the following papers referred to in the foregoing minutes is appended hereto.

Waiver of notice of meeting
Specimen certificate for shares
Resolution designating depository of funds

Figure 9.6
Minutes of Regular Meeting of the Board
Specimen Form

MINUTES OF REGULAR MEETING OF THE BOARD

MINUTES of the meeting of the Board held at the office of the Corporation at * * * on the * * day of * * 19 *, at * o'clock in the * * noon.

The President of the Corporation called the meeting to order.

The Secretary called the roll and the following Directors were found present: * * * * * * * *

The Secretary reported that Notice of the time and place of holding the meeting was given to each Director by mail in accordance with the By-Laws.

On motion duly made and carried, the notice was ordered filed with these minutes.

The President then stated that a quorum was present and the meeting was ready to transact business.

The minutes of the preceding meeting of the Board, held on the * * day of * * 19 * were thereupon read and adopted.

The President presented his report. * * * * * * *

On motion duly made and carried, the same was received and ordered filed with these minutes.

On motion duly made and carried, Messrs. * * * * * * * * were appointed a Committee to audit the books of the Treasurer before same are presented to the Shareholders.

On motion duly made and carried the meeting proceeded to the election of officers for the ensuing year.

The following officers were thereupon duly elected by ballot:
President:
Vice President:
Secretary:
Treasurer:

On motion duly made and carried, the salaries of the officers were fixed as follows: * * * *

There being no further business the meeting was adjourned.

Dated the * * day of * * 19 * .

_____
Secretary

Figure 9.7
Notice of Special Meeting of the Board
Specimen Form

NOTICE OF SPECIAL MEETING OF THE BOARD

PLEASE TAKE NOTICE that a special meeting of the Board of * * * will be held at the office of the Corporation at No. * * *, City and State of * * *, on the * * day of * * 19 *, at * * o'clock in the * noon, for the purpose of transacting the following business:

Dated the * * day of * * , 19 * .

_____
                                Secretary

**Figure 9.8
Written Consent of the Sole Shareholder
in Lieu of a Meeting
Specimen Form**

WRITTEN CONSENT
OF THE
SOLE SHAREHOLDER
in lieu of a MEETING

Pursuant to Section
of the

of the
State of

THE UNDERSIGNED, being the Sole Shareholder of   , a   corporation (the "Corporation"), who would be entitled to notice of the organization meeting of the   for the purpose of taking the action and adopting the resolutions set forth below, does hereby make the following statements, takes the following action and adopts the following resolutions by written consent to action without a meeting pursuant to Section   of the   of the State of   :

BE IT RESOLVED, that the Certificate of Incorporation of the Corporation was filed with the Department of State of the State of New York on the 13th day of December, 1976. A copy of said Certificate of Incorporation is hereby ordered permanently filed in the minute book of the Corporation; and be it further

RESOLVED, that the By-Laws annexed hereto are hereby adopted as and for the By-Laws of the Corporation, and a copy thereof is hereby ordered permanently kept in the minute book of the Corporation; and be it further

RESOLVED, that the following individuals be, and they hereby are elected as Directors of the Corporation, to hold such office until the First

Annual Meeting of Shareholders and until their successors are elected and qualify, or until their earlier death, resignation or removal:

IN WITNESS WHEREOF, the undersigned has signed this Consent at 280 Park Avenue, New York, New York 10017, as of the   day of   , 1977.

_____

Figure 9.9
Written Consent to Action of the Board of Directors
Without a Meeting
Specimen Form

WRITTEN CONSENT TO ACTION
OF THE BOARD OF DIRECTORS
WITHOUT A MEETING

Pursuant to Section 1701.54
of the
General Corporation Laws
of the
State of Ohio

THE UNDERSIGNED, being all of the Directors of   Inc., an Ohio corporation (the "Corporation"), who would be entitled to notice of a meeting of the Board of Directors for the purpose of taking the action and adopting the resolutions set forth below, do hereby take the following action and adopt the following resolutions by unanimous written consent to action pursuant to the General Laws of the State of Ohio:

WHEREAS, it has been proposed that the Corporation purchase certain computer equipment from   Corporation (" "), pursuant to the terms and conditions of a certain Purchase Agreement, dated September 29, 197 , by an between the Corporation and   (the "AGREEMENT"), and

WHEREAS, it is the judgment of this Board of Directors that it is desirable and in the best interests of the Corporation that the Corporation enter into the aforementioned Agreement,

NOW, THEREFORE,

BE IT RESOLVED, that in accordance with the foregoing preambles, the Board of Directors of the Corporation hereby approves and authorizes the purchase of the computer equipment (the "Equipment"), which is the subject of the Agreement; and that any one of the officers of the Corporation be, and they hereby are, authorized, empowered and directed to execute, deliver and perform the Agreement, in substantially the form annexed hereto and made a part hereof, with such changes thereto as they may, with the advice of counsel, deem necessary or appropriate; and be it further

RESOLVED, that the officers of the Corporation be, and they hereby are, jointly and severally authorized, empowered and directed to complete the purchase of the Equipment provided for in the Agreement and all of the transactions contemplated therein; and be it further

RESOLVED, that the officers of the Corporation be, and they hereby are, jointly and severally authorized, empowered and directed to execute, deliver and perform any and all agreements, certificates, instruments, documents or other writings, including, without limitation, assumption agreements, security agreements, financing statements, notes and notices, and do any and all other acts, necessary or convenient to the completion, or in furtherance of the Agreement and the transactions or matters provided for therein; and be it further

RESOLVED, that the officers of the Corporation be and they hereby are, jointly and severally authorized to borrow, in the name and on behalf of the Corporation, from   Corporation, the sole shareholder of the Corporation, a sum of money equal to the cash portion of the purchase price as set forth in the Agreement, upon such terms and conditions as they may deem appropriate; to sign, execute and endorse such documents as may be necessary or required by   Corporation to evidence the Corporation's indebtedness; and be it further

RESOLVED, that the proper officers of the Corporation be and they hereby are, authorized and directed to take all further action, to execute, deliver, and file all such other instruments and documents, and to do such further things, in the name and on behalf of the Corporation and under its corporate seal or otherwise, as in their judgment may be necessary or advisable in order to carry out the intent and purpose of the foregoing resolutions.

IN WITNESS WHEREOF, each of the undersigned has executed this Written Consent to Action of the Board of Directors as of this   day of September, 198 .

_____

_____

_____

_____

Figure 9.10
Minutes of Special Meeting of the Board
Specimen Form

MINUTES OF SPECIAL MEETING OF THE BOARD

Minutes of a special meeting of the Board held at the office of the Corporation at No. * *   City and State of * *   , on the * *   day of * *   19* , at * * o'clock in the * * noon.

The President called the meeting to order and directed the Secretary to call the roll of the Directors.

The following Directors answered present: * * * * * * *

The President then stated that this meeting was called especially at the request of * * Directors to consider the following business: * * * * * *

The Secretary then read the notice of meeting and stated that the same was sent to each and every director in accordance with the By-Laws.

On motion duly made and carried, the notice was ordered filed with these minutes.

The following business was thereupon taken up and transacted: * * * * * *

There being no further business the meeting was adjourned.

Dated the * * day of * * , 19* .

_____
Secretary

Figure 9.11
Minutes of the Annual Meeting of Shareholders
Specimen Form

MINUTES OF THE ANNUAL MEETING OF SHAREHOLDERS

MINUTES of the Annual Meeting of Shareholders held at No. * * * in the * * State of * * , on the * * day of * * 19 * , at * * o'clock, in the * * noon.

The meeting was duly called to order by the President, who stated the object of the meeting and requested the election of a Chairman.

On motion duly made and carried, the vote was taken viva voce and Mr. * * * was duly declared elected Chairman of the Meeting.

The Secretary then read the Notice of Meeting together with the Affidavit of service thereof, which were ordered filed. Such Affidavit and Notice are as follows: * * * * * * * * * * * * *

On motion duly made and carried, the same was received and ordered on file.

The Secretary reported that the list in said affidavit of mailing of notice of annual meeting contained the names of all the shareholders of the Corporation and their post-office addresses, as the same appear from the books of the Corporation.

The Chairman then directed the Secretary to call the roll of Shareholders from the Share-transfer book of the Corporation.

The following Shareholders were present in person:

NAMES OF SHAREHOLDERS	NO. OF SHARES
* * * * *	* * * *

The following Shareholders were present by proxy:

NAMES OF SHAREHOLDERS	PROXY	NO. OF SHARES
* * * * *	* *	* * * *

The Chairmen then requested all proxies to be filed with the Secretary.

The Chairman then stated that a Majority of the total number of outstanding shares of the Corporation was represented, and that the meeting was completely organized and ready to transact any business before it.

Figure 9.12
Resolution Re Qualification in Foreign State

SUGGESTED ADDITIONAL RESOLUTIONS

QUALIFICATION IN FOREIGN STATE

RESOLVED, that this Corporation qualify to do business in the State of * * * , and that the proper officers take all necessary steps to that end and cause to be executed and filed, upon instructions from counsel, all necessary documents therefor and to pay all necessary fees in connection therewith.

OFFICERS SALARIES

RESOLVED, that the salary of * * * , as * * * of this Corporation, hereby is fixed at the sum of * * * Dollars per annum beginning with the month of * * * , 19 * * , until further action by this Board of Directors.

ACQUIRING LEASE

WHEREAS, an offer has been made by * * * to this Corporation to lease to it for a period of * * * years the premises known as * * * , commencing on * * * and expiring on * * *, at a rental of * * * Dollars per annum; and

WHEREAS, it is the opinion of this Board of Directors that said premises are suitable and necessary for the purposes of this Corporation, and that said rental is reasonable;

NOW, THEREFORE, it is

RESOLVED, that the terms and conditions of the proposed lease presented to this meeting be and the same hereby are approved; and it is further

RESOLVED, that the President of this Corporation be and is hereby authorized to execute said lease on behalf of this Corporation in substantially the form approved at this meeting.

REGULAR MEETING OF BOARD OF DIRECTORS

RESOLVED, that the regular meeting of the Board of Directors of this Corporation be held on the * * * day of each and every month at the office of the Corporation at * * * o'clock in the * * noon.

PAYMENT OF ORGANIZATION FEES AND EXPENSES

RESOLVED, that the President of this Corporation be and he hereby is authorized to pay all charges and expenses incident to or arising out of the organization of this Corporation, including the bill of * * * * * Esq. for legal services and disbursements in connection therewith, and to reimburse any person who has made any disbursements therefor.

[¶903.1]   Give Paralegals Official Corporate Functions

Frequently, the legal assistant is elected as an assistant secretary with the result that the performance of certain ministerial duties can be properly delegated, including the certification of minutes and other corporate records. Some legal assistants have even been designated as registrars for the corporation's stock. In such circumstances it would be appropriate to bill for such services *in addition to* customary charges for legal services.

By establishing a full service corporate team of paralegals you are maximizing the "paralegal system" for your economic advantage. The corporate services described above and below will be accomplished within your own office, satisfying the needs of your corporate clients and rewarding you with higher gross billings. Moreover, all corporate matters will be unified within your office, delays will be avoided, filings centralized and retention of the corporate client will be better insured.

[¶904]   PARALEGALS CAN MAINTAIN THE STOCK TRANSFER LEDGER

Most jurisdictions do not require that stock transfers be performed by financial institutions. The resulting proliferation of private stock transfer agents indicates the development of a prosperous field of business endeavor. This business can be recaptured by the law firm through designation of an in-house legal assistant as the transfer agent. Of course, large public corporations would be unsuitable candidates for this business and small closely held corporations with limited transactions may consider this duty as an integral part of general corporate legal services, possibly included within a retainer arrangement. No matter how this service is to be translated in terms of the financial relationship with the client, it should be apparent that this particular service easily lends itself to being performed by a paralegal. A sample stock and bond transfer record is included on the following page.

[¶905]   HAVE PARALEGALS GATHER INFORMATION AND DRAFT AND FILE GOVERNMENT REPORTS

The myriad requirements imposed by Federal, State and City agencies are as varied as the number of bureaucratic agencies and departments that are

Figure 9.13
Stock and Bond Transfer Record

✓ To do   ✓ Done

B. STOCK AND BOND TRANSFER RECORD

Decedent No.	Company	Val	not Let Sent on	Trans Instr. Rec on.	6A CC Let	6B Con- sent	6C Stk Ass	6D CC Dth Cert	6E Aff Dom	Orig Sh Rec on	Doc Sent in on	New Sh Rec on	Sh del to Tr'ee
1	2	3	4	5	6A	6B	6C	6D	6E	7	8	9	10
B.1		✓											
B.2		✓											
B.3		✓											
B.4		✓											

Abbreviations:

1 Code number
2 Name of Company
3 Valuation to obtain/obtained (check items to obtain and cross-check when obtained)
4 Notification Letter sent on (date)
5 Transfer instructions received on (date)
6 Documents Needed (check items needed and cross-check when obtained)
   6A Certified copy of letters (testamentary, etc.)
   6B Consent to Transfer (or Inheritance Tax Waiver)
   6C Stock Assignment
   6D Certified copy of death certificate
   6E Affidavit of Domicile
7 Original shares received (date)
8 Documents sent in on (date)
9 New (Re-issued) shares received on (date)
10 Shares delivered to transferee on (date)

the mark of governmental participation in the daily affairs of business and personal relationships. Indeed, many public companies have recently elected "to go private" in order to escape the overwhelming burdens of "paper bureaucracy." The larger a corporation grows, the more dependent it becomes on its law firm to:

1. Keep them informed as to the applicability of existing and new laws in respect to the nature of their business; and
2. Provide the necessary assistance in processing and completing required forms and documents of compliance.

In the larger law firms in particular, paralegals can be trained to keep abreast of these filing requirements, and of course, to develop an expertise necessary to facilitate proper, efficient and timely filings.

One specialty area particularly appropriate for specialization by paralegals is the preparation and filing of the annual S.E.C. reports. These time-consuming reports require a high degree of special training but once mastered become uniquely suited for the paralegal whose labors should provide a profit for the firm.

[¶906] PARALEGALS SHOULD BE RESPONSIBLE FOR ASSEMBLING "BLUE SKY" MATERIALS

No more time-consuming task exists in the preparing of offering statements than the performance of due diligence including "Blue Sky" investigations. Although the attorney (law firm) must certify as to the performance of these requirements, the research and study procedures can be attended to most suitably by the paralegal.

Depending on the size of the offering and the number of states where the securities will likely be sold, compliance with the applicable rules and regulations will be extensive.

Essential to proper performance in meeting "Blue Sky" safeguards is the ability to analyze financial statements and to pursue independent verification of the accounting principles that may be employed. A knowledge of securities regulations is essential.

HELPFUL HINT: Compile a chart for each state indicating the disclosure requirements; filing dates; suspense date for receipt of letter of comments;

compliance with letter of comments; suspense date for receipt of "No Action Letter;" conference date scheduled, if required; final approval.

[¶907] PARALEGALS CAN PROVIDE EXTREMELY VALUABLE ASSSISTANCE IN THE PREPARATION OF REGISTRATION MATERIALS

It follows from the preceding paragraph that paralegals can also be trained to provide valuable assistance in the preparation of S.E.C. registrations. The prescribed formats require detailed disclosure which, on first draft, should be presented in narrative form. The process of encapsulating pertinent detail should await the first letter of comments. Each law firm has its own established system for preparing the registration filings in a team setting. However, over the years, with mounting legal costs measured in part by significantly higher starting salaries paid to recent law graduates, fierce competition has developed among the firms for this lucrative business. By training paralegals to perform within the team structure, a more efficient and economical system for performing this work will develop.

Example: The extensive editing and proofreading required before an offering statement is finalized has traditionally remained the province of the legal team, which usually spends countless hours poring over proofs and editing. Quite frankly, paralegals are often better schooled in English and grammar than young lawyers. The benefits of utilizing trained paralegals in the performance of these tasks is apparent. Indeed, some firms prefer to use non-lawyers who are less inclined to focus on the legal points and concentrate more on grammatical syntax. Paralegals who were college "English majors" have been found to be particularly beneficial in the performance of these details.

[¶908] BENEFITING BY USE OF PARALEGALS IN COMMERCIAL PRACTICE

The trend in commercial practice is to refer collection matters to collection agencies. The attraction of collection agencies is their practice of charging fees only contingent upon their success in recovering receivables. Their fees

Utilizing the Paralegal in Corporate Practice

are generally based upon a fixed percentage of the amounts collected ranging from 15 to 30 percent.

Many attorneys and law firms shy away from collection matters since they cannot compete with the collection agencies whose volume permits the fee arrangements referred to above. However, as part of the corporate practice, initial collection letters are usually included among the corporate services provided within the scope of the corporate retainer.

Basic form letters maintained by the paralegal staff can be tailored to the facts and circumstances of each matter. A tickler (suspense) follow-up file will be established, and telephone inquiries and responses can be maintained by the paralegal staff. Finally, communication with the client regarding settlement parameters and/or referral to collection agencies for suit are performed by the paralegal.

Docketing judgments, enforcement proceedings and issuing satisfactions and discharges are likewise performed by the paralegal. Further duties can include filing proofs of claims in bankruptcy proceedings and attending creditors meetings.

The entire process of preparing and filing U.C.C. statements to perfect a security interest may also be performed satisfactorily by the trained paralegal. These records are centralized for quick reference. Filing receipts are maintained in a system allowing for quick retrieval of information. Discharges or extensions become standard.

Figure 9.14
Form of U.C.C. Security Agreement
Specimen Form

SECURITY AGREEMENT, dated June   , 198 between   (the "Secured Party") and   Corporation (the "Debtor").

WITNESSETH

WHEREAS, the Secured Party and the Debtor, have entered into an agreement dated   , 198 (the "Purchase Agreement"); pursuant to which (i) the Secured Party has sold and assigned to the Debtor an undivided interest in the equipment listed and described in the Purchase Agreement (said undivided interest being hereinafter called the "Equipment"); (ii) the Secured Party has assigned to the Debtor an agreement of lease relating to such Equipment between the Secured Party and   , Inc. ("   ") dated   , 198 (the "   Lease"); and (iii) the Debtor has assumed the Secured Party's obligations under the   Lease; and

WHEREAS, the Purchase Agreement provides that the Purchase Price of the Equipment shall be paid by the delivery to the Secured Party of the Debtor's 6 percent recourse promissory note (the "Note") and certain other consideration;

NOW THEREFORE, in order to induce the Secured Party to enter into the Purchase Agreement and to accept the Note thereunder, the Debtor hereby agrees with the Secured Party as follows:

1. *Creation of Security Interest*

To secure the payment when due, of principal and interest under the Note and the payment and performance by the Debtor, when due, of all obligations and liabilities of the Debtor to the Secured Party under the Note, the Purchase Agreement, the assumption agreement referred to in Section 1.2(b) of the Purchase Agreement and this Security Agreement (such payment under the Notes, and such payment and performance of such obligations and liabilities are hereinafter referred to collectively as the "Obligations"), the Debtor shall and hereby does grant, convey, assign, and transfer to the Secured Party, subject and subordinate, however, to (i) the rights of holders of Liens (the "Senior Lienholders"), (ii) the rights of , Funding and Underlying Lessees (all as described in section 1.1 of the Purchase Agreement), a security interest in and to the Equipment and all additions, replacements and attachments thereto, all leases covering the same, all other contracts calling for the disposition of the Equipment or its use, and all proceeds (collectively, the "Collateral"), provided, however, that so long as no Event of Default shall have occurred, any Rent (as defined in the Lease) received by the Debtor as Lessor under the   Lease shall not be deemed part of the Collateral.

2. *Default.*

2.1 *Event of Default.* The term "Event of Default" as used herein shall mean the occurrence and continuation of any one or more of the following events:

(a) The failure of the Debtor to pay when due all payments due and payable under the Note;

(b) The failure of the Debtor promptly and faithfully to pay, observe and perform when due any of the Obligations other than those referred to in subsection (a) above which failure continues for 30 days after notice;

(c) If the Debtor shall:
  (i) admit in writing its inability to pay debts generally as they become due;
  (ii) file a petition in bankruptcy or a petition to take advantage of any bankruptcy or insolvency act;
  (iii) make an assignment for the benefit of its creditors;
  (iv) consent to the appointment of a receiver for itself or for the whole or substantially all of its property;
  (v) have a petition in bankruptcy filed against it, be adjudicated insolvent or a bankrupt; or
  (vi) file a petition or answer seeking reorganization or arrangement or other aid or relief under any bankruptcy or insolvency laws or any other law for relief of debtors.

(d) If a court of competent jurisdiction shall enter an order, judgment, or decree appointing, without the consent of the Debtor, a receiver for the Debtor or the whole or substantially all of its property, or approving a petition filed against it seeking reorganization or arrangement of the Debtor under any bankruptcy or insolvency laws or any other law for the relief of debtors, and such order, judgment or decree shall not be vacated or set aside or stayed within sixty (60) days from the date of entry thereof; or

(e) If, under the provision of any law for the relief of debtors, any court of competent jurisdiction shall assume custody or control of the Debtor or of the whole or any substantial part of its property without the consent of the Debtor, and such custody or control shall not be terminated or stayed within sixty (60) days from the date of assumption of such custody or control; or

(f) Sell, transfer or otherwise dispose of Collateral in violation of Section 4 below.

2.2 *Acceleration.* Upon the occurrence of an Event of Default the entire unpaid principal balance and all accrued but unpaid interest under the Note and all other amounts payable to the Secured Party pursuant to the Obligations shall, at the Secured Party's option, be accelerated and become and be immediately due and payable and the Secured Party shall have all the rights and remedies with respect to the Collateral of a secured party holding a purchase money security interest under the Uniform Commercial Code, provided, however, that such rights and remedies shall be subject and subordinate to the security and other interests and the rights and remedies of all Senior Lienholders. The Secured Party shall give the Debtor reasonable notice of the time and place of any public or private sale or other intended disposition of all or any portion of the Collateral. The Debtor agrees that the requirements of reasonable notice shall be met if notice is mailed to the Debtor at its address first above written not less than ten (10) business days prior to the sale or other disposition. Expenses of retaking, holding, preparing for sale, selling or the like, shall include, without limitation, the Secured Party's reasonable attorney's fees and other legal expenses. The Secured Party's rights and remedies, whether pursuant hereto or pursuant to the Uniform Commercial Code or any other statute or rule of law conferring rights similar to those conferred by the Uniform Commercial Code, shall be cumulative and not alternative.

Utilizing the Paralegal in Corporate Practice 253

3. *Notices.*

Any notice, request or other communication required or permitted to be given under any of the provisions of this Security Agreement, shall be in writing and shall be deemed given on the date the same is sent by certified or registered mail, return receipt requested, at the following address or at such other address as such party may hereafter designate to the other in a like notice:

If to the Secured Party:

        Suite 1400
        New York, New York 10004

If to the Debtor:

        New York, New York 10022

With a Copy to:

        New York, New York 10022

4. *Restrictions on Transfer.*

The Debtor shall not sell, transfer or otherwise convey all or any portion of the Collateral unless it (i) first delivers to the Secured Party an acknowledgment executed by the transferee to the effect that the transferee's interest in the Collateral transferred is subject and subordinate to the rights and interests of the Secured Party and all Senior Lienholders, (ii) delivers to the Secured Party an acknowledgment executed by the transferee to the effect that the transferee assumes all of the Obligations, and (iii) delivers to the Secured Party such documents and instruments of the transferee as the Secured Party may reasonably request to effectuate provisions (i) and (ii) above. In addition, the Debtor shall not sell, transfer or otherwise convey any portion of the Collateral if the documents creating the Existing Lien prohibits such transfer, unless it first obtains the written consent of the Senior Lienholders, as provided for in such documents.

5. *Miscellaneous.*

5.1 *Financing Statement.* The Debtor hereby authorizes the Secured Party from time to time to file financing or other statements in such form as may be necessary to perfect a security interest in the Collateral in any and all relevant jurisdictions and, in this regard, to execute such statements for itself, as secured party, and for the Debtor, as debtor, as its agent.

5.2 *Course of Dealing.* No course of dealing between the Debtor and the Secured Party, or any delay in exercising any rights or remedies hereunder or under any communication, report, notice or other document or instrument referred to herein, shall operate as a waiver of any of the rights and remedies of the Debtor and the Secured Party.

5.3 *Amendments.* This Security Agreement may be amended or varied only by a document, in writing, of even or subsequent date hereof, executed by the Debtor and the Secured Party.

5.4 *Governing Law.* This Security Agreement shall be governed by and interpreted under the laws of the State of New York applicable to contracts made and to be performed therein without giving effect to the principles of conflict of laws thereof.

5.5 *Successors and Assigns, Survival.* This Security Agreement shall be binding upon and inure to the benefit of the parties hereto and their respective successors, assigns and transferees.

5.6 *Severability.* The invalidity or unenforceability of any provision of this Security Agreement shall not affect the validity or enforceability of any other provision.

5.7 *Headings.* The descriptive headings in this Security Agreement are for convenience of reference only, and shall not be deemed to affect the meaning or construction of any of the provisions hereof.

IN WITNESS WHEREOF, the Debtor has set its hand and seal on the day and year first above written.

CORPORATION

By: _____
      President

[¶909] BENEFITING BY USE OF PARALEGALS IN EMPLOYEE BENEFIT PLAN PRACTICE

Paralegals working in this area of the law must be flexible and hard working. Changes occur with great frequency here. It may be difficult, but is absolutely necessary for the paralegal to understand each new provision, and be trained to adapt it to any current plan about to be submitted.

[¶909.1] Types of Plans

Legal assistants working in this field of the law must be familiar with the four principal types of plans. The three types of pension plans are:

1. Money purchase
2. Target benefit
3. Defined benefit

The fourth type of plan involves profit-sharing. Paralegals must know the various types of plans, and the laws and regulations that accompany each one of them.

[¶910] PARALEGALS CAN RESEARCH ELIGIBILITY AND VESTING REQUIREMENTS FOR VARIOUS PLANS UNDER ERISA

ERISA was basically enacted to enable the working class to participate in a pension plan. It was liberalized so that these employees would not have to wait as long as was previously the case to join a plan. Also, age changes were enacted so that more persons could qualify. These and other requirements must be understood by the paralegal, so that if asked to service a plan which would not qualify under the law, the legal assistant would be able to recognize the problem immediately.

To determine what percentage of a participant's monies have become vested, i.e., held completely without the possibility of forfeiture, the paralegal must be familiar with the term "account balance," and how it is derived. The legal assistant should be trained to determine the account balance, i.e., combination of contributions plus the earnings and losses of each participant to derive the participant's share of trust assets.

[¶911] HOW YOUR ERISA PARALEGAL WILL SPEND THE DAY[3]

The ERISA paralegal will spend much of his/her days with forms. We'd like to walk you through a typical day in the life of your paralegal in this field, assuming a new case has just come into your office.

The attorneys will usually prepare the trust document for the plan. They will provide the paralegal with a copy of same for submission to the Internal Revenue Service for approval. The paralegal must then:

1. Submit Form 5310 for either a Money Purchase or Target Benefit plan. Submit Form 5300 for the other types of plans. These forms must be submitted to the IRS together with the Trust Agreement. (See Appendix F: F.32, F.33, F.34.)

2. The office then receives a confirmation letter from the IRS stating that the plan has been received, and a determination as to its eligibility will be made shortly.

3. If the office will service the account after the plan has been approved, and it is a good annuity for a firm to do so, the paralegal will work with the client's accountants to determine the fiscal year of the plan.

4. When the tax return is due to be filed, the legal assistant can prepare it with a minimum of assistance, especially if you are fortunate in obtaining a paralegal with experience. The legal assistant will file a 5500C for a corporation with a plan, and a 5500K for individuals with a plan, usually of the Keogh type. To prepare this return, the legal assistant must work with the previously mentioned account balance, and determine the transactions that occurred in the Trust in the course of the year. If a distribution is made from the Trust, the legal assistant must prepare and file a 1099R. The purpose of this form is to determine the amount of the distribution that constitutes capital gain vs. ordinary income.

---

[3] The authors gratefully acknowledge the contribution of Monica Schlesinger, an ERISA paralegal in drafting this portion.

5. If the corporation has selected a Defined Benefit Plan, a PBGC must be filed (Premium Benefit Guarantee Corp.). However, this is not a requirement if a PC is involved.

6. Frequently, the client will ask the firm to determine what amount of surplus should be taken as salary and what portion as contribution to the plan. This is usually a legal determination, and is therefore determined by an actuary or attorney, but the paralegal should understand the mechanics of how this figure is derived.

7. The legal assistant should establish a ledger system so that the attorney can determine, at any moment, the status of any case which the office services. The legal assistant should call the clients to set up the time for their annual meetings when the attorneys can review the plan and ascertain whether any changes in the law necessitate the amending of the plan in any fashion. If it is determined that an amendment is necessary, the legal assistant prepares a Summary Plan Description (SPD), which takes the place of the former EBS1's which were required to be sent to the Department of Labor (DOL). The SPD's are sent at both the inception of the plan, and/or if any amendments should be required.

8. Should a participant leave, die, or retire, the legal assistant may be called upon to determine the vested amount due the participant or his estate.

[¶912] THE PARALEGAL IS YOUR GREATEST PUBLIC RELATIONS ASSET

The ERISA paralegal, because the field is one which requires such a high degree of technical skill, is often thought of as a behind-the-scenes worker. Nothing could be further from reality. When calculations must be made, information to draft the trust agreements, and the subsequent servicing of the account, the paralegal is on the telephone constantly doing your legwork. Rapport with the clients and their accountants is absolutely essential. Many a case is retained or lost due to the efforts or failure of the ERISA paralegal.
PRACTICAL TIP: Be certain that during the interview process, you keep in mind the requirements that your legal assistant must evoke a good public relations image, for the success of your practice in this area hinges directly on the legal assistant's ability to act in a professional manner at all times.

[¶913] SUMMARY REGARDING USE OF PARALEGALS IN THE LAW OFFICE

In complicated administrative areas, or in any of the complex series of tasks you may wish paralegals to perform, the systems approach really begins to demonstrate its value.

The concisely outlined sequence of tasks and ticklers, provides the clearest and most consistent type of practical training in legal support work, the kind of training that permits full development of skills that may eventually return to help improve the system.

When you first begin mixing a new system with paralegals, together with your old methods, there are bound to be a few bugs. But persistence and continual attention to improving the system's comprehensiveness and flow will quickly bring it into high gear and maximum efficiency.

These last four chapters outlining utilization of paralegals in the law office setting present only some examples of how a legal assistant can provide valuable services to your practice. Ultimately, the success or failure of a paralegal system will depend upon how many details of your practice (that *you* had been accustomed to handling) you are able to delegate with confidence to paralegals.

As your practice grows and the requirements on your time increase, the development of a paralegal system will reduce many of the pressures placed upon you. Larger firms are already experiencing the economic benefits of an efficient paralegal system. In the next chapter we will explore the benefits derived through the use of paralegals outside of the private law practice sector—documenting current state-of-the-art employment of paralegals and showing how you stand to gain from it.

10

Benefiting From Utilization of Paralegals Outside the Private Law Sector

[¶1001] PARALEGALS GAIN INVALUABLE EXPERIENCE WORKING FOR GOVERNMENT AGENCIES

Agencies of the U.S. Government, at all levels, utilize more legal assistants than any other single employer in the country. Along with large corporations and smaller law-intensive service businesses, they have recognized the benefits of employing paralegals, and have placed full confidence in paralegals' work.

Aside from adding food for thought to our thesis—that the key to success for a firm today is effective employment of paralegals—they have been actively contributing a wealth of practical training and experience to the paralegal work force. You can tap this tremendous and continually enlarging source within your respective fields of practice.

[¶1001.1] The U.S. Attorney's Office Offers a Wide Range of Duties to Paralegals[1]

Paralegals in the Justice Department wear many hats, among them research analyst, intelligence analyst, and paralegal specialist.

Similar to the law firm counterpart who may be involved in an anti-trust case for years, large cases occupy paralegals for comparable long periods in the Department of Justice. In addition to anti-trust matters, civil rights cases tend to be in discovery for long periods; the current record is six years and still going strong.

The government places paralegals in the non-professional group of employees. This has generated hard feelings, and although there are constant movements afoot to have this designation changed, all attempts thus far have been unsuccessful.

[¶1001.2] Paralegals' Litigation Work is About the Same as for a Private Firm

Litigation at the U.S. Attorney's Office resembles litigation anywhere else. There is the necessary digesting of depositions and legal precedents. *Law Week* is an essential reference work which must be checked weekly for all cases dealing with matters on hand. Legal memoranda requiring legal research must be performed.

No government legal assistant is required to type as a condition of employment. All work is sent to a typing pool. An exception would be an urgent case, when both legal assistants and U.S. Attorneys will sit at the typewriter and with two fingers produce the copy. Because all persons work together at times of crisis, which usually manages to occur at about 4:30 p.m. on a Friday afternoon, there can be a real camaraderie between the legal and the paralegal staff.

---

[1] Co-author Rita K. Gilbert interned at the U.S. Attorney's Office, Southern District of New York, for the academic year 1978–1979.

[¶1001.3] The Paralegal as "Intelligence Analyst"

At the U.S. Attorney's Office for the Southern District of New York, most paralegals attend all pre-trial conferences. Indeed, many of them prepare all the prior work for them. At this early stage, a subpoena or writ will be issued to extract certain information to determine whether a full-scale prosecution should ensue.

An intelligence analyst, a pseudonym for a legal assistant working in the area of organized crime, has three main tasks. These include:

1. Getting information concerning organized crime from diverse sources.
2. Analyzing the data received.
3. Disseminating this information to the proper individuals and agencies.

Other paralegals are involved with labor union issues, *i.e.*, to determine if there have been pension fund abuses, or other types of fraud perpetrated on the public.

Examples include worthless land being sold under false pretenses in the case of the *Rio Rancho* prosecution, or the odometer rollback cases. The area of consumer protection is also still expanding with the result that an increasing number of legal assistants are concentrating their time in consumer law as a specialty.

[¶1001.4] Paralegals' "Trial Work" for the U.S. Attorney's Office

Although not permitted to conduct the trial itself, paralegals are important in trial strategy. A paralegal trial specialist often interviews the witnesses, and after consultation with the attorney, determines the order in which witnesses will be called to testify. Expert witnesses will often come under the supervision of the legal assistant, who arranges for their court appearance after first interviewing them, usually in the presence of the trial attorney.

[¶1002]   **OTHER VALUES OF THE PARALEGAL TO GOVERNMENT EMPLOYERS**

In 1975, the Civil Service Commission developed a new Paralegal Assistant Program designed to expand the paralegal's responsibilities to include:

☐ analyzing legal materials and preparing digests of points of law for internal governmental agency use;
☐ maintaining legal reference files and furnishing attorneys with citations of pertinent decisions;
☐ selecting, assembling, summarizing, and compiling substantive information on statutes and treatises on specific legal subjects;
☐ collecting, analyzing, and evaluating evidence concerning activities under specific federal laws before an agency hearing or determination;
☐ analyzing facts and legal questions presented by personnel administering specific federal laws;
☐ answering questions by collecting interpretations of applicable legal provisions, regulations, precedents, and agency policy;
☐ preparing informational and instructional material for general use;
☐ performing other paralegal duties "requiring discretion and independent judgment" in applying specialized knowledge of particular laws, regulations, precedent, or agency practices based thereon.[2]

Paralegals are currently employed by the National Labor Relations Board, the Federal Trade Commission, Equal Employment Opportunity Commission, Department of Health, Education and Welfare as well as the Department of Justice.

[¶1003]   **SUMMARY—ANOTHER LOOK AT THE WIDE-RANGING WORK PARALEGALS DO FOR THE GOVERNMENT**

To summarize the role of the government paralegal, the following may be taken as key responsibilities:

---

[2] Neil T. Shayne, *The Paralegal Profession—A Career Guide*, Oceana Publications, Inc., Dobbs Ferry, 1977 at 5 et seq.

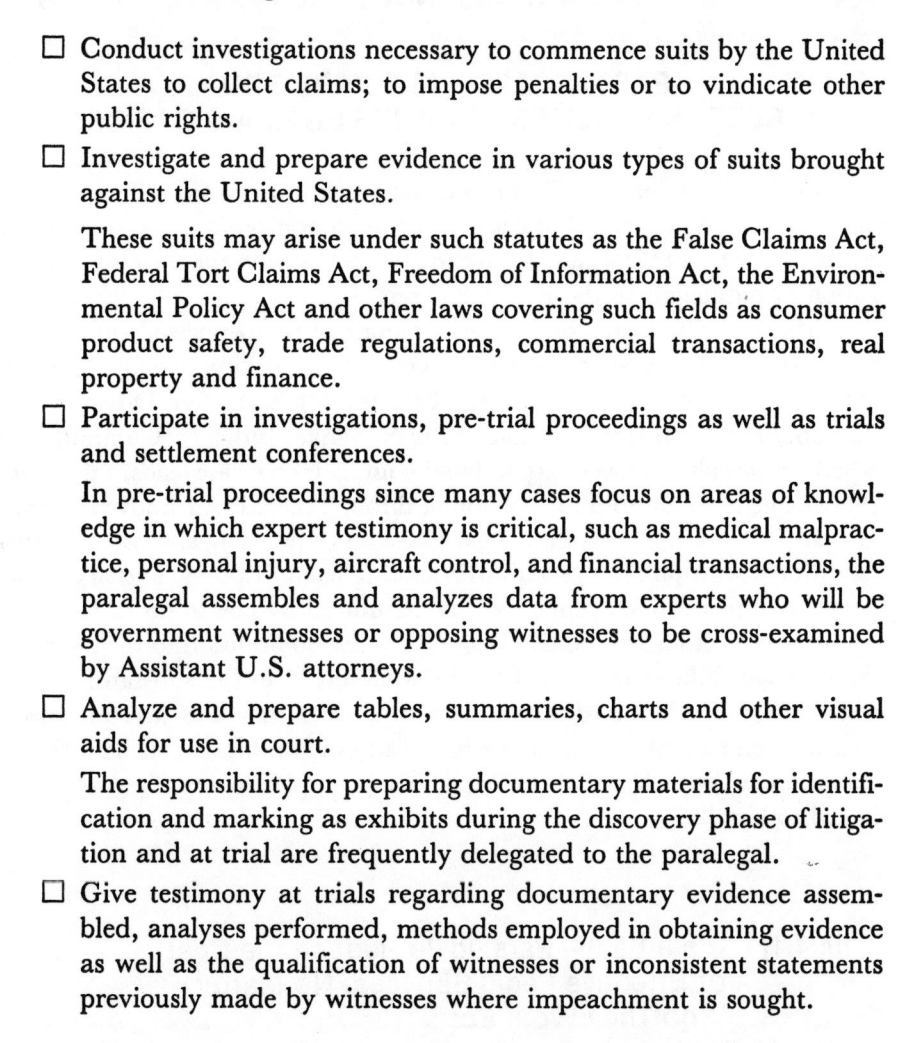

Utilization of Paralegals Outside the Private Law Sector

- ☐ Conduct investigations necessary to commence suits by the United States to collect claims; to impose penalties or to vindicate other public rights.
- ☐ Investigate and prepare evidence in various types of suits brought against the United States.

  These suits may arise under such statutes as the False Claims Act, Federal Tort Claims Act, Freedom of Information Act, the Environmental Policy Act and other laws covering such fields as consumer product safety, trade regulations, commercial transactions, real property and finance.
- ☐ Participate in investigations, pre-trial proceedings as well as trials and settlement conferences.

  In pre-trial proceedings since many cases focus on areas of knowledge in which expert testimony is critical, such as medical malpractice, personal injury, aircraft control, and financial transactions, the paralegal assembles and analyzes data from experts who will be government witnesses or opposing witnesses to be cross-examined by Assistant U.S. attorneys.
- ☐ Analyze and prepare tables, summaries, charts and other visual aids for use in court.

  The responsibility for preparing documentary materials for identification and marking as exhibits during the discovery phase of litigation and at trial are frequently delegated to the paralegal.
- ☐ Give testimony at trials regarding documentary evidence assembled, analyses performed, methods employed in obtaining evidence as well as the qualification of witnesses or inconsistent statements previously made by witnesses where impeachment is sought.

In the job description of a Paralegal Specialist, the Department of Justice recognizes the independence of the legal assistant. The conclusion of the job description provides:

"Incumbent works almost entirely on personal initiative and responsibility and without specific supervision. Incumbent must be capable of independently carrying out assignments and exercising a high degree of judgment and discretion."

[¶1004] PARALEGALS HAVE VERY BROAD RESPONSIBILITIES IN MANY LEGAL AID OFFICES

Until 1971, the training of paralegals for work in legal aid offices was done on-the-job. The National Paralegal Institute, a non-profit corporation funded by the OEO and HEW, was begun in 1972 to assist in the training and utilization of paralegals in the public law sector.

Many public sector paralegals maintain their own case loads, and are specialists in areas such as social security, disability, welfare law, and workmen's compensation. William Fry, former Executive Director of the National Paralegal Institute, told the U.S. Senate Judiciary Committee that where paralegals are specialists and maintain their own case loads, "they represent clients in cases from the beginning through the administrative hearing."[3]

In OEO Legal Services, legal assistants interview clients, investigate cases, deal with public agencies in resolving legal disputes, and argue cases before administrative agencies where permitted by law to do so.[4]

In areas other than OEO Legal Services, in addition to the aforementioned legal skills, paralegals become well-versed in the substantive law in welfare, family, landlord-tenant, poverty, consumer and juvenile law, as well as elements of community organization. Paralegals can handle small claims cases, which no attorney, publicly employed or otherwise, could afford to handle.

[¶1004.1] It's a Fact—Paralegals Reduce the Cost of Effective Legal Services, No Matter Who They Work For

It has been reported in figures submitted by California's Legal Services program to the Senate Judiciary Committee's Hearing on Paralegal Assistants, that the cost to the state for an attorney handling a welfare hearing was $189.89 per case as opposed to a paralegal cost of $93.31 for the same

---

[3] Susan Lerner, "Paralegal Paranoia," 4 *Student Lawyer* 9 (Oct. 1975).

[4] Victoria Watenmaker, "The Impact of the Legal Assistant on the Delivery of Legal Services," 10 *Beverly Hills Bar Asso. J.* 45 (Nov.–Dec. 1976).

Utilization of Paralegals Outside the Private Law Sector 265

service performed. In addition to these substantial savings experienced by the State, the win-loss record remained the same.[5]

Another factor that helps assure the success of the public sector paralegal is that part of the staff may be neighborhood personnel who enjoy a good rapport with their "clients."

One paralegal we spoke with, who was working in the Civil Division of the Legal Aid Society of Westchester County, New York in the matrimonial field, interviews all of her clients personally. She also writes all the complaints and will even go to court on occasion, but only in the company of the attorney in charge, should any unforeseen legal problems occur. A full-time paralegal in this office interviews a new client every day. This heavy case load is possible due to the fact that all legal processes have been reduced to forms and much typing is saved by copying the forms and just filling in the blanks.[6] Lastly, since it is now possible to do a non-contested divorce solely by affidavit, a great deal of court time is eliminated, permitting an increased case load. To enable a client who meets the income qualifications to obtain a divorce for $8.00 plus court costs (the former being the charge for the initial interview) the use of paralegals is absolutely essential.

[¶1005]   PARALEGALS ARE VALUED EMPLOYEES OF FINANCIAL INSTITUTIONS

The banking field does not easily lend itself to formal paralegal training. Closest to training in this field is probably the area of business corporations, but this is obviously far afield from the requirements of this industry. Hence, most paralegals here are trained in-house.

A paralegal working in banking may assume the following responsibilities:

1. Comply with subpoenas, i.e., receive service of subpoena and direct it to the proper channels within the bank.
2. Perform legal research relating to litigation.

---

[5] Lerner, op. cit. at 10.
[6] See Chapter 5 for the complete story on office systematization.

3. Maintain current awareness of all recent legal developments in the banking area and prepare memos disseminating new developments.
4. Answer customer inquiries preceding legal determinations.

[¶1005.1] Paralegals and Finance-Related Work

Although prior training of paralegals working for financial institutions is rare, some legal work does lend itself to formalized training, as the following task inventory for program graduates indicates:[7]

**Figure 10.1
Task Inventory for Some Paralegal Work
in Banking Areas**

Handling banker matters and wage earner plan—

☐ Collect personal financial information about bankruptcy
☐ Compile initial bankruptcy schedules
☐ Survey court records of lawsuits and judgments re bankruptcy
☐ File bankruptcy schedules and fee with court bankruptcy
☐ Collect and organize data for bankruptcy hearing
☐ Collect data for credit proof of claim regarding bankruptcy
☐ Compile credit proof of claim regarding bankruptcy
☐ Compile initial schedules for bankrupt wage earner plan
☐ File wage earner plan, schedule, and fee at bankruptcy court
☐ Collect information for bankruptcy hearing
☐ Compile data for credit proof claim for wage earner plan
☐ Write credit proof of claim for wage earner plan

Of course there is another shiny side to this coin. You will find that there are a great many paralegals working for financial institutions who have

---

[7] We gratefully acknowledge the permission of Harold C. Hart, Lead Instructor, Legal Assistant Program, to publish the task inventory designed at Portland Community College.

Utilization of Paralegals Outside the Private Law Sector

developed a good deal of valuable experience in some highly specialized areas—such as municipal finance, for example—through practical, on-the-job training.

PRACTICAL TIP: You may be able to locate highly experienced paralegals in other law-related professional service businesses. If your area of specialization interfaces with such a business, you should consider carefully whether a well-trained legal assistant could handle some work you personally do right now. You'd be free to concentrate on the most technical aspects of the work, and handle additional clients as well.

[¶1006] PARALEGALS PERFORM IMPORTANT AND DIVERSE WORK IN TITLE COMPANIES

Paralegals employed by title companies usually hold one of three positions. These are known as Title Examiner, Title Reader, and Account Manager. The first position mentioned is typically the first encountered by the paralegal employed by a title company.

The Title Examiner locates records, searches a chain of title, and sometimes prepares the Title Report for the attorney's inspection. The Title Reader examines the information obtained from the Examiner and usually abstracts it. Lastly, the Account Manager includes jobs in the back office area where the research and other problems are resolved, to public relations where the paralegal deals with the public.

Since the principle applied in this industry is one of risk prevention rather than risk assumption, the title researchers must consider all the facts and circumstances surrounding the chain of title, and raise all the necessary exceptions under which the title policy might not protect the client.

In summary, paralegals working in this field are part customer-relations specialists and part administrative persons. They must review and sometimes write the Title Reports, check the Surveyor's Report which also includes verification of the Surveyor's credentials, and if a closing date is fast approaching, ascertain that all necessary information has been obtained, and the Title Report is complete. Banks always get preferential treatment so dates are changed to suit their convenience. This often places additional pressures on title companies, which paralegals must accept as an occupational hazard.

[¶1006.1] Sample Job Descriptions for Paralegals in Several Title Insurance Company Positions

A. TITLE READER: SUMMARY—Analyzes title examinations, determines the insurability of title, raises appropriate exceptions in accordance with company policies and procedures, and writes the preliminary title report.

DUTIES—Analyzes title examinations, or searches of title in accordance with company procedures to determine the condition of title and the effect of standard deeds, mortgages, quitclaim deeds, easements, tax liens, assessments, mechanics' liens, probates and other conveyances, encumbrances and legal proceedings necessary in writing the title reports. May be required to prepare legal descriptions and read surveys supplied to the company into the reports.

Review customer requirements to determine whether instructions can be met within the limits of the policy requested.

Certifies titles based upon examination showing vesting, legal description and all encumbrances affecting the property. Reconciles customer's instructions with conclusions of examination.

B. TITLE OFFICER: ORGANIZATIONAL RELATIONSHIPS—Reports to Supervisory Title Officer or Area/Branch Manager.

JOB SUMMARY—Determines the insurability of a variety of moderately complex title orders involving high liability or involved property interests within company policies. Interprets customer instructions and adapts company procedures accordingly. May train and distribute work to others.

JOB ACCOUNTABILITY—

1. Analyzes title examinations or searches of title in accordance with company procedures to determine the condition of title and the effect of moderately complex deeds, mortgages, quitclaim deeds, easements, tax liens, assessments, mechanics' liens, probates and other conveyances and encumbrances. Writes the title reports, raising the proper exceptions. May be required to prepare difficult legal descriptions and read into title reports surveys supplied to the company.

2. Review customer requirements to determine whether instructions can be met within the limits of company policy. May work with Senior Title Officer or Counsel to develop solutions.
3. Certifies title based upon examination showing vesting, legal description and all encumbrances affecting the property. Reconciles customer's instructions with conclusions of examination.
4. May be assigned to assist in claims research.

C. ACCOUNT MANAGER: ORGANIZATIONAL RELATIONSHIPS—

Reports to: Branch Manager or Area Manager.

Supervises Directly: Personnel in training status or supporting typing personnel.

Internal Contacts: Frequently with all levels of supervision at assigned office or other offices concerning clearance of titles.

External Contacts: Frequently with customers concerning exceptions to title raised by company personnel. Contact with other title companies concerning clearance of titles of mutual interest.

JOB SUMMARY—Provides contact with customers for the purpose of disposing of exceptions to title as set forth in the certificate of title prior to or during the closing of title.

JOB ACCOUNTABILITY—

1. Advises customers concerning documents and procedures required to dispose of exceptions to title raised by company personnel. Such advice may vary in complexity from explaining lien dates regarding taxes to more complex matters.
2. Reviews and authorizes sufficiency of affidavits and other proof submitted to dispose of title exceptions.
3. Receives requests for affirmative insurance and may draft the preliminary wording thereof to conform to the limits of the policy and the scope of services rendered by the company, subject to the approval of Counsel.
4. Authorizes the omission or deletion of, and revises the wording of, title exceptions for the purpose of clarification or limitation.

5. Answers questions asked by customers concerning title insurance or matters preliminary to entrance of a title. Refers legal questions to Counsel.
6. Authorizes within prescribed limits escrows and letters of undertaking as necessary in title transactions and signs checks for the disposition of escrow funds after confirming appropriate documentation.
7. Contacts other title companies to acquire and pass on sufficiency of proof contained in their files to clear title exceptions and examines company records to supply reciprocal information to other companies. Arranges for an exchange of letters of indemnity or letters of indemnity with letter of performance as necessary and with approval of Branch Manager or Counsel.
8. Advises company closers on policy and procedural matters for the removal of exceptions to title. Conducts closings when other closers are not available. Prepares write-up on letter closings received from attorneys who have conducted their own closings.
9. Reads surveys into titles if they are received after a title has been reported. Considers correctness of descriptions and takes appropriate action to initiate corrections. Considers possible violations of covenants, encroachments, possession problems, etc.
10. Investigates claims, obtaining title information from sources both inside and outside the company and submits a report to Counsel with any appropriate recommendations for resolution.
11. Keeps informed of changing real estate laws, technical procedures, local economics and business conditions affecting the title industry.

D. CUSTOMER SERVICE SUPERVISOR: ORGANIZATIONAL RELATIONSHIP—

Reports to: Area/County Manager, Assistant Area/County Manager, Title Operations Manager or Searching Manager.

Supervises Directly: Searchers, Senior Searchers; Title Information Searchers, Senior Title Information Searchers; Auto Messengers; and supporting clerical staff.

Total Supervised: Seven to twelve nonexempt employees

JOB SUMMARY—Supervises the operations of a section providing a variety of customer service functions and title processing support.

Utilization of Paralegals Outside the Private Law Sector 271

JOB ACCOUNTABILITY—
1. Supervises a variety of operations of a section providing:
   a) Specialized title information requested by customers. This information can include identification and verification of names of parties to a transaction, legal descriptions, recording date of action, type of action, status relative to superior and municipal court cases, civil actions, etc.
   b) Some title processing support, including the overseeing of recording procedures, maintenance of general index records, processing of reconveyances, and typing of new orders.
   c) Special searching and examining services such as grantor-grantee property inspections, assignment endorsements, judgment lien guarantees, mechanic lien clearances and appraisal information searches.
   d) May include messenger services between company office and customers.
2. Analyzes practices and procedures of section supervised, recommending changes as needed. Implements such changes upon approval.
3. Confers with customers such as developers, brokers, attorneys, etc., regarding unusual or complicated requests for special title information, searches, endorsements, or guarantees. Cooperates with other management personnel in providing and securing information relative to areas of accountability.

[¶1007] USE OF PARALEGALS BY INSURANCE COMPANIES

Many of the large insurance companies also employ a substantial number of paralegals. Their services are generally well-utilized in supporting insurance defense litigation. In these positions, paralegals can perform substantially the same litigation support tasks we outlined in Chapter 7.

[¶1008] CORPORATE USE OF PARALEGALS IS INCREASING

Individual clients are not the only people concerned with the rising costs of legal services today. There is an increasing trend among corporations—who have been reviewing their expenditures on outside legal counsel—to attract top caliber personnel to their in-house corporate staff.

Recently, many large and prestigious law firms have suddenly found themselves in competition with these corporations for top law school graduates, and are even fighting to retain their experienced associates. Right along with the expansion of the corporate law departments has come an increasing use of paralegals.

A paralegal's work load in the corporate sector varies greatly, from assisting an attorney in the patent field (where the company handles its patent work in-house), for example, to the many facets of company litigation. As more corporations are becoming cost conscious, either out of necessity or in response to shareholders' demands, more legal work is being handled in-house resulting in an increase in positions for paralegals within the corporate sector.

[¶1008.1] Sample Job Descriptions for Paralegals Assisting Corporate Counsel

A. LEGAL ASSISTANT TO CORPORATE COUNSEL: BASIC PURPOSE—To assist the lawyers in providing legal advice and legal services to the corporation, its subsidiaries, and affiliates.

NATURE OF WORK—Under the supervision and guidance of the lawyers the legal assistant performs all professional functions of a lawyer for which the legal assistant is trained and qualified but which do not constitute the practice of law.

Specific examples of what the legal assistant may be expected to handle follow:

- ☐ Review and report on pending laws and regulations and recent cases.
- ☐ Research the law on given subjects and prepare memoranda with citations.
- ☐ Make full use of law library resources in general, including statutes, decisions, treaties, loose-leaf services, digests, indexes, and Shepard's.

Utilization of Paralegals Outside the Private Law Sector

- ☐ Collect, organize, and maintain all documents, papers, correspondence, and evidence which may relate to a pending case, matter, or subject.
- ☐ Draft documents and provisions in frequent or periodic use, such as commercial agreements, patent and trademark licenses, minutes, resolutions, notices, waivers, deeds, leases, and options.
- ☐ Prepare forms and filings for federal and state regulatory agencies having jurisdiction over corporations with respect to, among other things, doing business, selling stock, issuing securities or franchises, and reporting on business activities (e.g., Securities and Exchange Commission, state Blue Sky authorities).
- ☐ Prepare security agreements and financing statements under the Uniform Commercial Code and attend to perfecting the security interest of record.
- ☐ Review advertising and marketing copy for compliance with predetermined criteria.
- ☐ Interview personnel and outsiders and prepare statements for witnesses.
- ☐ Participate in the process of discovery, prepare interrogatories and answers to interrogatories.
- ☐ Arrange for depositions and make requests for the inspection of documents.
- ☐ Draft simple pleadings, motions, and notices.
- ☐ Summarize and index depositions, transcripts, and documentary material.
- ☐ Appraise attitudes of potential judges, arbitrators, and outside lawyers, based primarily on previous decisions.
- ☐ Assist lawyers generally in their active conduct of litigation and arbitration.
- ☐ Maintain dockets or records on status of pending litigation and arbitration.
- ☐ Maintain records on identity and compensation of outside counsel.
- ☐ Assist lawyers in preparing applications for, securing, and maintaining patents and trademarks, domestic and foreign.
- ☐ Monitor timely compliance with legal requirements affecting patent and trademark practice.

- Attend meetings of management committees which deal with corporation's patent and trademark estates.
- Attend bar association and similar meetings as observer and reporter.
- Generally correspond and communicate within and outside the corporation for the lawyers as directed.

This position requires training as a legal assistant (paralegal).

B. LEGAL ASSISTANT TO FOREIGN PATENT SPECIALIST: BASIC PURPOSE—A professional person educated and trained to assist the attorney in handling the heavy work load by working independently on matters ordinarily handled by an attorney.

NATURE AND SCOPE—The legal assistant/Foreign Patents is not a secretary, lawyer or patent agent, but assists the Foreign Patent Specialist by working directly with foreign patent agents and in maintaining a foreign estate of 1,000 patents. The legal assistant, under the supervision of the Patent Specialist, performs broad and varied duties as follows:

- Communicates directly and independently with foreign agents on all correspondence relating to filing, prosecuting and paying taxes on foreign patents.
- Must be knowledgeable and conversant on foreign patent laws in each country, as well as procedures for filing in the various countries.
- Provides legal research and opinion on patent law questions in individual foreign countries.
- Must be capable of advising if foreign filing of invention is possible.
- Communicates directly and independently with members of the International Patent Committee and advises on foreign filing possibilities and costs involved.
- Rewrites U.S. applications for foreign filing in each country in conformance with patent law in that individual country.
- Prepares drafts of contracts, secrecy agreements and patent license agreements.
- Prepares all formal documents, assignment, oath, agency power, etc., for foreign filing.
- Maintains docket of deadlines for filing foreign convention cases.

Utilization of Paralegals Outside the Private Law Sector

- ☐ Arranges for timely decision on foreign filing of all convention cases.
- ☐ Prepares agenda for, attends, and must be capable of directing the Foreign Filing Committee meetings.
- ☐ Prepares and updates status reports on the corporations' foreign patent holdings.
- ☐ Must respond independently and be capable of working with other corporate patent attorneys and coordinators on patent problems.
- ☐ Must be capable of monitoring and controlling costs of foreign patents within budget restraints forecast.

PRINCIPAL ACCOUNTABILITY—The legal assistant/Foreign Patents is responsible for the *daily operation* of filing, prosecuting, and paying taxes on foreign patents amounting to a cost of $400,000. Failure to respond to a patent office communication, filing of an application, or payment of a tax prior to its deadline, will result in a loss of valuable patent rights.

[¶1008.2] How Does the Corporate Paralegal's Role Differ From the Law Firm Legal Assistant?

The work of corporate paralegals differs from that of their law firm counterparts in several ways. One of the most significant, according to the paralegals interviewed, is the lack of client contact which many law firm paralegals enjoy and miss when they cross over into the corporate area. Naturally, since the corporation is the "client," there is not client contact, as such. However, many are able to compensate by maintaining personal contact with firms working in those areas where the corporation prefers to refer to outside counsel.

In the corporate sector the transition from a specialty in "Business Corporations" to the real world corporation seemed an especially easy one. While more law firm legal assistants we talked to seemed to have been trained in-house, the corporate paralegals tended to be graduates of paralegal institutions.

Also, many of the corporate paralegals we interviewed expressed frustration at not being generally included in attorney staff meetings. They felt that the management process was "passing them by" and the interaction between paralegal and attorney that had been successfully achieved in many law firms had not yet been reached in the corporate sector.

[¶1008.3] Similarities Between Law Firm and Corporate Paralegals

Litigation paralegals in both the private law firms and corporate sectors do enjoy similar responsibilities. The legal assistant will calendar cases, index them, digest depositions, research interrogatories, write legal memoranda on points of law, and in general will stay with the case until it is either tried or settled, when they must remain in the background in accordance with the Canon of Ethics.

Paralegals working in corporate legal departments also engage in routine claim activites, such as workmen's compensation and unemployment claims.

Where the corporation is under contract to the United States government, paralegals are especially useful in reviewing government requirements with respect to contract provisions to be certain that the government requirements have been complied with.

[¶1009] TAP THE EVER-DEEPENING POOL OF PARALEGAL EXPERIENCE

From the discussions in this chapter and in the preceding four chapters, it should be clear that paralegals have justifiably earned the trust and confidence of their employers in a wide variety of legal assistance endeavors. They represent an undeniable source of talent and experience that you can and should put to work for you and your clients.

If you employ the systems approach presented in Chapter 5, the benefits that will accrue are clear cut: greater efficiency throughout the office, greater productivity, lower per-client billing plus capability of handling a greater number of clients for increased total billings, and greater freedom to reach your full professional potential by virtue of the ability to concentrate on the technical complexities of the areas in which you've chosen to work.

Now that we have examined paralegals' capabilities, and contributions to their employers, we will present some specific methods that you can use in evaluating the effect they produce in your office.

Part Three

Evaluating and Refining the Paralegal System in Your Office

11

Evaluating Your Paralegal Program

[¶1101] ASSESSING THE ACCOMPLISHMENTS OF THE PARALEGAL SYSTEM IS NECESSARY MAINTENANCE

A system must be constantly updated to continue to serve you wisely and well. While a good law office system will retain its basic structure indefinitely, some of its elements must change due to substantive adjustments made in the law. Certainly, someone who has worked with the system long enough will discover that a step might be eliminated or modified. When this occurs, welcome the necessary changes as part of your ability to adapt to modern advances in law office management.

In addition to developing your paralegal system, this chapter deals with the trends which have already begun to develop as the result of the increased use of paralegals in the legal sphere. These trends include:

- ☐ The growth of employment agencies that specialize in the procurement of "paralegal temps" when your work load is suddenly increased, or a vacuum is created by the loss of a trained paralegal.

280   EVALUATING AND REFINING THE PARALEGAL SYSTEM

☐ The proliferation of free-lance paralegals who enjoy working for many firms without tying themselves down to one of them.

☐ The upsurge of legal clinics and their need to hire paralegals to keep costs at a minimum.

[¶1102]   THREE-STEP SYSTEM FOR RATING YOUR USE OF PARALEGALS

In this context you need some methods for evaluating the performance and value to the firm of your paralegals as individual employees, as well as your entire paralegal system—including supervisors. To get an accurate picture of how things are going, you'll have to perform three separate evaluations. Start with the employee, to measure in both quantitative and qualitative terms the changes paralegals have brought into your office.

[¶1102.1]   Step One: Evaluate Employees With This Sample Form

Utilize the following Employee Evaluation Form, or develop a similar one so that all your employees will be subject to the same criteria.[1] There should be uniformity in the evaluation methods.

Figure 11.1
Sample Employee Evaluation Form[1]

Attorney's or
Supervisor's Name _____   Date _____
Employee's Name _____   Date of Last Review _____

Please place an "X" mark on each rating scale, over the descriptive phrase which most nearly expresses your overall judgment on each quality of the individual being rated. The care and accuracy with which this appraisal is made will determine its value to you, to the employee and to the firm.

---

[1] The authors gratefully acknowledge the permission of Suzanne K. Mahel (Nelson & Harding) and the Practicing Law Institute to utilize the following material.

Evaluating Your Paralegal Program

Confidentiality: Has ability to maintain confidential information re client, firm, section, attorney.

Has ability to maintain confidential material in all aspects of work.	Quite conscientious about client and firm confidentiality.	Usually careful in speaking about firm, section, client, and attorney matters.	Sometimes neglects firm, section, client and attorney confidentiality.	Has no sense of confidentiality.

Professional Appearance: Consider professional appearance individual makes on others.

Presents an excellent professional appearance.	Presents a good professional appearance (good grooming and cleanliness).	Conscientious about appearance.	Careless about personal appearance.	Needs to improve in dress and grooming.

Ability to learn new duties. Consider the speed with which the employee masters new routine and grasps explanations. Consider also the ability to retain the knowledge.

Exceptionally fast to learn and adjust to changed conditions.	Learns rapidly Retains instructions.	Instructions occasionally need to be repeated but does well once routine is mastered.	Requires a great deal of supervision.	Learns slowly. Does not retain instructions.

Communication: Consider ability to express ideas, information.

Communicates ideas across easily and with tact. Listens carefully to others.	Usually communicates well; usually expresses thoughts/questions clearly.	Expresses thoughts/questions adequately.	Seems to have some difficulty comprehending and being understood.	Requires much explanation and cannot communicate own thoughts clearly.

Leadership: Suggests new ideas, imaginative and able to answer questions when asked.

Has confidence and sufficient knowledge of section procedures to train others effectively; uses excellent judgment.	Has the ability and confidence to handle *most* section responsibilities; able to train some people; uses good judgment.	Has ability to handle most individual duties well; sometimes needs assistance.	Needs prodding often; lacks self confidence.	Continually needs encouragement and assistance.

282 EVALUATING AND REFINING THE PARALEGAL SYSTEM

Attitude: Consider attitude toward job.

Employee has a genuine interest in all phases of employment; always willing to work overtime; readily volunteers assistance.	Has genuine interest in *most* phases of work; will use judgment on overtime.	Shows only an adequate interest in work environment; will assist when asked; works overtime if specifically asked.	Shows only a passive interest in work environment; often complains.	Continually shows displeasure of work environment. Is a constant complainer.

Stability: Consider the ability to withstand pressure and to remain calm in crises situations.

Remains calm and works efficiently under pressure.	Tolerates most pressure. Can handle crises.	Has passable tolerance for crises; usually remains calm.	Occasionally "blows up" under pressure; is easily irritated.	Goes "to pieces" under pressure; is "jumpy" and nervous.

Judgment and Common Sense: Does the employee think intelligently and make logical decisions? Is employee accountable for decisions that he/she makes?

Rapid and sound decision maker.	Thinks logically before making decisions.	Thinks intelligently but sometimes makes hasty decisions.	Inclined to make hasty and illogical decisions.	Totally unreliable.

Cooperation: Consider manner of handling business relationships.

Cooperates with everyone. Wants to get job done right.	Works well with co-workers.	Cooperates only when necessary to get work done.	Shows reluctance to cooperate.	Does not work well with fellow co-workers.

Quality of Work: Consider neatness and accuracy regardless of volume.

Exceptionally accurate with very few mistakes.	Accurate and seldom makes mistakes.	Acceptable accuracy. Occasional errors.	Work sometimes unacceptable. Frequent errors.	Large amount of errors. Work frequently unacceptable.

Evaluating Your Paralegal Program

Quantity of Work: Consider the volume of work produced under normal conditions; ability to recognize and organize priorities.

Superior work production. Full effort put into work.	Industrious. Puts forth more than required.	Puts out a satisfactory amount of work.	Does only enough work to get by.	Doesn't meet minimum work production.

Attendance: Consider absenteeism and tardiness.

Prompt and regular in attendance.	Usually present and on time. Has good reason when absent.	Occasionally late but causes few problems.	Lax in attendance and/or reporting for work.	Often late; chronic absenteeism. Intolerable.

Based on the appraisal you have made above, please answer the following questions:
Do you see any need for improvement? ☐ Yes ☐ No (If "yes" please explain) _____
_____
_____

What would be your overall evaluation of the employee? (Please circle one)

    Excellent   Good   Satisfactory   Fair   Poor

Additional comments: _____
_____
_____
_____
_____
_____

PRACTICAL TIP: Employers who feel that their employees should be shown their weak points as well as their strong ones, should review the employee evaluation form with the paralegal. It is necessary for a paralegal, as well as your other employees to know how they measure up to the standards expected of them. Should an employee's performance be totally unsatisfactory, spending additional time reviewing work habits will prove a waste of your valuable time. However, for those who appear to be career employees, this joint review of the evaluation form should prove a beneficial and enlightening experience. It allows both parties to discuss any aspirations or expectations which might prove unrealistic.

284 EVALUATING AND REFINING THE PARALEGAL SYSTEM

The more lawyers can delegate work to competent assistants, the more efficient and productive they'll become. Greater profitability is achieved. Having evaluated your employee, it is necessary to evaluate yourself in the managing and motivating of employees.

[¶1102.2] Step Two: Evaluate Yourself and/or Your Supervisory Staff With the Following Criteria[2]

The authors do not suggest that an "Employer Evaluation Form" be given to your employees, but something similar to that below will be valuable for *your* own use in the office.

A. SELECTION OF QUALIFIED STAFF PERSONNEL

☐ Do you spend as sufficient an amount of time seeking qualified legal assistants as you do in working for an important client? The time spent need not be your own if the group interview techniques have been implemented but rather that of your staff.

☐ Do you tend to hire people who are content to follow directions or do you make a deliberate effort to select only those who show a promise of initiative, creativity and resourcefulness?

B. MANAGING AND MOTIVATING EMPLOYEES

☐ Have you provided an environment where staff employees:
a) feel a friendship among those in the office;
b) enjoy a keen sense of belonging to an office in which they take pride; and
c) feel that they are accepted as peers on a *team* working together to serve clients?

☐ Have you endeavored to help each staff person to achieve a position of adequate status by:
a) recognition of exceptional performance;

---

[2] The authors gratefully acknowledge the permission of Kline D. Strong, Esq. to quote this material, which appeared on pages 339-340 of his book *Practicing Law Profitably*, published by American Press, Reynolds & Reynolds, 8th Edition, 1979.

Evaluating Your Paralegal Program

       b) intellectual acknowledgment of their contribution to the office; and
       c) personal identification with and recognition of each individual as an important person in the office?
- Have you endeavored to provide realistic means for your staff personnel to make satisfying contributions to the office and to achieve worthwhile goals such as:
  a) giving that individual an opportunity to learn and develop personally, rather than merely to follow directions;
  b) giving an opportunity to achieve through more challenging and rewarding tasks; and
  c) extending to staff personnel an opportunity to participate in all those phases of management that will affect the work they do?
- Have you allowed your staff the opportunity to experience self-fulfillment by permitting them to work as independently as is feasible and as creatively as possible, challenging their intellectual skills and talents as well as their mechanical abilities?

PRACTICAL TIP: Allow the forms and systems we discussed in Chapter 5 to work. Instead of always having to dictate a (often long and rambling) memorandum on the next matter you expect a paralegal to handle, you can simply refer them to the forms and procedures you have systematized, and allow them to use some creativeness in answering the expected challenge. Don't tell the paralegal where to dot every "i" and cross every "t" and you will soon be pleasantly surprised at the finished work product.

[¶1102.3] Step Three: Evaluate How the System Itself Works

Now that you have some information regarding performance of your employees and yourself, how does your system stand up as a unified framework for your activities?

1. When a new case comes into the office, does pandemonium reign, or does the system demonstrate how to set up a new file accurately for a case in this area?

2. Does the system alert your legal assistant to all important dates that must be meticulously adhered to; are constant reminders built into the system to alleviate any possibility of missed deadlines?

286   EVALUATING AND REFINING THE PARALEGAL SYSTEM

3. When a new legal assistant is hired, must you personally spend a great deal of time providing instructions on the use of your system, or is it for the most part self-explanatory?

4. Can you leave your office for extended periods with the peace of mind necessary to do your trial work or other activities?

If your rating is high for yourself, your employees, and your system, you have much to be proud of. Your increased profitability will reward you for your efforts.

[¶1103]   HOW TO ASSESS YOUR NEEDS AND PLAN TO IMPROVE YOUR SYSTEM

The legal profession has a very low capital-to-labor ratio. This indicates that management principles applicable to people-training programs may be your key to future success and profitability. Hence, when you take inventory to determine needs and establish plans think in terms of people principles that will help win lawsuits.

For instance:

- ☐ Tell your legal assistants the number of billable hours their work is expected to generate.
- ☐ Screen your new cases carefully to be certain there is enough support personnel and lawyer competence to do an excellent job for your client.

PRACTICAL TIP: Be certain that there are at least two persons competent in every area of the law you handle. Therefore, if one person drafts the document, another must be ready to check the draft. These two persons can be one attorney and one paralegal who respect each other as professionals.

- ☐ Budget for your paralegal on an annual basis, but be certain that increases in productivity will translate into greater remuneration.

Evaluating Your Paralegal Program

[¶1103.1] Improving Case Handling Procedures— Work Flow Changes

Law students are imbued with the notion that in a general partnership, each partner has equal authority. The law graduate of today eventually becomes the partner of tomorrow, and translates this theory of partnerships into principles of partnership management, violating the unity of command principle, and wasting an inordinate amount of time.[3] If you follow the suggestions in Chapter 4 on hiring a legal assistant coordinator, this problem can be eliminated. When there is finally one chief, repetitious tasks can be eliminated, with the result that your office will be better and more profitably run. By this rather simple work-flow change, a new vista of productivity may be realized.

[¶1104] NEW TRENDS IN THE PROFESSION MAY BENEFIT YOU

Kline Strong, in his book cited in footnote one, has a chapter entitled "When 2 + 2 = 5." In this chapter he demonstrates how the synergistic effect of using the legal assistant along with office systems allows your profitability to rise in geometric progressions. We would now like to illustrate some trends that reinforce Mr. Strong's perceptions as well as our own theme: That paralegals can be the key to your success—in many different ways.

[¶1104.1] Temporary Paralegal Service Agencies Are Increasingly Useful

If your firm should receive a sudden influx of work that requires additional trained personnel immediately, don't panic. There are paralegal personnel agencies who will send you "paralegal temps" who are well-trained in indexing and digesting of depositions, as well as the other myriad tasks that must be done on short notice. This group of temporary personnel will

---

[3] Kline D. Strong, *Practicing Law Profitably*, 8th Edition, 1979, at 351.

leave quietly after their special project has been completed, with no additional overhead incurred by the employer for personnel no longer needed. Thus, a sudden "tender-offer" which can be likened to a hurricane—arriving with a sweeping wind and blowing out as quickly as it came—does not lead to total disruption of staff. In this situation, a "one-shot big deal" recommends use of temporary support staff, over the illogical expense of hiring and training new people for short periods of time.

[¶1104.2] Free-Lance Paralegals Can Handle Specific Work for You

The free-lancing paralegal has really "caught on" in California, and the trend is beginning to shift eastward. Free-lance paralegals enjoy greater freedom of movement in that they work for any number of attorneys at one time. They can accept or reject work as their schedules permit. Several former full-time paralegals have taken this route shortly after beginning their families, and do most of their work at home while the children nap.

Some full-time free-lance paralegals, however, have never worked harder in their lives than they are right now. For example, Linda Harrington, in San Francisco, California, has installed her own computer in her office. She estimates it has cut down computation time enormously, allowing her to handle estate work for her client-firms in less than half the time than had previously been the case.

Although all paralegals must work under the supervision of attorneys, and must have all work checked by their employers, the freedom enjoyed by the free-lancers, together with the tax incentives available for establishing their own businesses portend much success for these professionals.

[¶1104.3] More and More Legal Clinics Have Large Paralegal Staffs

Consider this announcement in a Westchester County, New York newspaper:[4]

"(A)nother addition to the Mall will be a legal clinic. . . Attorney Melvin Evans said the clinic will provide at low rates, simple legal services—such as

---

[4] *The Standard Star*, Gannett Westchester Newspapers, January 19, 1980 at Section 3.

drawing up a will in which estates are less than $100,000, marriage separations, real estate transactions and negligence cases which can be settled out of court. The clinic will be staffed by a paralegal and a secretary with an attorney on call and available by appointment. . ."

The need to provide legal services to the masses has led to the great proliferation of legal clinics. As competition increases, the pressures to lower prices may lead to many more clinics being staffed by legal assistants. Perhaps by not showing a sensitivity to costs in the past, we in the legal profession have fostered this movement ourselves, and we will now have to learn to practice in a new environment of competition.

[¶1105]   A PLEA FOR CONTINUING EDUCATION

In addition to recommending articles and books such as this one, we feel that local bar associations should help organize seminars that will encourage *attorneys* to tell their fellow professionals how to employ paralegals effectively. As one legal assistant succinctly stated: "If the paralegals conduct the seminars, the attorneys won't go."

What we feel many paralegals have mistaken as lack of interest on the part of their employers was really ignorance of their training and capabilities. The "no-win" or "Catch 22" dilemma of the paralegal must be addressed. This syndrome translates into the following:

"If you are very bright, the attorney feels he will lose you to law school, so why bother training you. If you aren't too bright, the attorney doesn't want to bother with you so you get stuck with the dull, repetitive jobs."

To extricate themselves from this "no-win" situation, paralegals sometimes feel forced to leave the profession just to save face. If they're told often enough that they are overqualified to be a paralegal, they begin to believe it and feel pressured to leave the career and pursue other avenues of endeavor. It is our hope that none of our readers will be found guilty of perpetuating this dilemma.

It's apparent from the previous discussions that it's possible—preferable actually—to systematize evaluation of your staff and even the systems themselves.

Once you've got a clear idea of how *your* paralegals are performing, you might be interested in comparing your salary structure with that of other firms. In Chapter 12 we review the comparative salary scales for paralegals throughout the United States—using a number of separate, local surveys.

12

Compensation and Fringe Benefits

[¶1201] DETERMINING COMPENSATION AND FRINGE BENEFITS FOR YOUR PARALEGAL

Once you have hired a paralegal, an important question will obviously be: "Am I paying enough, too much, etc., and how does this salary compare with those of other firms and corporations in this area?" This chapter's goal is to help you answer these questions, and we'll also discuss other benefits received by practicing paralegals in your area.

Many paralegal associations throughout the United States have conducted their own surveys—in an attempt to compile and interpret statistics that relate to paralegals in their region, and discern trends within the profession. The authors are most grateful for permission to quote the published statistics obtained by the various associations included herein.[1]

---

[1] The authors gratefully acknowledge the permission of The Philadelphia Association of Paralegals, 1979; The National Capital Area Paralegal Association, 1979; The Georgia Association of Legal Assistants, 1978 and 1979; The Kansas City Association of Legal Assistants, 1979; The Washington Legal Assistants Association, 1977 and 1978; The San Francisco

Compensation and Fringe Benefits

Because salaries are defined differently throughout the country—yearly or monthly—the figures quoted in the surveys are also different. For ease of comparison, we have always included the salary in both forms. The figures used in the actual surveys are always given first, and the converted figures—whether to yearly or monthly form—follow in parentheses. Please note, in addition, that we have sometimes rounded off the survey results to give a more consistent, though less precise, basis for comparison.

Most of these surveys reflect salary levels form 1977 to 1979. While they can provide some valuable information and criteria, you may wish to obtain more recent information pertinent to your geographical location. A partial list of local and national paralegal associations, with addresses, is included in Appendix B. It's most probable that you can obtain more up-to-date information by contacting them.

[¶1202] NATIONWIDE LOOK AT PARALEGAL COMPENSATION

Before proceeding to the chart that compares many compensation factors, we would like to offer a brief overview of some of the regional differences we encountered. Following the chart (Figure 12.1), let us take a look at some interesting factors that were examined in only a limited number of the surveys we reviewed.

[¶1202.1] Survey of Paralegal Compensation in the Eastern United States

As might be expected, *some* of the highest salaries paid to paralegals can be found in this area, although the average salary is similar to the nationwide mean. Of the twenty paralegals we personally interviewed in the New York City area and its environs, the average current salary (1979) was $16,476 ($1,373) with an average starting salary of $10,550 ($879). The current salary, while seemingly high, is indicative of the career opportunities available in this field. While there was an unspoken salary limit of $20,000

Association of Legal Assistants, 1978; The East Bay Association of Legal Assistants, 1978; to quote the results of their surveys; and to Mary Guinan and Cornelia Ferguson for use of their material, based on the 1977 survey conducted by them and the 1978 survey conducted by Cornelia Ferguson for paralegals working in the New York area.

292   EVALUATING AND REFINING THE PARALEGAL SYSTEM

($1,667) for Wall Street paralegals, this barrier has been shattered by career-minded paralegals who have become invaluable to their firms.

[¶1202.2]   Survey of Paralegal Compensation in the Midwestern United States

The Midwestern portion of the United States has been in the forefront of the development of paralegal systems—particularly in terms of training future law office managers and administrators. Lee Turner and Kline Strong are Midwestern "products," and much activity has centered in this area of our country which saw the incorporation of the Kansas City Association of Legal Assistants in 1975.

[¶1202.3]   Survey of Paralegal Compensation in the Western United States

While the California area employs some of the highest-paid legal assistants, the responsibilities they enjoy are commensurate with their remuneration. Of the paralegals we observed, those in the estate planning field draft all documents, including wills and trusts; those in the litigation area draft and take command of a case till it is either settled or tried in a court of law when they must of necessity take a back-row seat; those in law office management are responsible for the entire paralegal work force, which can number as many as sixty legal assistants.

The average salary enjoyed by legal assistants we interviewed in the San Francisco area was $20,450 ($1,704); this figure can*not* be used as a guidepost, however, because those persons interviewed had been paralegals for many years, and were really at the pinnacle of the profession.

[¶1203]   SOME ADDITIONAL FACTORS OF IMPORTANCE IN PARALEGAL COMPENSATION AND STATUS

Despite the comprehensive look at paralegal compensation afforded by the comprehensive chart, there are a few other noteworthy factors worthy of consideration.

Figure 12.1
Nationwide Look at Paralegal Compensation

Survey Data Category	Philadelphia	New York City	Wash., D.C.	Georgia	Kansas/Missouri	Wash. State	San Francisco	Oakland
I. BACKGROUND AND DEMOGRAPHICS								
Number of Respondents	172	93	258	186	61	153	255	35
Female Respondents	97%			94%		81%	85%	94%
Age Categories	20-22 yrs 16% 22-24 yrs 34% 25-27 yrs 32% 27-30 yrs 8%			avg. 28 yrs	18-35 yrs 79%	26-35 yrs ½ % 21-20 yrs 68%	40 + yrs 39%	
Complete or Partial Training in Formal Program	71%	50%	73%	74%	56%	18%	66%	40%
Bachelors Degree	99%		73%	76%	89% completed high school	50%	65%	43%
Graduate Work	75%			20%		50%	18% Masters	20% Masters 3% Ph.D.
Previously Legal Secretaries				20%	43%	32%	27%	29%
Work for Private Firms	87%		76%	71%	82%		85%	91%
Work Outside Private Firms	10% corporate		19%	20% corporate				
Size of Firms	18% 1-10 12% 11-25 12% 26-50		25% 50 +		46% 36-50			

293

Figure 12.1
Nationwide Look at Paralegal Compensation (Continued)

Survey Data Category	Philadelphia	New York City	Wash., D.C.	Georgia	Kansas/Missouri	Wash. State	San Francisco	Oakland
II. COMPENSATION								
Starting Salary	$10,000-$10,400 ($833-$875)	$10,000-$10,999 ($833-$916)	$12,750 ($1,063) for 0-2 yrs	Atlanta $10,345 ($ 862) Outside Atlanta $ 9,033 ($ 753)		$ 745 ($8,940)		$750-$850 ($ 9,000-$10,200)
Salary After Two Years	$12,500-$12,999 ($ 1,042-$1,083)	$16,476 ($1,373) for 3 + yrs	$15,500 ($1,292) for 2-5 yrs	Atlanta $12,578 ($ 1,044) Outside Atlanta $ 9,980 ($ 832)	57% make $900 + per mo $10,800-$14,838	$1,036 ($12,432)	47% earn $ 800-$1,323 ($ 9,600-$15,876) 5% earn $1,300-$1,324 $15,600-$15,876	$1,133 ($13,596) for 2 yrs 2 mo +
Salary After Five Years	$15,000-$15,499 ($1,250-$1,292)		18,300 ($1,525)	Atlanta $17,308 ($1,442) Outside Atlanta $12,100 ($1,008) for 6 + yrs				
III. FRINGE BENEFITS								
Salary Increases: % Who Receive	90% annual	2 in first yr	81% annual	51% annual	52% annual 28% semi-annl	53% annual 23% semi-annl	64% annual	45% annual

294

Figure 12.1
Nationwide Look at Paralegal Compensation (Continued)

Survey Data Category	Philadelphia	New York City	Wash., D.C.	Georgia	Kansas/Missouri	Wash. State	San Francisco	Oakland
Average Increase	$1,000-$1,500 for 32% of paralegals	average 10% of salary			$1,257 average			
Bonus Pay			47% receive	$398 per yr average $25-$4,000 range		$397 per yr average	50% receive	37% receive
Receive Overtime Pay	53%	small %	52%	30%		46%	76%	52
Employer Pays for Professional Association Dues	79%			47%			34%	
Paid Employee Benefit Plans:								
Life Insurance	87%	majority	No % given	89%	81%	30%	74%	6%
Medical	63% Full 35% Partial	Blue Cross (majority) Maj. Medical (majority)	No % given	62% Full 32% Partial	81% Full	48% Full	89% Full	77% Full
Dental	11%		No % given	27%	24%	3%	34%	14%
Pension	55%		No % given	51%	65%		49%	60%
Profit Sharing	28%			13% get stock option	14%		20%	60%
Full Disability Insurance	38%		No % given		36%			
Vacations	28% 2 wks 48% 3 wks			avg 2 wks		avg 2 wks	50% 2 wks 33% 3 wks	69% 2 wks 23% 3 wks

Figure 12.1
Nationwide Look at Paralegal Compensation (Continued)

Survey Data Category	Philadelphia	New York City	Wash., D.C.	Georgia	Kansas/ Missouri	Wash. State	San Francisco	Oakland
Sick Days	52% get unlimited sick days					25% get unlimited sick days		
IV. WORKING CONDITIONS								
Billing Paralegal Time: % Who Bill Time	78%			84%		✓	83%	85%
Hours Per Day Billed	6	7		5.4	13% 4-5 8% 5-6 9% 6-7			
Average Fee	$25-$30			$26		$27		
Must Bill Minimum Hours Per Week	7 hrs						46% must bill	19% must bill
Private Office	39%	11%		67%		60%	62%	64
Shared Office	42%	89%		12%		20%		
Have Their Own Secretary	5%							
Share a Secretary				68%		89%	37%	
Perform Own Typing	10%	1%					18% have a typing pool	17%
V. AREAS OF SPECIALIZATION								
Litigation	46%	34%		48%		31%	64%	
Estates, Trusts and Probate	16%	12%		19%		37%	15%	
Corporate	12%	12%				16%	17%	

[¶1203.1] Training and Education

The Philadelphia survey indicated that only 15 percent of paralegals were being fully-trained on the job. In a survey conducted three years earlier, this figure was 20 percent higher. The trend toward requirement of some formal paralegal training seems pretty clear here. Perhaps this may be due to the increasing demands made on paralegals, as well as the increasing competition for the available positions. Those with formal degrees would seem to have an easier time obtaining positions in the current job market.

In a New York survey conducted separately from our own, all but one of ninety-three respondents had received a bachelors degree, and twenty-three of the paralegals had attended or were attending graduate school.

In San Francisco, 27 percent of the respondents had formerly been legal secretaries, and 70 percent of this group had tacked formal paralegal training on to their work experience. This type of background would seem to be the most desirable you could hope for in a candidate for employment.

[¶1203.2] Period of Employment as Paralegals

In Philadelphia, 10 percent of the survey participants had been in their present position less than six months; 20 percent were employed between one and one-half years; 8 percent were employed in this field for over seven years.

Some 25 percent of the participants in the survey of Kansas and Missouri paralegals had been employed as legal assistants for between two and four-and-a-half years.

In the New York survey, a very large percentage of paralegals had been hired rather recently, and this affected the average salary for the New York area. Twenty-five percent of the respondents had been working at their present position less than six months, and 22 percent were presently employed from six months to one year.

This leaves roughly one-half of the respondents employed in their jobs for one year or less, and thus, the salary scale is presently toward the lower end of the spectrum.

[¶1203.3] Fringe Benefits

In Philadelphia some available benefits included maternity leave (where applicable), tuition refunds (62 percent) for continuing education, and expense accounts for travel. In Washington State 59 percent of respondents indicated that they were reiumbursed by employers for attendance at classes or seminars. In San Francisco, this figure was 55 percent.

In Washington, D.C., the percentage of paralegals receiving the usual fringe benefits for that area varied with respect to the length of time they'd been employed, and with the type of employer. In Georgia, on the other hand, time employed played less of a role—at least in terms of vacation. The average vacation after one year was two weeks; after three years of employment, the average vacation was still only two weeks and two days. Also in Georgia, 13 percent of respondents indicated that stock options were available as a fringe benefit.

[¶1203.4] Paralegals' Status and Participation in the Firm

In New York, 51 percent of respondents indicated that they are included in the activities of their firm or corporation, *i.e.*, meetings, seminars, etc., on the same basis as attorneys.

In Georgia, 25 percent of respondents said they were provided with business cards; 75% of this group use the title "legal assistant" on their cards.

[¶1203.5] Billing Paralegal Time

The New York Survey showed that most often it was only law firms, and not corporate or other employers, who expected their legal assistants to account for their time via the billing mechanism. When a specific amount of billing was required, it was usually seven hours per day.

In Washington State there are several figures related to billing—of those paralegals who did bill work to clients:

- ☐ 13 percent billed between 76 and 100 hours monthly;
- ☐ 8 percent billed between 101 and 125 hours monthly; and
- ☐ 9 percent billed between 126 and 150 hours monthly.

The average billing rate to clients was $27 per hour.

In San Francisco, 83 percent of respondents regularly record time spent on client matters, and 46 percent must record a minimum number of billable

Compensation and Fringe Benefits

hours. The survey did not report on what the minimum number of hours is, or at what rate paralegals' time was billed.

SOME PRACTICAL ARITHMETIC: The following is based on the compensation and billing figures in the chart with regard to the Philadelphia survey.

On a yearly basis, 1625 hours at $27.50 per hour translates into a gross income to the firm of $44,687.50. If the starting salary averages $10,250 ($854), and even after adding an additional 50 percent for overhead, fringe benefits and increases, it is obvious that the paralegal is a true money-maker for any employer.

[¶1203.6] Professional Development of Legal Assistants

In Philadelphia, 93 percent of the participating legal assistants said they were permitted to attend educational seminars, and 62 percent said employers picked up the tab for such activities. Seventy-nine percent of the employers paid for membership dues in the Philadelphia Association of Paralegals, and 69 percent paid luncheon costs for the educational luncheons sponsored by the association.

In San Francisco, 55 percent of the respondents reported that they received reimbursement for attending courses or seminars. One really discouraging statistic in the area of professional development was that 27% of the respondents here had decided not to continue in the paralegal profession. Their reasons ranged from "the work tends to be whatever the attorneys or secretaries don't want to do," to "legal assistants are grossly underpaid for the thankless menial tasks they perform." Not all comments were negative in tone, however, and remarks such as "paralegals serve a worthwhile purpose to demystify the legal profession" must give hope to those legal assistants who intend to remain within the profession.

In Washington State, 49 percent of participants clearly indicated that they wanted to be career legal assistants.

[¶1203.7] Who Are Paralegal Employers?

In Philadelphia, almost the same percentage of paralegals were employed by firms with only 1-5 paralegals (29 percent), as by firms employing more than thirty paralegals (27 percent).

300   EVALUATING AND REFINING THE PARALEGAL SYSTEM

The Washington, D.C. survey indicated the following:

- ☐ 25 percent of respondents were employed by firms with fifty or more attorneys;
- ☐ 16 percent were employed by government agencies;
- ☐ 3 percent were employed by public interest groups.

Larger firms have obviously found it easiest to train and assimilate legal assistants into the profession. They could also more easily afford to attract the top-quality person who was a bit more rare ten years ago than now.

If you run a small firm or even a solo practice, however, you can no longer ignore the practical arithmetic we ran through in ¶1203.4. You can employ paralegals successfully.

[¶1204]   BUDGETING FOR YOUR PARALEGAL COST SAVINGS

Hal Cornelius, in the Law Office Management and Operations column of the *New York Law Journal*[2] estimates that delegable tasks can be performed by paralegals for as little as one-fourth the cost for the same work performed by an attorney. If your office can be staffed by part-time paralegals in the early evening hours, additional monies may be saved.

The legal assistant's work has traditionally been deemed general overhead. The paralegal was considered a part of the non-profit support service to the attorney, much like a piece of equipment that would only enable the lawyer to charge for his own services. This concept has been totally changed in modern law office management schemes. Paralegals' services are akin to the lawyer's own services, and should be billed for accordingly. In many firms, today's paralegal is required to keep complete and accurate time records. Paralegal work is billed to clients at $20 and up per hour, depending on the skill and experience brought to the job. These latter factors also determine the paralegal's salary level which in turn often determines the billing

---

[2] Hal Cornelius, "Paralegals, Outside Special Services Aids to Cost Efficiency." *New York Law Journal*, October 18, 1977 at p. 4.

Compensation and Fringe Benefits

rate to clients. Hence, legal assistants are viewed as an independent service of the law office and *not* as a non-profit service facility.

[¶1204.1] How to Bill Your Paralegals' Time

Billing legal services by the hour is only one method of approaching the problem. Performing services for a fixed fee, *i.e.*, $300 to form a corporation, $100 to write a will, or placing a set fee on a retainer basis to handle all legal work generated by a client are other common ways of handling the billing procedure.

The following examples illustrate and compare billings for the same work performed using 1) the traditional office staff approach and 2) a legal assistant system. You can use the overall model to assess how a paralegal system can improve your own office economics, substituting 1981 figures for those utilized by Kline Strong in 1971.[3]

ASSUME THE FOLLOWING FACTS:

- ☐ A fixed fee of $300 will be charged.
- ☐ The hourly rate for the lawyer is $40.
- ☐ If the lawyer were not forming this corporation, he could be serving other clients on other matters.
- ☐ In the first case, the secretary receives $3 per hour; in the second case, the legal assistant receives $5 per hour.

---

[3] Kline Strong, "Utilization of Legal Assistants by Law Firms in the United States," ABA, Special Committee of Legal Assistants, Preliminary Draft, June, 1971.

Figure 12.2
Billing Comparison for Office With and Without Paralegal Staff

	CASE I— The Traditional Approach		CASE II— The Legal Assistant Approach	
	Time Consumed (Hours)		Time Consumer (Hours)	
	Lawyer	Secretary	Lawyer	Legal Assistant
Functions:				
Interviewing client	1.0	0.0	0.5	0.5
Advising and counseling	1.0	0.0	1.0	0.0
Obtaining information	1.0	0.0	0.0	1.0
Preparing papers	2.0	4.0	0.5	3.5
Executing and filing papers	1.0	0.5	0.5	0.5
	6.0	4.5	2.5	5.5
Cost (measured by economic input)	$240.00	$13.50	$100.00	$27.50

Total Cost	$253.50
Fee	300.00
Net Gain over standard hourly rate	$46.50

Total Cost	$127.50
Fees:	
Corporation	300.00
Other client work "saved" × $40 per hour	140.00
	$440.00
Profit through use of legal assistant	$312.50

WHAT TO DO: If you are quoting a flat fee for performing a job, be certain that your paraprofessional costs, along with an appropriate profit factor, are built into your quoted fee.

[¶1204.2] Sample Budget

The sample budget reproduced on the next page should prove helpful in determining how to allocate monies for paralegals:

Figure 12.3
Sample Budget for a Legal Assistant

I. Legal Assistant (Probate)	Min. Hrs of Expected Billing	Rate Per Hour	Gross Dollar Value
	1625 (6.5 hrs per day × # of days per week 5 = 32.5 × 50 (# of weeks per year)	$25	$40,625
	Salary and Overhead $22,000		Profit $18,625

These figures can be multiplied by the number of legal assistants needed to generate the billable hours in the various phases of your law practice and from this chart, it can easily be seen again that the legal assistant can be a vital component to your firm's profitability.

[¶1205] PROVIDE INCREMENTAL SALARY INCREASES BASED UPON MERIT AND INFLATION

Incremental salary increases must be given on the basis of merit and inflation. If the employee knows that he or she will obtain a 6 percent increase regardless of the work performed, what incentive is there to improve output and performance? On the other hand, if every time your employee does a "super" job a raise is forthcoming, you will be working for your employees and not vice versa. To achieve a happy medium, you should have a salary review either annually or semi-annually, at which time the incremental increase should be based on both merit and inflation.

[¶1206] EVALUATING YOUR COMPENSATION PROGRAM

If you are experiencing a high turnover of personnel, perhaps your compensation program needs some revamping. Many local surveys are available such as those discussed in this chapter, to enable you to judge more effectively the appropriate salary scale for your paralegal employees. Maybe a colleague you meet at the next bar association dinner, whose office is within a close proximity to yours, has just hired a new paralegal employee. What is his salary scale? And, how much more would he pay for an experienced paralegal as opposed to an inexperienced one? Is it very difficult, if not impossible, to discuss salary scales on anything but a very general plane. But once you learn what your competition is paying, you may feel your own offering salary is in need of some revision.

13

Ethical and Accepted Uses of the Paralegal

[¶1301] **INTRODUCTION**

The ethical guidelines established by the American Bar Association for the use of legal assistants have changed surprisingly little through the years. The various State Bar Associations however have set their own guidelines regarding paralegals employed in their respective states. The use of lay persons to assist lawyers is expressly permitted by EC 3-6 of the *Code of Professional Responsibility* which reads:

> "(A) lawyer often delegates tasks to clerks, secretaries, and other lay persons. Such delegation is proper if the lawyer maintains a direct relationship with his client, supervises the delegated work, and has complete professional responsibility for the work product. This delegation enables a lawyer to render legal service more economically and efficiently."

Most State Bar Associations provide more detailed guidelines than the American Bar Association, but where conflicts exist, the State Code controls. At the October 17, 1975 New York Bar Foundation sponsored "Equal Justice Under Law Conference," it was concluded that:

> "(D)efinitional niceties aside, it is clear that appropriately trained and supervised non-lawyers can be enormously helpful in assisting lawyers in fact gathering, preparation of documents, organizing files, providing information and status reports to clients, and in a myriad of other tasks which are necessary to the efficient operation of a law office which do not require the independent exercise of an attorney's judgement. Particularly in the context of law office systems, paralegals can perform many duties which have traditionally (and for little more reason than tradition) been carried out by lawyers."

Each of the two major paralegal associations—National Association of Legal Assistants (NALA) and National Federation of Paralegal Associations (NFPA)—has developed a comprehensive Paralegal Code of Responsibility as guidelines for their members. Both codes, reproduced in Appendix E, reflect the seriousness and dedication with which paralegals view their professional responsibilities.

[¶1302]   PROHIBITIONS: THE FOUR DON'TS

A legal assistant is basically a non-lawyer who performs lawyerly tasks, except:

1. A legal assistant may not accept a case independently.
2. A legal assistant may not set a fee.
3. A legal assistant may not give legal advice.
4. A legal assistant may not represent a client in court.

Letterheads, partnership and legal advice—what do they have in common? In *most* jurisdictions, all three are prohibited by state bar associations. Thus, despite the loosening of prohibitions in the publicity and commercial advertising fields, letterheads, partnerships and the dispensing of legal advice are still deemed the special domain of attorneys, but even these long-standing proscriptions are beginning to falter.

[¶1302.1] You May NOT Put a Paralegal's Name on Your Letterhead—Except in New York

A legal assistant's name may not appear on your letterhead, except in New York. In New York Ethics Opinion #500, New York broke with the long-standing tradition of no non-legal names on a firm's letterhead. It is thought by most states that the appearance of a non-lawyer's name would confuse clients and tend to give "lawyer-like" status to those who are not members of the profession. This is still the majority view.

In breaking with tradition, the *New York Committee on Professional Ethics* stated that where non-lawyer's activities are relevant to the firm's work, those persons' names could appear on the firm's letterhead. The Committee went on to say that this decision was necessary "to disseminate information designed to educate the public to an awareness of legal needs, and to provide information relevant to the selection of the most appropriate counsel.[1] Thus, lawyers in New York may include the names of their non-lawyer employees whenever inclusion of such names would not be deceptive and might reasonably be expected to supply information relevant to the selection of counsel.

BE CAREFUL: You must be certain that the non-lawyer status is clearly stated. In summation, inclusion of a non-lawyer's name on your letterhead is still prohibited in most jurisdictions and must therefore be included under the "don'ts" category. With greater acceptance of the paralegal concept, the likelihood of a change from this prohibition appears certain.

[¶1302.2] A Paralegal Cannot Assume the Role of a Lawyer

A paralegal cannot give legal advice. However, the definition of "legal advice" is not always uniform. For example, a legal assistant may not supervise the *execution* of a will.[2] This is regarded as providing legal counseling to a client. This Ethics opinion goes on to state that:

---

[1] *State Bar News*, December, 1978 at page 1.
[2] *New York State Ethics Opinion* 343 (1974).

"Not only is strict compliance with the Statute required, but the presence of an attorney provides added assurance that the Will was properly executed by a competent testator."

It is the majority view that the execution of a will requires professional judgment which can't be delegated. On the other hand, the same restriction does not hold true with regard to will *drafting*. After the attorney interviews the client and determines the necessary clauses to be contained therein, it is often the paralegal who drafts the Will and gives it to the attorney upon completion for final approval.

[¶1302.3] A Paralegal May Never Be a Partner in Law Firm

The third generally recognized prohibition is that a lawyer cannot form a partnership with a legal assistant if any part of the firm's activities consist of the practice of law. This comes under the general prohibition that a lawyer shall not share his fees with a non-lawyer. This prohibition does not apply however to retirement plans, even though the plan may be based on a profit-sharing arrangement.[3] This exception to the general principle is thought permissible because it does not aid or encourage laymen to practice law.

[¶1303]   THE THREE DO'S

Business cards, recognition for work done in brief preparation, and signing correspondence with non-lawyer status clearly delineated are three privileges for which paralegals have fought, and won their case.

[¶1303.1] Paralegals May Use Business Cards That Connect Them With Their Firm

Formal Opinion 1185 issued by the *American Bar Association* permits a legal assistant to possess a business card, provided that the non-lawyer status

---

[3] DR 3-102(A)—This is an exception to the aforementioned Disciplinary Rule (ABA Code of Professional Responsibility) which reads as follows:
   "(3) A lawyer or law firm may include non-lawyer employees in a retirement plan, even though the plan is based in whole or in part on a profit-sharing arrangement."

is clearly stated. The Opinion states that a business card is assigned only to identify the legal assistant and her/his firm of employment, and the business card is thus approved in form and substance by the lawyer-employer. However, this is not always the case. In areas where paralegals have joined together to form paralegal firms and free-lance for many attorneys, the latter has no direct supervision over the content of the legal assistant's business cards. Apparently, the free-lancing of paralegals is such a new phenomena that the bar associations have not addressed themselves to the issue.

[¶1303.2] Recognition Can Be Given on Legal Documents to Paralegals Involved in Their Preparation

In New York it is now permissible to give a paralegal recognition for work performed on a brief.[4] The opinion suggests that this be done especially where the contribution of a legal assistant has been of particular significance. But, the paralegal's non-lawyer status must be made crystal clear. The opinion states that this recognition is especially appropriate when the legal assistant has been involved in pro bono matters.

[¶1303.3] In Certain States the Paralegal May Sign Correspondence for the Firm

A legal assistant may sign her own letters on the law firm's stationery, but must clearly designate her/his status as a non-lawyer in New York, Maine, and Michigan. Georgia will permit the legal assistant to sign correspondence *only* if it's to a non-adversary party. New Jersey will permit the legal assistant to do this *only* if the correspondence involves an administrative request, *i.e.*, routine requests for documents from officials, court stenographers, law firms, parties, or agents of parties.[5]

---

[4] New York State Ethical Opinion 299 (1973) Association of the Bar of the City of New York Ethics Opinion 884 (1974).
[5] "How Much Can Legal Assistants Write?" 17 *Law Office Economics and Management* 397 (1976).

[¶1304]   CONCLUSIONS REGARDING ETHICS

The wide disparity of views demonstrates the need to achieve uniformity to permit mobility of employment of paralegals as state boundaries continue to give in the flow of national commerce. Presently, ethics committees from fifty states are issuing opinions on identical issues which are decided in different ways. An attempt to conform more closely to the *American Bar Association's Code of Professional Responsibility* is overdue. In the meantime the authors can only sugest that if you are in doubt concerning the "do's" and "don'ts" permitted your paralegal employee, consult the Ethics Committee in your jurisdiction.

It is certain that the responsibility for supervising the legal assistant must be borne by attorneys. They must be certain that legal assistants operate within the Guidelines of the State Bar Association. If a member of the state bar permits a paralegal to perform functions that amount to the unauthorized practice of law, the bar is authorized to discipline this attorney.[6]

In summary, a properly directed legal assistant can do many things a lawyer can do except dispense legal advice or appear in court.[7]

These restrictions should not impede the use of legal assistants in your practice but rather serve to enlighten you as to the ethical boundaries within which a paralegal system can aid and assist you in developing a more productive practice.

[¶1305]   MIXING PARALEGALS WITH SYSTEMS: GAME PLAN FOR A REWARDING EXPERIENCE

Behind you now is the undeniable economic rationale, and the details of why and how to put paralegals to work for the benefit of your firm, your clients and yourself. Before you is the challenge of implementation. It's up to you to blend the elements we've offered—systematization (Chapter 5) using the great talents and experience of paralegals (Chapters 6-10)—with the most comfortable and efficient aspects of your current office organization.

---

[6] Disciplinary Rule 3-101(A) of the ABA Code.
[7] 59 *ABA Journal* 449 (December, 1973).

Ethical and Accepted Uses of the Paralegal

You can develop a system and tailor it to function with maximum efficiency in *your own* office, with your present staff and paralegal support. Our parting contribution is a broad game plan. Use it starting right now, to give your practice the extra edge that will mean smooth operations, growth capability and greater, well-earned profits.

- ☐ Select your major area of practice (or specialization) and begin systematizing your work immediately. (Chapter 5)
- ☐ Begin preparing an office manual immediately. (Chapter 4)
- ☐ Start a casual effort at locating paralegals qualified to do your work. (Chapter 2)
- ☐ Conduct interviews and hire a paralegal or paralegals. (Chapter 3)
- ☐ Train the paralegal and simultaneously polish your systems approach. (Chapters 4, 6-10)
- ☐ Systematize other significant areas of your practice. (Chapters 5, 6-10)
- ☐ After six months to a year, evaluate your staff, your system, and yourself. (Chapter 11)
- ☐ Plan improvements. (Chapters 11, 5)

We are fortunate to be part of a most exciting profession. Legal assisting is such a new area when you consider how long the legal profession has been in existence. The excitement which you first felt after learning you had passed the bar exam in your state should still be more than a memory, rather it should be the reason for getting up and going to work in the morning. Imagine that you can once again recapture the enchantment that motivated your going to law school by returning to the true practice of law, leaving behind the administrative headaches. The romance of the law can once again be a source of great fulfillment. And you can reach this goal through the proper utilization of legal assistants. Use the paralegal system wisely and you will be richly rewarded!

Appendices

		Page
A.	Paralegal Schools and Training Programs	315
B.	State and Local Paralegal Associations in the United States	335
C.	Alternate Letters of Rejection for Paralegal Position Applicants	341
D.	National Federation of Paralegal Associations (NFPA), *Affirmation of Responsibility*; National Association of Legal Assistants (NALA), *Code of Ethics and Professional Responsibility*	345
E.	Forms and Documents That Paralegals May Draft or Complete in Assisting the Attorney With Corporate Work	351

Appendix A
Paralegal Schools and Training Programs

The number of training and CLE training programs for paralegals is continuing to grow as this book goes to press. Occasionally, of course, a program at a college or university is discontinued, or a private institute shuts down. The list of schools below is as up-to-date as possible.

Most paralegal training programs are connected with colleges, universities and law schools. If a program is university affiliated, it may be run through the law school or the adult education curriculum. There are also a number of proprietary programs operated by business and secretarial schools, in addition to those institutes that concentrate exclusively on paralegal training.

The majority of schools in this list are ABA *approved*, though for a variety of reasons many are not. NOTE: the ABA does not "accredit" paralegal training programs, as it does law schools.

APPENDIX A

PREPARED BY
NATIONAL FEDERATION OF PARALEGAL ASSOCIATIONS
Ben Franklin Station   P.O. Box 14103   Washington, D.C. 20044

The schools on this list have indicated that they offer paralegal training programs or individual classes relating to law and our justice system. The National Federation of Paralegal Associations makes no guarantees or representations as to the existence or quality of the programs. This list is for informational purposes only and should not be construed to be approval or endorsement of any of the programs. Additional information on these courses may be obtained directly from the schools.

PARALEGAL TRAINING PROGRAMS
REGION I (WESTERN UNITED STATES)

ALASKA

University of Alaska
The Justice Center
Anchorage, AK 99501

ARIZONA

Academy for Legal Assistants
  and Paralegals
Luhrs Central Building
Suite L
132 S. Central Avenue
Phoenix, AZ 85003

Mesa Community College
1833 West Southern Avenue
Mesa, AZ 85202

Navajo Community College
Tsaile, AZ 86556

Northern Arizona University
Box 15044
Flagstaff, AZ 86011

The Paralegal Institute, Inc.
5350 N. 16th Street
Suite 104
Phoenix, AZ 85016

Phoenix College
Business Department
1202 West Thomas Road
Phoenix, AZ 85013

Scottsdale Community College
Pima and Chaparral Roads
P.O. Box Y
Scottsdale, AZ 85252

Sterling School, Inc.
1010 E. Indian School Road
Phoenix, AZ 85014

Paralegal Schools and Training Programs

CALIFORNIA

American College of Para-
  Medical Arts & Sciences
1800 N. Broadway
Santa Ana, CA 92706

American Legal Services Institute
2719 Canada Boulevard
Glendale, CA 92108

American River College
4700 College Oak Drive
Sacramento, CA 95841

California College of Paralegal Studies
6832 Van Nuys Boulevard
Van Nuys, CA 91405

California State University
Carson, CA 90747

California State University
Chico, CA 95929

California State University
Continuing Education Office
Administration 710
Los Angeles, CA 90032

California State University
Political Science Department
5500 State College Parkway
San Bernardino, CA 92407

Canada College
4200 Farm Hill Boulevard
Redwood City, CA 94061

Cerritos College
1110 East Alondra Boulevard
Norwalk, CA 90650

City College of San Francisco
50 Phelan Avenue
San Francisco, CA 94112

Coastline Community College
10231 Slater Avenue
Fountain Valley, CA 93708

Dominican College of San Rafael
San Rafael, CA 94901

El Camino College
16007 Crenshaw Boulevard
Via Torrance, CA 90506

Empire College
37 Old Court House Square
Santa Rosa, CA 95404

Fresno City College
1101 E. University
Fresno, CA 93741

Glendale College of Legal Arts
220 N. Glendale Avenue
Glendale, CA 91206

Golden Gate University
536 Mission Street
San Francisco, CA 94105

Golden West College
15744 Golden West
Huntington Beach, CA 92647

Humphreys College
6650 Inglewood Drive
Stockton, CA 92507

Imperial Valley College
Hwy. 111 and Corner Aten Road
P.O. Box 158
Imperial, CA 92251

Lake Tahoe Community College
P.O. Box 14445
So. Lake Tahoe, CA 95702

Los Angeles City College
855 N. Vermont Avenue
Los Angeles, CA 90029

Los Angeles Southwest College
1600 W. Imperial Highway
Los Angeles, CA 90047

Merritt College
12500 Campus Drive
Oakland, CA 94619

Orange Coast College
2701 Fairview Road
Costa Mesa, CA 92626

Pasadena City College
Business Department
1570 E. Colorado Blvd.
Pasadena, CA 91106

Pepperdine University
8035 Vermont Avenue
Los Angeles, CA 90044

Saint Mary's College of California
P.O. Box 52
Moraga, CA 94575

San Francisco State University
Continuing Education
1600 Holloway
San Francisco, CA 94132

San Jose State University
Continuing Education
San Jose, CA 95192

Santa Ana College
Seventeenth at Bristol
Santa Ana, CA 92706

Sawyer College of Business
6832 Van Nuys Boulevard
Van Nuys, CA 91405

Skyline Community College
3300 College Drive
San Bruuno, CA 94066

University of California, Berkeley
2232 Fulton Street
Berkeley, CA 94720

University of California, Irvine
Certificate Program in Legal
   Assistantship
Irvine, CA 92717

University of California, Los Angeles
10995 LeConte Avenue
Suite 214
Los Angeles, CA 90024

University of California, Santa Cruz
Legal Assistantship Program
Santa Cruz, CA 95064

University of La Verne
1950 Third Street
La Verne, CA 91750

University of San Diego
Graduate Career Programs
Alcala Park
San Diego, CA 92110

University of Santa Clara
Continuing Education Center
261 Bannan Hall
Santa Clara, CA 95053

Paralegal Schools and Training Programs

University of Southern California
Continuing Education
CES Building #9
Los Angeles, CA 90007

University of West Los Angeles
10811 Washington Boulevard
Culver City, CA 90230

West Valley College
1400 Fruitvale Avenue
Saratoga, CA 95070

HAWAII

Kapiolani Junior College
620 Pensacola
Honolulu, HI 96814

IDAHO

Boise State University
1910 University Drive
Dept. No. 077-A001
Boise, ID 83725

NEVADA

Reno Business College
258 Wonder
Reno, NV 89502

OREGON

Chemeketa Community College
4000 Lancaster Drive, N.E.
Salem, OR 97309

Clackamas Community College
Business Education Dept.
19600 S. Molalla Avenue
Oregon City, OR 97045

Lane Community College
Business Department
4000 E. 30th Avenue
Eugene, OR 97405

Portland Community College
12000 Southwest 49th Avenue
Portland, OR 97219

Rogue Community College
3345 Redwood Highway
Grants Pass, OR 97526

UTAH

University of Utah
Div. of Continuing Education
Carlson Hall
Salt Lake City, UT 84112

Utah Technical College
1200 South 800 West
Orem, UT 84057

WASHINGTON

Bellevue Community College
Bellevue, WA 98007

Central Washington University
Program in Law & Justice
Ellensburg, WA 98926

City College
Lyon Building
Seattle, WA 98104

Edmonds Community College
20000 68th Avenue West
Lynnwood, WA 98036

Fort Steilacoom Community College
9401 Farwest Drive S.W.
Tacoma, WA 98498

Highline Community College
240th and Pacific Highway South
Midway, WA 98031

Lower Columbian College
Longview, WA 98632

Olympic College
Bremerton, WA 98310

Spokane Community College
Evening Division
1810 N. Greene Street
Spokane, WA 99207

PARALEGAL TRAINING PROGRAMS—REGION II (CENTRAL UNITED STATES)

COLORADO

Arapahoe Community College
5900 S. Santa Fe Drive
Littleton, CO 80120

Colorado Paralegal Institute
609 W. Littleton Boulevard
Suite 306
Littleton, CO 80120

Community College of Denver
Auraria Campus
Room CA-313
1111 W. Colfax
Denver, CO 80204

Denver Paralegal Institute
908 Central Bank Building
1108 Fifteenth Street
Denver, CO 80202

El Paso Community College
2200 Bott Street
Colorado Springs, CO 80904

Otero Junior College
18th and Colorado
La Junta, CO 81050

Southern Colorado State College
Behavioral & Social Sciences
900 W. Ormon
Pueblo, CO 81001

University of Denver
College of Law
200 W. 14th Avenue
Denver, CO 80204

ILLINOIS

Illinois State University
Political Science Department
Normal, IL 61761

Paralegal Schools and Training Programs

MacCormac Junior College
327 S. LaSalle Street
Chicago, IL 60604

Mallinckrodt College
Legal Assistant Program
1041 Ridge Road
Wilmette, IL 60091

Midstate College
Jefferson at Liberty
Peoria, IL 61602

National College-Chicago
18 South Michigan Avenue
Chicago, IL 60603

National College-Evanston
2840 Sheridan Road
Evanston, IL 60201

National College-New Trier
3013 Illinois Road
Wilmette, IL 60091

Roosevelt University
430 S. Michigan Avenue
Chicago, IL 60605

William Rainey Harper College
Algonquin and Roselle Roads
Palatine, IL 60067

IOWA

Des Moines Area Community College
20006 Ankeny Boulevard
Ankeny, IA 50021

Iowa Lakes Community College
300 S. 18th Street
Estherville, IA 51334

Marshalltown Community College
3700 South Center
Marshalltown, IA 50158

Marycrest College
1607 W. 12th Street
Davenport, IA 52804

KANSAS COLLEGE

Barton County Community College
Great Bend, KS 67530

Hutchinson Community Junior College
1300 N. Plum Street
Hutchinson, KS 67501

Johnson County Community College
Business and Economics
College Blvd. at Quivira
Overland Park, KS 66210

Washburn University
Communications Arts Dept.
1700 College
Topeka, KS 66621

Wichita State University
Business Administration
Box 88
Wichita, KS 67208

MICHIGAN

Baker Junior College of Business
1110 Eldon Baker Drive
Flint, MI 47507

Charles Stewart Mott Community
  College
1401 E. Court Street
Flint, MI 48503

Ferris State College
Big Rapids, MI 49307

Grand Valley State Colleges
Public Service School
Allendale, MI 49401

Henry Ford Community College
22586 Ann Arbor Trail
Dearborn Heights, MI 48127

Hillsdale College
33 College Street
Hillsdale, MI 49242

Kellogg Community College
450 North Avenue
Battle Creek, MI 49016

Lansing Community College
419 North Capitol
P.O. Box 40010
Lansing, MI 48901

Macomb County Community College
14500 Twelve Mile Road
Warren, MI 48093

Madonna College
26600 Schoolcraft Road
Livonia, MI 48150

Mercy College of Detroit
8200 W. Outer Drive
Detroit, MI 48219

Michigan Paraprofessional Training
  Institute, Inc.
1720 David Stott Building
Detroit, MI 48226

Michigan Paraprofessional Training
  Institute, Inc.
21700 Northwestern Highway
Suite 515
Southfield, MI 48075

Muskegon Business College
141 Hartford
Muskegon, MI 49442

Oakland University
Continuing Education
Rochester, MI 48063

Saginaw Valley State College
2250 Pierce Road
University Center, MI 48603

Washtenaw Community College
4800 East Huron River Drive
Ann Arbor, MI 48107

MINNESOTA

Inver Hills Community College
8445 College Trail
Inver Grove Heights, MN 55071

North Hennepin Community College
7411 85th Avenue
North Minneapolis, MN 55445

University of Minnesota
106 Nicholson Hall
216 Pillsbury Drive, S.E.
Minneapolis, MN 55455

Winona State University
Paralegal Program
Winona, MN 55987

Paralegal Schools and Training Programs

MISSOURI

Avila College
Business and Economics
11901 Wornall Road
Kansas City, MO 64145

Central Missouri State University
Warrensburg, MO 64903

Columbia College
Columbia, MO 65216

Florissant Valley Community College
3400 Perhall Road
St. Louis, MO 63135

Hannibal La Grange College
College Heights
Hannibal, MO 63401

Marysville College
13550 Conway Road
St. Louis, MO 63110

Missouri Southern State College
Social Sciences
Joplin, MO 64801

Missouri Western State College
4525 Downs Drive
St. Joseph, MO 64507

Penn Valley Community College
Administration of Justice
3201 Southwest Trafficway
Kansas City, MO 64111

Rockhurst College
Evening Division
5225 Troost Avenue
Kansas City, MO 64110

St. Louis Community College at Meramec
Business Division
11333 Big Bend Boulevard
Kirkwood, MO 63122

Southeast Missouri State University
Cape Girardeau, MO 63701

William Woods College
Social Sciences Department
Fulton, MO 65251

NEBRASKA

Lincoln School of Commerce
1821 "K" Street
P.O. Box 82826
Lincoln, NE 68501

Metropolitan City College
4469 Farham Street
Omaha, NE 68131

University of Nebraska
Omaha, NE 68132

NEW MEXICO

University of New Mexico
Law School
1117 Standard, N.E.
Albuquerque, NM 87131

SOUTH DAKOTA

Yankton College
Yankton, SD 57078

WISCONSIN

Lakeshore Technical Institute
1290 North Avenue
Cleveland, WI 53015

Madison Area Technological College
211 N. Carroll Street
Madison, WI 53703

Milwaukee Area Technological College
1015 N. Sixth Street
Milwaukee, WI 53203

PARALEGAL TRAINING PROGRAMS—REGION III (SOUTHERN UNITED STATES)

ALABAMA

Auburn University Montgomery
Criminal Justice Dept.
Montgomery, AL 36193

Gadsden State Junior College
Gadsden, AL 35903

Samford University
800 Lakeshore Drive
Birmingham, AL 35209

Spring Hill College
Legal Studies Program
Mobile, AL 36608

University of South Alabama
Continuing Education Division
307 University Boulevard
Mobile, AL 36688

Wallace State Community College
P.O. Box 250
Hanceville, AL 35077

DELAWARE

Delaware Technical Community
   College
Southern Campus
Georgetown, DE 19947

Golden Beacon College
Pike Creek Valley Campus
P.O. Box 5047
Wilmington, DE 19808

Wesley College
Paralegal Studies Program
Dover, DE 19901

DISTRICT OF COLUMBIA

Antioch School of Law
1624 Crescent Place, N.W.
Washington, DC 20009

Georgetown University
Continuing Education
36 and "N" Streets
Washington, DC 20057

Paralegal Schools and Training Programs

George Washington University
College of General Studies
2130 H Street, N.W.
Library, Suite 621
Washington, DC 20052

George Washington University
Institute of Law & Aging
2025 "I" Street, N.W.
Suite 514
Washington, DC 20006

Southeastern University
501 Eye Street, S.W.
Washington, DC 20024

FLORIDA

Barry College
11300 N.E. Second Avenue
Miami, FL 33161

Florida Atlantic University
Continuing Education
Boca Raton, FL 33431

Florida Technological University
P.O. Box 25000
Orlando, FL 32816

Hillsborough Community College
P.O. Box 22127
Tampa, FL 33622

Langley Paralegal Institute
315 Hyde Park Avenue
Tampa, FL 33606

Manatee Junior College
P.O. Box 1849
Bradenton, FL 33506

Miami Dade Community College
300 N.E. 2nd Avenue
Miami, FL 33312

Palm Beach Junior College
4200 Congress Avenue
Fort Worth, FL 33461

St. Petersburg Junior College
P.O. Box 13489
St. Petersburg, FL 33733

Santa Fe Community College
P.O. Box 1530
3000 Northwest 83 Street
Gainesville, FL 32602

Southern Career Institute
1580 N.W. Second Avenue
Suite #9
P.O. Drawer 2158
Boca Raton, FL 33432

University of Central Florida
Allied Legal Services
Orlando, FL 32816

University of Miami
Continuing Studies
P.O. Box 248005
Coral Gables, FL 33124

Valencia Community College
P.O. Box 3028
Orlando, FL 32802

GEORGIA

Fort Valley State College
Fort Valley, GA 31030

Gainesville Junior College
Business Division
Gainesville, GA 30501

Institute of Paralegal Training
c/o Columbia Southern College of Law
4544 Memorial Drive
Decatur, GA 30032

Kennesaw College
Marietta, GA 30061

The National Center for Paralegal
  Training
3376 Peachtree Road, N.E.
Suite 430
Atlanta, GA 30326

KENTUCKY

Eastern Kentucky University
Wallace 317
Political Science Dept.
Richmond, KY 40475

Elizabethtown Community College
Elizabethtown, KY 42701

Midway College
Paralegal Studies Dept.
Midway, KY 40347

Murray State University
Murray, KY 42071

LOUISIANA

Louisiana State University in
  Shreveport
Conferences & Institutes
8515 Youree Drive
Shreveport, LA 71115

Northeast Louisiana University
Monroe, LA 71209

St. Mary's Dominican College
7214 St. Charles Avenue
New Orleans, LA 70118

MARYLAND

Catonsville Community College
800 So. Rolling Road
Baltimore, MD 21228

Community College of Baltimore
2901 Liberty Heights Avenue
Baltimore, MD 21215

Dundalk Community College
7200 Sollers Point Road
Baltimore, MD 21222

Harford Community College
401 Thomas Run Road
Bel Air, MD 21014

Para-Legal Institute
914 Silver Spring Avenue
Silver Spring, MD 20910

University of Maryland
University College
College Park, MD 20742

Villa Julie College
Green Spring Valley Road
Stevenson, MD 21153

Washington Business School
5454 Wisconsin Avenue, N.W.
Chevy Chase, MD 20015

Paralegal Schools and Training Programs

MISSISSIPPI

Meridian Junior College
Para-Legal Technology
Meridian, MS 39301

Mississippi Gulfcoast Junior College
P.O. Box 47
Perkinston, MS 39573

Northeast Mississippi Junior College
Box 1837
Booneville, MS 38829

Northwest Mississippi Junior College
300 No. Panola Street
Senatobia, MS 38668

Pearl River Junior College
Poplarville, MS 39470

University of Mississippi
University, MS 38677

University of Southern Mississippi
Southern Station
P.O. Box 9267
Hattiesburg, MS 39401

NORTH CAROLINA

Central Carolina Technical College
1105 Kelly Drive
Sanford, NC 27330

Davidson County Community College
P.O. Box 1287
Lexington, NC 27292

Durham Technological Institute
P.O. Box 11307, E. Durham
Durham, NC 27703

Fayetteville Technical Institute
P.O. Box 5236
Fayetteville, NC 28303

Greensboro College
Legal Administration
Greensboro, NC 27420

Pitt Technical Institute
P.O. Drawer 7007
Greenville, NC 27834

Southwestern Technical Institute
P.O. Box 95
Sylvia, NC 28779

OKLAHOMA

Oscar Rose Junior College
Business Division
6420 S.E. 15th
Midwest City, OK 73110

Tulsa Junior College
10th and Boston
Tulsa, OK 74119

University of Oklahoma Law Center
Continuing Legal Education
300 Timberdell Road
Room 314
Norman, OK 73019

SOUTH CAROLINA

Greenville Technical College
P.O. Box 5616
Greenville, SC 29606

Midlands Technical College
Business Division
Box 2408
Columbia, SC 29202

TENNESSEE

Cleveland State Community College
Legal Services Program
P.O. Box 1205
Cleveland, TN 37311

East Tennessee State University
Johnson City, TN 37601

Memphis State University
University College
Memphis, TN 38152

University of Tennessee
Stokely Management Center (SMC) 6
Knoxville, TN 37916

TEXAS

Del Mar College
Baldwin and Ayers
Corpus Christi, TX 78404

El Centro College
Main and Lamar
Dallas, TX 75202

Houston Community College System
Legal Assistant Program
4310 Dunlavy Avenue
Houston, TX 77006

Lamar University
P.O. Box 10008
Beaumont, TX 77710

Le Tourneau College
P.O. Box 7001
Longview, TX 75602

San Antonio College
San Antonio, TX 78212

Southwest Texas State University
Political Science Dept.
San Marcos, TX 78666

Southwestern Paralegal Institute
999 One Main Plaza
Houston, TX 77002

Texas Paralegal School
608 Fannin, Suite 1903
Houston, TX 77002

Texas Women's University
Denton, TX 76204

Tyler Junior College
Tyler, TX 75701

University of Texas
Arlington, TX 76010

West Texas State University
Business Division
Canyon, TX 79016

VIRGINIA

Ferrum College
Ferrum, VA 24088

J. Sargent Reynolds Community
  College
P.O. Box 12084
Richmond, VA 23241

Paralegal Schools and Training Programs

James Madison University
Political Science Dept.
Harrisonburg, VA 22807

Para-Legal Institute
6801 Whittier Avenue
McLean, VA 22101

Thomas Nelson Community College
P.O. Box 9407
Hampton, VA 23670

Tidewater Community College
State Route 135
Portsmouth, VA 23703

University of Richmond
University College
Evening School
University of Richmond, VA 23173

Virginia Western Community College
3095 Colonial Avenue, S.W.
Roanoke, VA 24015

WEST VIRGINIA

Community College of Marshall
  University
Huntington, WV 25701

PARALEGAL TRAINING PROGRAMS—REGION IV (NORTHEASTERN UNITED STATES)

CONNECTICUT

Goddard College
Plainfield, CT 05667

Hartford College for Women
The Counseling Center
1283 Asylum Avenue
Hartford, CT 06105

Manchester Community College
P.O. Box 1046
Manchester, CT 06040

Mattatuck Community College
Public Service & Social Sciences
Division
750 Chase Parkway
Waterbury, CT 06708

Norwalk Community College
333 Wilson Avenue
Norwalk, CT 06854

Post College
Applied Arts and Sciences
800 Country Club Road
Waterbury, CT 06708

Quinnipiac College
Mount Carmel Avenue
Hamden, CT 06518

Sacred Heart University
P.O. Box 6460
Bridgeport, CT 06606

University of New Haven
300 Orange Avenue
West Haven, CT 06516

INDIANA

Ball State University
Muncie, IN 47306

Indiana Central University
1400 E. Hanna Avenue
Indianapolis, IN 46227

University of Evansville
Paralegal Studies Program
P.O. Box 329
Evansville, IN 47702

Vincennes University
Division of Public Service
1002 N. First Street
Vincennes, IN 47591

MASSACHUSETTS

Anna Maria College
Sunset Lane
Paxton, MA 01612

Assumption College
Paralegal Studies
500 Salisbury Street
Worcester, MA 01609

Bay Path Junior College
588 Longmeadow Street
Longmeadow, MA 01106

Becker Junior College
61 Sever Street
Worcester, MA 01609

Bentley College
Continuing Education
Beaver and Forrest Streets
Waltham, MA 02154

Boston State College
Continuing Education
625 Huntington Avenue
Boston, MA 02115

Hampshire College
Amherst, MA 01002

Middlesex Community College
Continuing Education
P.O. Box T
Bedford, MA 01730

Mt. Ida Junior College
777 Dedham Street
Newton Centre, MA 02159

Newbury Junior College
921 Boylston Street
Boston, MA 02115

Northeastern University
Center for Continuing Education
303 Wyman Street
Waltham, MA 02154

Regis College
Special Programs
Weston, MA 02115

Paralegal Schools and Training Programs

University of Massachusetts–Boston
Center for Legal Educational Services
100 Arlington Street
Boston, MA 02116

Worcester State College
486 Chander Street
Worcester, MA 01602

NEW HAMPSHIRE

Notre Dame College
2321 Elm Street
Manchester, NH 03104

Rivier College
Paralegal Studies
Nashua, NH 03060

University of New Hampshire
Continuing Education
Verrette House
6 Garrison Avenue
Durham, NH 03824

NEW JERSEY

Bergen Community College
400 Paramus Road
Paramus, NJ 07652

Burlington County College
Pemberton-Brown Mills Road
Pemberton, NJ 08068

Cumberland County College
P.O. Box 517
Vineland, NJ 08360

First School of Secretarial & Paralegal
  Studies
516 Main Street
East Orange, NJ 07018

Mercer County Community College
P.O. Box B
Trenton, NJ 08690

Middlesex County College
9 Ennis Drive
Hazlet, NJ 07730

Ocean County College
Business Department
Toms River, NJ 08753

The Plaza School
Garden State Plaza
Route 17 and Route 4
Garden State Parkway
Paramus, NJ 07652

Upsala College
Continuing Education
East Orange, NJ 07019

NEW YORK

Adelphi University
Lawyer's Assistant Program
Garden City, NY 11530

Corning Community College
Social Sciences Division
Corning, NY 14830

Erie Community College
1309 Main Street
Buffalo, NY 14209

Herkimer County Community College
Reservoir Road
Herkimer, NY 13350

Hilbert College
5200 South Park Avenue
Hamburg, NY 14075

Junior College of Albany
140 New Scotland Avenue
Albany, NY 12208

Long Island University/APS
Continuing Education, Room M1
LIU Brooklyn Center
Brooklyn, NY 11201

Long Island University
Greenvale, NY 11548

Manhattanville College
Purchase, NY 10577

Marist College
History and Political Science
North Road
Poughkeepsie, NY 12601

Nassau Community College
Stewart Avenue
Garden City, NY 11530

New York University
Continuing Education
11 West 42nd Street
New York, NY 10036

Paralegal Institute
132 Nassau Street
New York, NY 10038

Schenectady County Community
  College
Washington Avenue
Schenectady, NY 12305

Suffolk County Community College
533 College Road
Senden, NY 11784

OHIO

Antioch College
Yellow Springs, OH 45387

Capital University
2199 E. Main Street
Columbus, OH 43209

Clark Technical College
Box 570
Springfield, OH 45501

College of Mt. St. Joseph
Mt. St. Joseph, OH 45051

Dyke College
1375 E. Sixth Street
Cleveland, OH 44114

Ohio Paralegal Institute
Ten-O-One Euclid Avenue
Cleveland, OH 44115

Sinclair Community College
444 W. 3rd Street
Dayton, OH 45402

The University of Toledo Community
  and Technical College
Business Technology Dept.
2801 West Bancroft Street
Toledo, OH 43606

Paralegal Schools and Training Programs

PENNSYLVANIA

Allegheny Community College
808 Ridge Avenue
Pittsburgh, PA 15212

Cedar Crest College
Legal Assistant Program
Allentown, PA 18104

Central Pennsylvania Business School
College Hill Road
Summerdale, PA 17093

Edinboro State College
Edinboro, PA 16444

Gannon College
Lawyer Assistant Program
Erie, PA 16505

Harrisburg Area Community College
3300 Cameron Street Road
Harrisburg, PA 17110

The Institute for Paralegal Training
235 S. 17th Street
Philadelphia, PA 19103

Kings College
Wilkes-Barre, PA 18711

Lackawanna Junior College
Linden Street at Jefferson
Scranton, PA 18503

Main Line Paralegal Institute
121 W. Wayne Avenue
Wayne, PA 19087

Manor Junior College
Fox Chase Manor
Philadelphia, PA 19046

Marywood College
Scranton, PA 18509

Northampton County Area
  Community College
3835 Greenpond Road
Bethlehem, PA 18017

Peirce Junior College
1420 Pine Street
Philadelphia, PA 19102

Pennsylvania State University
P.O. Box 519, Route 119 North
Uniontown, PA 15401

Pennsylvania State University
1031 Edgecomb Avenue
York, PA 17403

Pennsylvania State University
University Drive
McKeesport, PA 15132

Pennsylvania State University
Fogelsville, PA 18051

Pennsylvania State University
310 Business Administration Bldg.
University Park, PA 16802

Robert Morris College
Continuing Education
610 Fifth Avenue
Pittsburg, PA 15219

Widener University
Paralegal Studies
Chester, PA 19013

Wilson College
Chambersburg, PA 17201

RHODE ISLAND

Johnson & Wales College
Abbott Park Place
Providence, RI 02903

Roger Williams College
Bristol, RI 02809

University of Rhode Island
Legal Assistant Program
Newport, RI 02840

VERMONT

Woodbury Associates
School of Legal and Continuing
    Education
659 Elm Street
Montpelier, VT 05602

Appendix B
State and Local Paralegal Associations in the United States

Members of the National Association of Legal Assistants (NALA) and the National Federation of Paralegal Associations (NFPA) represent a significant percentage of professional legal assistants. NALA is a single, national organization; NFPA is a national organization comprised of a number of local associations throughout the United States.

Paralegal associations are forming and growing at a steadily increasing rate. As of the printing of this book, even the following was only a partial list.*

---

* The authors gratefully acknowledge the cooperation of the National Federation of Paralegal Associations (NFPA) for their permission to reproduce this list. The NFPA has published a guide entitled *The Formation of Paralegal Associations: An Organizational Manual*. This provides comprehensive information on the various aspects to be considered in this process, such as drafting by-laws, preparing newsletters, electing officers, organizing committees, and defining responsibilities of the leadership. It is available for $10.00 from the National Federation of Paralegal Assistants, Ben Franklin Station, P.O. Box 14103, Washington, DC 20044.

LIST OF LOCAL AND STATE PARALEGAL ASSOCIATIONS
(Prepared by National Federation of Paralegal Associations, Ben Franklin Station, Post Office Box 14103, Washington, DC 20044)

ARIZONA

Northern Arizona Paralegal Association
Northern Arizona University
Post Office Box 7692
Flagstaff, AZ 86001

CALIFORNIA

California Alliance of Paralegal Associations
Post Office Box 26383
San Francisco, CA 94126

California Public Sector Paralegal Association
c/o N.P.I.
1714 Stockton Street, Suite 400
San Francisco, CA 94133

* East Bay Association of Legal Assistants
Post Office Box 424
Oakland, CA 94604

* Los Angeles Paralegal Association
Post Office Box 24350
Los Angeles, CA 90024

Paralegal Association of Santa Clara County
Post Office Box 26736
San Jose, CA 95159

* Sacramento Association of Legal Assistants
Post Office Box 453
Sacramento, CA 95802

* San Diego Association of Legal Assistants
Post Office Box 1649
San Diego, CA 92112

* San Francisco Association of Legal Assistants
Post Office Box 26668
San Francisco, CA 94126

COLORADO

Legal Assistants of Colorado
P.O. Box 628
Gunnison, CO 81230

* Rocky Mountain Legal Assistant Association
Post Office Box 304
Denver, CO 80201

CONNECTICUT

Connecticut Association of Paralegals
Post Office Box 134
Bridgeport, CT 06604

State and Local Paralegal Associations

DELAWARE

Delaware Paralegal Association
Post Office Box 1362
Wilmington, DE 19899

FLORIDA

Florida Legal Assistants, Inc.
5420 SW 88th Place
Miami, FL 33165

GEORGIA

* Georgia Association of Legal
   Assistants
  Post Office Box 1802
  Atlanta, GA 30301

HAWAII

Hawaii Association of Legal
   Assistants
Post Office Box 674
Honolulu, HI 96809

ILLINOIS

* Illinois Paralegal Association
  Post Office Box 857
  Chicago, IL 60690

INDIANA

* Indianapolis Paralegal Association
  Post Office Box 44518
  Federal Station
  Indianapolis, IN 46204

IOWA

Iowa Legal Assistants Association
c/o Carol Coufal
Davis Hockenberg Law Firm
2300 Financial Center
Des Moines, IA 50309

KANSAS

Kansas Legal Assistant Society
c/o Laurine R. Kreipe
8129 S.E. 2nd Street
Tecumseh, KS 66542

KENTUCKY

Louisville Association of Paralegals
Post Office Box 962
Louisville, KY 40201

Kentucky Association of Legal
   Assistants
c/o Carol Pulliam
192 Sunset Drive
Frankfort, KY 40601

LOUISIANA

Louisiana Association of Legal
   Assistants
c/o Joyce E. Ludwig
305 Baronne Street, 9th Floor
New Orleans, LA 70112

MAINE

Maine Association of Paralegals
c/o Megan Perry
28 Driftwood Lane–Pine Point
Scarborough, Maine 04074

MARYLAND

Baltimore Associaiton of Legal
   Assistants
c/o Claire M. Kittridge
Mercantile-Safe Deposit & Trust
   Company
Two Hopkins Plaza
Post Office Box 2257
Baltimore, MD 21203

MASSACHUSETTS

* Massachusetts Paralegal Association
Post Office Box 423
Boston, MA 02102

MICHIGAN

Michigan Association of Legal
   Assistants
2477 Bratton
Bloomfield Hills, MI 48013

MINNESOTA

* Minnesota Association of Legal
   Assistants
Main Post Office
Post Office Box 3712
St. Paul, MN 55165

MISSOURI

* Kansas City Association of Legal
   Assistants
Post Office Box 13223
Kansas City, MO 64199

St. Louis Association of Legal
   Assistants
Post Office Box 8705
St. Louis, MO 63102

NEBRASKA

Nebraska Association of Legal
   Assistants
Post Office Box 81434
Lincoln, NE 68501

NEW JERSEY

New Jersey Legal Assistant
   Association
Central Jersey Paralegal Division
Post Office Box 403
U.S. Highway 130
Dayton, NJ 08810

New Jersey Paralegal Association
c/o Russell Gale
232 Inza Street
Highland Park, NJ 08904

NEW YORK

* New York City Paralegal
   Association
FDR Station, Post Office Box 5143
New York, NY 10022

Paralegal Association of Rochester
Post Office Box 9673
Midtown Station
Rochester, NY 14604

State and Local Paralegal Associations

Western New York Paralegal
  Association
c/o Margaret Dick
Jaeckle, Fleischman & Mugel
700 Liberty Bank Building
Buffalo, NY 14202

NORTH CAROLINA

North Carolina Paralegal
  Association
Post Office Box 238
Greensboro, NC 27402

Raleigh-Wake Paralegal Association
Post Office Box 10096
Raleigh, NC 27605

OHIO

Akron Paralegal Association
c/o Marian K. O'Hear
Segedy & Umbaugh
40 East Mill Street
Akron, OH 44308

* Cleveland Association of Paralegals
Post Office Box 95527
Cleveland, OH 44101

* Legal Assistants of Central Ohio
Post Office Box 15182
Columbus, OH 43216

Toledo Association of Legal
  Assistants
Post Office Box 1842
Central Station
Toledo, OH 43612

OKLAHOMA

* National Association of Legal
  Assistants
3005 East Skelly Drive
Suite 122
Tulsa, OK 74105

OREGON

* Oregon Legal Assistants
  Association
Post Office Box 8523
Portland, OR 97207

PENNSYLVANIA

Pennsylvania Association of Legal
  Assistants
c/o Janet Brown
Robin Hill Apartment 1507
4th and Preson Avenue
Voorhees, NJ 08043

* Philadelphia Association of
  Paralegals
Post Office Box 55
Philadelphia, PA 19105

* Pittsburgh Paralegal Association
Post Office Box 1053
Pittsburgh, PA 15230

RHODE ISLAND

Rhode Island Paralegal Association
Post Office Box 1003
Providence, RI 02901

TEXAS

Capitol Area Paralegal Association
Post Office Box 12552
Capitol Station
Austin, TX 78711

* Dallas Association of Legal Assistants
Post Office Box 50812
Dallas, TX 75250

Houston Legal Assistants Association
Post Office Box 52241
Houston, TX 77052

Texas Association of Paralegals
c/o Marilyn Abbott
4811 South Congress
Austin, TX 78745

VIRGINIA

Paralegal Association of Virginia
Post Office Box 3922
Norfolk, VA 23514

WASHINGTON

* Washington Legal Assistants Association
Post Office Box 2114
Seattle, WA 98111

WASHINGTON, DC

* National Capital Area Paralegal Association
Post Office Box 19505
Washington, DC 20036

WISCONSIN

Paralegal Association of Wisconsin
Post Office Box 246
Milwaukee, WI 53202

---

* Member, National Federation of Paralegal Associations

Appendix C
Alternate Letters of Rejection for Paralegal Position Applicants

Because the precise situations of firms seeking to employ paralegals will differ vastly, we offer the following alternate responses to your unsuccessful applicants. You may or may not, in fact, wish to retain some résumés and applications for future reference—though probably not all of them. At times you may receive unsolicited applications. These letters may be useful under such circumstances.

C.1   Rejection Letter for Application
Received in Response to Classified Advertisement
(Application Retained on File)

Name and Applicant's Address   Date

_____

_____

Dear _____:

Thank you for responding to our recent advertisement.

Your background is impressive but, unfortunately, not what we are seeking for this position. Your application will remain active for ninety days. Should an appropriate position become available, we will contact you directly.

Best wishes for success in your career pursuit.

                    Sincerely,

                    _____
                    X, Y & Z
                    Attorneys at Law

C.2 Alternate Rejection Letter for Application Received in Response to Classified Advertisement (Application Not Retained on File)

Name and Applicant's Address   Date
_____
_____

Dear _____:

Thank you for your interest in our recent advertisement.

At the present time we are interviewing a few individuals whose backgrounds seem most related to our needs. If we do not make a placement from this group we may contact you, However, if we do not contact you, I would like to take this opportunity to thank you for applying for employment, and wish you success in your current endeavors.

Sincerely,

_____
X, Y & Z
Attorneys at Law

C.3   Rejection Letter in Response to Unsolicited Application
(Application Not Retained on File)

Name and Applicant's Address   Date
_____
_____

Dear _____:

    Thank you for your inquiry in which you outlined your qualifications and interests for our consideration.

    We would like very much to be able to utilize your abilities in our firm. However, we find that at present we have no suitable openings for someone with your particular qualifications.

    Your interest in our firm is appreciated. Best wishes for success in locating the type of opportunity you are seeking.

                                Sincerely,

                                _____
                                X, Y & Z
                                A Professional Corporation

C.4   Alternate Rejection Letter in Response to Unsolicited Application (Application Retained on File)

Name and Applicant's Address   Date
_____
_____

Dear _____:

    Your recent employment inquiry has been referred to me for consideration.
    We note with interest your background and experience; however, we regret we do not have an opening at this time and your application is not under active consideration. If the situation should change, we will be happy to contact you for an interview.
    Let me thank you for your interest, and wish you success in your current endeavors.

                                                Sincerely,

                                                _____
                                                X, Y & Z
                                                Attorneys at Law

Appendix D
National Federation of Paralegal Associations (NFPA), *Affirmation of Responsibility*; National Association of Legal Assistants (NALA), *Code of Ethics and Professional Responsibility*

Two major, national paralegal associations have set general standards of professional responsibility and ethics for their members. Both sets of standards are reproduced here, as an adjunct to the discussions in Chapter 13.

For individual situations where you are in some doubt about the ethics of involving paralegals in particular work, we suggest that you consult the regulations and opinions issued by your state bar association. Because the profession of paralegal or legal assistant is growing not simply by increase of members overall, but through expansion of skills and capabilities of so many of those members, situations are bound to continue arising where state bars must render specific opinions, upon request, about ethical uses of paralegals.

The authors gratefully acknowledge the kind permission of the National Federation of Paralegal Associations (NFPA) to reproduce their *Affirmation of Responsibility*, and also the kind permission of the National Association of Legal Assistants (NALA) to reprint their *Code of Ethics and Professional Responsibility*.

Affirmation of Responsibility of the National Federation of Paralegal Associations

Preamble

The paralegal profession is committed to responsibility to the individual citizen and the public interest. In reexamining contemporary institutions and systems and in questioning the relationship of the individual to the law, members of the paralegal profession recognize that a redefinition of the traditional delivery of legal services is essential in order to meet the expressed needs of the general public.

This Affirmation of Responsibility asserts that the principles recognized by the National Federation of Paralegal Associations are essential to the continuing work of the paralegal.

Through this Affirmation of Responsibility, the National Federation of Paralegal Associations recognizes the responsibility placed upon each paralegal and encourages the dedication of the paralegal to the development of the profession.

I. Professional Responsibility

The paralegal is dedicated to the development of the paralegal profession and endeavors to expand the responsibilities and the scope of paralegal work.

Discussion: There is room for a great deal of growth in the paralegal profession and an opportunity to tap human resources to assist an overburdened legal system. This Affirmation of Responsibility aims to establish a positive attitude through which the paralegal may perceive the importance, responsibility and potential of the paralegal profession and work toward enhancing its professional status.

II. The Role of the Paralegal and the Unauthorized Practice of Law

The paralegal performs all functions permitted under law which are not in violation of the unauthorized practice of law statutes within the applicable jurisdiction.

Discussion: The increase in the number of paralegals has given rise to much discussion concerning what the paralegal may or may not do. This development has prompted new interpretations as to what constitutes the practice of law, and thus it is unwise to delineate exactly or to restrict the types of tasks which the paralegal may perform.

However, this Affirmation of Responsibility insists on compliance with regulations governing the practice of law as determined by the applicable jurisdiction. It is not within the scope of the Affirmation of Responsibility to change or challenge any of these statutes.

Whenever the paralegal performs tasks related to the delivery of legal services, it is the responsibility of the paralegal to insure that the applicable unauthorized practice of law statutes are not violated and that the best interests of the public are met. To this end, it is the responsibility of the paralegal to be aware of legislation affecting the paralegal profession and the legal welfare of the public.

III. Competence and Education

The paralegal maintains integrity and promotes competence through continuing education.

Discussion: The growth of a profession and the attainment and maintenance of individual competence require an ongoing incorporation of new concepts and techniques. Continuing education enables the paralegal to become aware of new developments in the field of law and provides the opportunity to improve skills used in the delivery of legal services.

The paralegal recognizes the importance of maintaining an interest in the development of continuing paralegal education. Professional competence is each paralegal's responsibility. The exchange of ideas and skills benefits the profession, the legal community, and the general public.

IV. Client Confidences

The paralegal is responsible for maintaining all client confidences.

Discussion: The paralegal is aware of the importance of preserving all client confidences. Such information is understood to be a vital part of the relationship between the paralegal and the client, facilitating the delivery of legal services. The confidentiality of this information is respected at all times.

V. Protection of the Public Interest

The paralegal upholds the responsibility of protecting public interests by contributing to the delivery of quality legal services and by maintaining a sensitivity to public needs.

Discussion: The paralegal should make every effort to educate the public as to the services and tasks that paralegals may render. Such services may be performed within the setting of a law firm, public agency, governmental agency, business or within a defined program specifically addressing the needs of increased legal services to the public, including *pro bono* work.

The paralegal should inform the public of the scope of duties that the paralegal may perform and should encourage the public to examine issues and to explore innovative means by which an increased availability of moderate cost legal services may be obtained. It is also within the responsibility of the paralegal to maintain an interest in the development and continuation of paralegal education programs that address the public interest.

VI. Support of Professional Association

The paralegal recognizes the necessity of membership and participation in the professional association.

Discussion: One of the hallmarks of any profession is its professional association, founded for the purpose, among many others, of determining standards and guidelines for the growth and development of the profession. The paralegal profession is in a dynamic stage of growth. The ability of individual paralegals to determine the direction and quality of that growth depends largely upon the success of the paralegal association in providing effective representation of and communication among members of the profession. Through the professional association, the paralegal is able to promote a cooperative effort with members of the legal community, paralegal educators and the general public to improve the quality of paralegal participation in the delivery of legal services.

The role which the paralegal occupies in the legal system is, to some extent, the result of the cumulative and cooperative efforts of paralegals working through the paralegal association. The continued and increased contribution of paralegals to the delivery of legal services is dependent upon a further delineation of their skills, qualifications and areas of responsibility. It is, therefore, incumbent upon each paralegal to promote the growth of the profession through support of and participation in the endeavors of the paralegal association.

Code of Ethics and Professional Responsibility of National Association of Legal Assistants, Inc.

Preamble

It is the responsibility of every legal assistant to adhere strictly to the accepted standards of legal ethics and to live by general principles of proper conduct. The performance of the duties of the legal assistant shall be governed by specific canons as defined herein in order that justice will be served and the goals of the profession attained.

The canons of ethics set forth hereafter are adopted by the National Association of Legal Assistants, Inc., as a general guide, and the enumeration of these rules does not mean there are not others of equal importance although not specifically mentioned.

Canon 1. A legal assistant shall not perform any of the duties that lawyers only may perform nor do things that lawyers themselves may not do.

Canon 2. A legal assistant may perform any task delegated and supervised by a lawyer so long as the lawyer is responsible to the client, maintains a direct relationship with the client, and assumes full professional responsibility for the work product.

Canon 3. A legal assistant shall not engage in the practice of law by accepting cases, setting fees, giving legal advice or appearing in court (unless otherwise authorized by court or agency rules).

Canon 4. A legal assistant shall not act in matters involving professional legal judgment as the services of a lawyer are essential in the public interest whenever the exercise of such judgment is required.

Canon 5. A legal assistant must act prudently in determining the extent to which a client may be assisted without the presence of a lawyer.

Canon 6. A legal assistant shall not engage in the unauthorized practice of law and shall assist in preventing the unauthorized practice of law.

Canon 7. A legal assistant must protect the confidences of a client, and it shall be unethical for a legal assistant to violate any statute now in effect or hereafter to be enacted controlling privileged communications.

Canon 8. It is the obligation of the legal assistant to avoid conduct which would cause the lawyer to be unethical or even appear to be unethical, and loyalty to the employer is incumbent upon the legal assistant.

Canon 9. A legal assistant shall work continually to maintain integrity and a high degree of competency throughout the legal profession.

Canon 10. A legal assistant shall strive for perfection through education in order to better assist the legal profession in fulfilling its duty of making legal services available to clients and the public.

Canon 11. A legal assistant shall do other things incidental, necessary, or expedient for the attainment of the ethics and responsibilities imposed by statute or rule of court.

Canon 12. A legal assistant is governed by the American Bar Association Code of Professional Responsibility.

Adopted May 1, 1975

Appendix E
Forms and Documents That Paralegals May Draft or Complete in Assisting the Attorney With Corporate Work

The paralegal can be a very key person if your practice includes corporate work. You can provide a very broad range of corporate start-up and maintenance services to clients through the auspices of your paralegals. There's no reason why you should have to let this work slip out of your domain, when you can provide very effective service to clients at the most reasonable fee they'll be able to locate (predominantly your paralegal's billing rate).

The following forms can all be either drafted, completed or maintained by paralegals who've developed their experience with corporate matters.

Contents of Appendix E:

1. Letter to Client Re Stock Assignment
2. Transmittal Letter
3. (A) Corporate Minutes of Organization Meeting, Sole Incorporator
   (B) Corporate Minutes of Organization Meeting, Multi-Incorporator
4. Copy of Certificate of Incorporation
5. Certification as to Resolution That Corporate Name Does Not Conflict
6. Resolution Fixing Salaries
7. Oath of Inspectors of Election
8. Corporate By-Laws
9. Waiver of Notice of First Meeting of Shareholders

The authors gratefully acknowledge the permission of Kathleen Commins to reproduce some of the forms she furnished, which appear in this Appendix and in Chapter 9.

10 Minutes of First Meeting of Shareholders
11 Notice of Annual Meeting
12 Affidavit of Mailing of Notice of Annual Meeting
13 Notice of Regular Meeting of Board of Directors
14 Proxy—Shareholders Meeting
15 Resolution Re Execution of Lease
16 Resolution Re Ratification of Shareholders Agreement
17 Form of Corporate Certification of a Shareholders Agreement
18 Plan to Offer Shares Qualifying Under Section 1244 of the IRC
19 Form of Plan of Merger
20 Form of Letter to the Office of the Secretary of State Requesting Review of Decision to Refuse Reservation of Corporate Name
21 Form of Letter to the Office of the Secretary of State Advising Corporate Approval of the Use of a Similar Name
22 Form of Letter to the Office of the Secretary of State Releasing the Reservation of a Corporate Name
23 Form of Letter to the State Franchise Tax Department Concerning Payment of Taxes
24 Form of Designation of a Limited Partnership of the Secretary of State to Act as Agent as Required by Law
25 Form of Business Certificate for Partners
26 Form of Certificate of Limited Partnership
27 Form of Consent and Guarantee
28 Form of Assumption Agreement
29 Form of General Assignment
30 Form of Bill of Sale
31 Form of General Release

E.1 Letter to Client Re Stock Assignment

(Letterhead)

We are ready to transfer the shares of stock noted on the enclosed stock assignments. It is necessary that the stock assignments be signed by you before a bank official and your signature guaranteed.

Please return the stock assignments to us, together with the original shares of stock and we will forward them for transfer to you.

Very truly yours, *SPECIMEN FORM*

Enclosure

LETTER TO CLIENT RE STOCK ASSIGNMENT

FOR VALUE RECEIVED, _____

as _____

hereby sell, assign and transfer unto _____

_____ (S.S. # _____)

_____ (_____) shares of

_____ stock of _____

now standing in the name(s) of _____

_____ on the books of said corporation representing by the following certificates:

_____   _____

_____   _____

_____   _____

herewith and do hereby irrevocably constitute and appoint _____ attorney to transfer the said stock on the books of the within named corporation with full power of substitution in the premises.

Dated: _____   _____

In the presence of: Signature Guaranteed:

_____   _____

Assignment Separate From Certificate

APPENDIX E

E.2 **Transmittal Letter**

(Letterhead)

SPECIMEN FORM **TRANSMITTAL LETTER**

Subject: _____ shares in name(s) of _____

Company _____

Enclosed for reissuance per instructions below are:

No. Shares   **Certif. No.**   **Date Issued**   **Type of Shares**

Also enclosed are:

Where Shares in Name of Decedent

_____ Certified Copy of Letters (Dated within 60 days)

_____ Stock Assignment (Signature guaranteed)

_____ Affidavit of Domicile

Where Shares in Joint Tenancy

_____ Certified Copy of Death Certificate

_____ Consent to Transfer

_____ Stock Assignment (Signature guaranteed)

_____ Affidavit of Domicile

Transfer Instructions

Please reissue the shares as follows and forward the reissued shares to our office

No. Shares   **Name and Social Security No.**   **Address (include Zip)**

Forms and Documents That Paralegals May Draft

E.3(A) Corporate Minutes of Organization Meeting, Sole Incorporator

SPECIMEN FORM

MINUTES OF ORGANIZATION MEETING OF
_____

The undersigned, being the sole incorporator of this corporation, held an organization meeting at the date and place set forth below, at which meeting the following action was taken:

It was resolved that a copy of the certificate of incorporation together with the receipt issued by the department of state showing payment of the statutory organization tax and the date and payment of the fee for filing the original certificate of incorporation be appended to these minutes.

By-laws regulating the conduct of the business and affairs of the corporation, as prepared by:

counsel for the corporation were adopted and ordered appended hereto.

The persons whose names appear below were named as directors.

The board of directors was authorized to issue all of the unsubscribed shares of the corporation at such time and in such amounts as determined by the board and to accept in payment money or other property, tangible or intangible, actually received or labor or services actually performed for the corporation or for its benefit or in its formation.

The principal office of the corporation was fixed at

Dated at
the   day of   19   _____
                                        Sole incorporator

The undersigned accept their nomination as directors.

Type director's name	Signature
_____	_____
_____	_____

The following are appended to the minutes of this meeting:
    Copy of certificate of incorporation, filed on
    Receipt of department of state
    By-laws

E3(B) Corporate Minutes of Organization Meeting, Multi-Incorporator

MINUTES OF ORGANIZATION MEETING OF

_____

The organization meeting of the incorporators was held at

on the   day of   19   at   o'clock   M.

The following were present:

being a quorum and all of the incorporators.

One of the incorporators called the meeting to order. Upon motion duly made, seconded and carried,
was duly elected chairman of the meeting and
duly elected secretary thereof. They accepted their respective offices and proceeded with the discharge of their duties.

A written waiver of notice of this meeting signed by all the incorporators was submitted, read by the secretary and ordered appended to these minutes.

The secretary then presented and read to the meeting a copy of the certificate of incorporation and reported that on the   day of   19   , the original thereof was duly filed by the department of state.

Upon motion duly made, seconded and carried, said report was adopted and the secretary was directed to append to these minutes a copy of the certificate of incorporation together with the original receipt issued by the department of state, showing payment of the statutory organization tax, the filing fee and the date of filing of the certificate.

The chairman stated that the election of directors was then in order.

The following were nominated as directors:

Upon motion duly made, seconded and carried, it was unanimously
RESOLVED, that each of the above named nominees be and hereby is elected a director of the corporation.

Forms and Documents That Paralegals May Draft

Upon motion duly made, seconded and carried, and by the affirmative vote of all present, it was

RESOLVED that the board of directors be and it is hereby authorized to issue all of the unsubscribed shares of the corporation at such time and in such amounts as determined by the board, and to accept in payment money or other property, tangible or intangible, actually received or labor or other services actually performed for the corporation or for its benefit or in its formation.

The chairman presented and read, article by article, the proposed by-laws for the conduct and regulation of the business and affairs of the corporation as prepared by

counsel for the corporation.

Upon motion duly made, seconded and carried, they were adopted and in all respects, ratified; confirmed and approved, and as for the by-laws of this corporation.

The secretary was directed to cause them to be inserted in the minute book immediately following the receipt of the department of state.

Upon motion duly made, seconded and carried, the principal office of the corporation was fixed at

County of   State of New York.

Upon motion duly made, seconded and carried, and by the affirmative vote of all present, it was

RESOLVED, that the signing of these minutes shall constitute full ratification thereof and waiver of notice of the meeting by the signatories.

There being no further business before the meeting, the same was, on motion, duly adjourned.

Dated the   day of   19   .

_____
Secretary of meeting

_____

_____
Chairman of meeting

_____

_____

_____

The following are appended to the minutes of this meeting:
    Waiver of notice of organization meeting
    Copy of certificate of incorporation
    Receipt of department of state
    By-laws

E.4   Copy of Certificate of Incorporation

CERTIFICATE OF INCORPORATION
OF

———————

SPECIMEN FORM

[Under Section 402 of the Business
Corporation Law of the State of New York]

The undersigned, desiring to form a corporation pursuant to the provisions of the Business Corporation Law of the State of New York, hereby certifies as follows:

1. The name of the corporation is   (the "Corporation").
2. The purposes for which the Corporation is formed are as follows:

To prospect for, explore, purchase, acquire, take, hold, own, establish, maintain, supervise, develop, drill, work, exploit, sell, convey, transfer, assign, pledge, mortgage, and dispose of, lease as lessor and lessee, license the use of as licensor and licensee, obtain, collect, grant, and assign royalties, options, interests, and rights on and in respect of, and generally to deal in and with, as principal, agent, broker, or in any other lawful capacity, any and all kinds of gas-bearing, petroleum-bearing, oil-bearing, water-bearing, salt-bearing, and other mineral-bearing lands, properties, deposits, wells, mines and sites, and any and all interests whatsoever therein or thereto, and to engage generally in the business of extracting, producing, mining, refining, processing, purchasing, distributing, importing, exporting, and generally dealing and trading in and with petroleum, and other minerals and the products, by-products, components and resultants thereof.

other indications of origin and ownership granted under the laws of the United States of America or of any state or subdivision thereof, or of any foreign country or subdivision thereof, and all rights connected therewith or appertaining thereunto:

(c) franchises, licenses, grants and consequences.

The foregoing clauses shall be construed as objects and powers in furtherance and not in limitation of the general powers conferred upon corporations by the laws of the State of New York; and it is hereby expressly provided that the foregoing enumeration of specific powers shall not be held to limit or restrict in any manner the powers of the Corporation and that the Corporation may do all and everything necessary, suitable or appropriate for the accomplishment of any of the purposes or objects hereinbefore enumerated and for the exercise of any of its general powers, either alone or in association with other corporations, firms, or individuals, to the same extent and as fully as individuals might or could do either as principals or as agents, contractors or otherwise.

3. The office of the Corporation in the State of New York is to be located in the City of New York, County of New York.

4. The aggregate number of shares which the Corporation shall have the authority to issue is one million (1,000,000) Common Shares of the par value of one cent ($.01) per share and one million (1,000,000) Preferred Shares of the par value of one cent ($.01) per share.

5. The designations, relative rights, preferences and limitations of the shares of each class are as follows:

A. *Dividends*

The holders of record of the Preferred Shares shall be entitled to receive, when and as declared by the board of directors of the Corporation, out of funds legally available for the payment thereof, preferential cash dividends at the rate of four per centum (4%) on the par value thereof, per annum and no more, payable annually, semi-annually or quarterly on such dates as may be determined by the board of directors before any dividend shall be declared or paid upon or set apart for the Common Shares. Such dividends upon the Preferred Shares shall be cumulative from the date of issue thereof so that if dividends for any past dividend period at the rate of four per centum (4%) on the par value thereof, per annum shall not have been paid thereon, or declared and a sum sufficient for payment thereof set apart, the deficiency shall be fully paid or set apart but without interest, before any dividend shall be paid upon or set apart for the Common Shares. Whenever the full dividends upon the Preferred Shares for any past dividend periods shall have been paid, and the full dividend thereon for the then current dividend period shall have been paid or declared and a sum sufficient for the payment thereof set apart, dividends upon the Common Shares may be declared by the board of directors out of the remainder of the assets available therefor.

B. *Liquidation*

In the event of any liquidation, dissolution or winding up of the affairs of the Corporation, whether voluntary or involuntary, the holders of record of the Preferred Shares shall be entitled to be paid the full par value of such Preferred Shares together with a sum of money equivalent to dividends at the rate of four per centum (4%) per annum on the par value thereof, from the date or dates upon which dividends on such Preferred Shares became cumulative to the date of payment thereof, less the amount of dividends theretofore paid thereon.

After payment to the holders of Preferred Shares of the amount payable to them as aforesaid, the remaining assets of the Corporation shall be payable to and distributed pro rata among the holders of record of the Common Shares.

If, upon such liquidation, dissolution or winding up, the assets of the Corporation distributable as aforesaid among the holders of the Preferred Shares shall be insufficient to permit the payment to them of said amount, the entire assets shall be distributed ratably among the holders of the Preferred Shares.

C. *Redemption*

The Corporation may not redeem the whole or any part of the issued and outstanding Preferred Shares.

D. *Conversion*

The Preferred Shares of the Corporation shall not be convertible into any other securities issued or to be issued by the Corporation.

E. *Sinking Fund*

The Corporation shall not be required to establish or maintain any sinking or purchase fund with respect to the Preferred Shares.

F. *Voting*

The holders of the Preferred Shares shall not be entitled to vote, except as otherwise provided for in the Business Corporation Law of the State of New York, and this provision shall prevail in all elections and in all proceedings over the provisions of any statute which authorizes any action by a vote or written consent of the holders of all of the shares or a specific proportion of the shares of the Corporation entitled to vote thereon, and all rights to vote shall be vested exclusively in the Common Shares.

6. No holder of stock or any other security of the Corporation shall be entitled as such, as a matter of right, to subscribe for or purchase any part of any new or additional issue of any class of stock of the Corporation, whether now or hereafter authorized and whether issued for cash or other consideration or by way of dividend.

7. The Secretary of State of the State of New York is hereby designated as the agent of the Corporation upon whom any process in any action or proceeding against the Corporation may be served, and the address to which the

Secretary of State shall mail a copy of any process against the Corporation served upon him is c/o   ,   Avenue, New York, New York   , Attn: .

8. The accounting period which the Corporation intends to establish as its first calendar or fiscal year for reporting the franchise tax on business corporations imposed by Article nine-a of the tax law is the period ending May 31st.

IN WITNESS WHEREOF, I have executed this Certificate of Incorporation and affirm and verify that the statements herein, are true under the penalties of perjury this * * day of * *, 19 * *.

_____
Incorporator

New York, New York

E.5 Certificate as to Resolution That Corporate Name Does Not Conflict

SPECIMEN FORM

CERTIFICATE AS TO RESOLUTION
CORPORATE NAME DOES NOT CONFLICT

The following is a true copy of a resolution duly adopted by the Board of Directors of * * * at a meeting of the said board duly held at * * * on * * *:

"WHEREAS, there has been proposed the formation of a corporation pursuant to the laws of the State of * * * under the name * * * and the Secretary of State has requested the expression of an opinion by this board concerning the similarity of the proposed name to that of this corporation;
Now, therefore be it
RESOLVED, that in the opinion of this Board the above mentioned proposed name is not the same name as, or so similar to the name of this corporation, as to tend to confuse or deceive."

Dated:

_____
President

_____
Secretary

(Corporate Seal)

E.6 Resolution Fixing Salaries

RESOLUTION FIXING SALARIES

RESOLVED, that the salary of * * * as president of this corporation hereby is fixed at the sum of $ * * * per month beginning with * * * until the further action of this board of directors.

E.7   Oath of Inspectors of Election

OATH OF INSPECTORS OF ELECTION OF * * *

STATE OF   )
) ss.:
COUNTY OF   )

SPECIMEN FORM

    We, the undersigned, being duly sworn, each for himself deposes and says, promises and agrees that he will faithfully, truly, honestly and well execute and perform the duties of Inspector of Election of the election of Directors, held at the meeting of the Shareholders of the * * * on the * * day of * * 19* , with strict impartiality and according to the best of his understanding, judgment, knowledge and ability.

                                                _____
                                                Inspectors

Severally sworn to before me
this * * day of * * 19* .

E.8   Corporate By-Laws

BY-LAWS
of
_____

SPECIMEN FORM

ARTICLE I—OFFICES

The principal office of the corporation shall be in the   of   County of   State of New York. The corporation may also have offices at such other places within or without the State of New York as the board may from time to time determine or the business of the corporation may require.

ARTICLE II—SHAREHOLDERS

1. *Place of Meetings.*

Meetings of shareholders shall be held at the principal office of the corporation or at such place within or without the State of New York as the board shall authorize.

2. *Annual Meeting.*

The annual meeting of the shareholders shall be held on the   day of   at   M. in each year if not a legal holiday, and, if a legal holiday, then on the next business day following at the same hour, when the shareholders shall elect a board and transact such other business as may properly come before the meeting.

3. *Special Meetings.*

Special meetings of the shareholders may be called by the board or by the president and shall be called by the president or the secretary at the request in writing of a majority of the board or at the request in writing by shareholders owning a majority in amount of the shares issued and outstanding. Such request shall state the purpose or purposes of the proposed meeting. Business transacted at a special meeting shall be confined to the purposes stated in the notice.

4. *Fixing Record Date.*

For the purpose of determining the shareholders entitled to notice of or to vote at any meeting of shareholders or any adjournment thereof, or to express consent to or dissent from any proposal without a meeting, or for the purpose of determining shareholders entitled to receive payment of any dividend or the allotment of any rights, or for the purpose of any other action, the board shall fix, in advance, a date as the record date for any such determination of shareholders. Such date shall not be more than fifty nor less than ten days before the date of such meeting, nor more than fifty days prior to any other action. If no record date is fixed it shall be determined in accordance with the provisions of law.

5. *Notice of Meetings of Shareholders.*

Written notice of each meeting of shareholders shall state the purpose or purposes for which the meeting is called, the place, date and hour of the meeting and unless it is the annual meeting, shall indicate that it is being issued by or at the direction of the person or persons calling the meeting. Notice shall be given either personally or by mail to each shareholder entitled to vote at such meeting, not less than ten nor more than fifty days before the date of the meeting. If action is proposed to be taken that might entitle shareholders to payment for their shares, the notice shall include a statement of that purpose and to that effect. If mailed, the notice is given when deposited in the United States mail, with postage thereon prepaid, directed to the shareholder at his address as it appears on the record of shareholders, or, if he shall have filed with the secretary a written request that notices to him be mailed to some other address, then directed to him at such other address.

6. *Waivers.*

Notice of meeting need not be given to any shareholder who signs a waiver of notice, in person or by proxy, whether before or after the meeting. The attendance of any shareholder at a meeting, in person or by proxy, without protesting prior to the conclusion of the meeting the lack of notice of such meeting, shall constitute a waiver of notice by him.

7. *Quorum of Shareholders.*

Unless the certificate of incorporation provides otherwise, the holders of a majority of the shares entitled to vote thereat shall constitute a quorum at a meeting of shareholders for the transaction of any business, provided that when a specified item of business is required to be voted on by a class or classes, the holders of a majority of the shares of such class or classes shall constitute a quorum for the transaction of such specified item of business.

When a quorum is once present to organize a meeting, it is not broken by the subsequent withdrawal of any shareholders.

The shareholders present may adjourn the meeting despite the absence of a quorum.

8. *Proxies.*

Every shareholder entitled to vote at a meeting of shareholders or to express consent or dissent without a meeting may authorize another person or persons to act for him by proxy.

Every proxy must be signed by the shareholder or his attorney-in-fact. No proxy shall be valid after expiration of eleven months from the date thereof unless otherwise provided in the proxy. Every proxy shall be revocable at the pleasure of the shareholder executing it, except as otherwise provided by law.

9. *Qualification of Voters.*

Every shareholder of record shall be entitled at every meeting of shareholders to one vote for every share standing in his name on the record of shareholders, unless otherwise provided in the certificate of incorporation.

10. *Vote of Shareholders.*

Except as otherwise required by statute or by the certificate of incorporation:

(a) directors shall be elected by a plurality of the votes cast at a meeting of shareholders by the holders of shares entitled to vote in the election;

(b) all other corporate action shall be authorized by a majority of the votes cast.

11. *Written Consent of Shareholders.*

Any action that may be taken by vote may be taken without a meeting on written consent, setting forth the action so taken, signed by the holders of all the outstanding shares entitled to vote thereon or signed by such lesser number of holders as may be provided for in the certificate of incorporation.

ARTICLE III—DIRECTORS

1. *Board of Directors.*

Subject to any provision in the certificate of incorporation the business of the corporation shall be managed by its board of directors, each of whom shall be at least 18 years of age and   be shareholders.

2. *Number of Directors.*

The number of directors shall be   . When all of the shares are owned by less than three shareholders, the number of directors may be less than three but not less than the number of shareholders.

3. *Election and Term of Directors.*

At each annual meeting of shareholders, the shareholders shall elect directors to hold office until the next annual meeting. Each director shall hold office until the expiration of the term for which he is elected and until his successor has been elected and qualified, or until his prior resignation or removal.

4. *Newly Created Directorships and Vacancies.*

Newly created directorships resulting from an increase in the number of directors and vacancies occurring in the board for any reason except the removal of directors without cause may be filled by a vote of a majority of the directors then in office, although less than a quorum exists, unless otherwise provided in the certificate of incorporation. Vacancies occurring by reason of the removal of directors without cause shall be filled by vote of the shareholders unless otherwise provided in the certificate of incorporation. A director elected to fill a vacancy caused by resignation, death or removal shall be elected to hold office for the unexpired term of his predecessor.

5. *Removal of Directors.*

Any or all of the directors may be removed for cause by vote of the shareholders or by action of the board. Directors may be removed without cause only by vote of the shareholders.

6. *Resignation.*

A director may resign at any time by giving written notice to the board, the president or the secretary of the corporation. Unless otherwise specified in the notice, the resignation shall take effect upon receipt thereof by the board or such officer, and the acceptance of the resignation shall not be necessary to make it effective.

7. *Quorum of Directors.*

Unless otherwise provided in the certificate of incorporation, a majority of the entire board shall constitute a quorum for the transaction of business or of any specified item of business.

8. *Action of the Board.*

Unless otherwise required by law, the vote of a majority of the directors present at the time of the vote, if a quorum is present at such time, shall be the act of the board. Each director present shall have one vote regardless of the number of shares, if any, which he may hold.

9. *Place and Time of Board Meetings.*

The board may hold its meetings at the office of the corporation or at such other places, either within or without the State of New York, as it may from time to time determine.

10. *Regular Annual Meeting.*

A regular annual meeting of the board shall be held immediately following the annual meeting of shareholders at the place of such annual meeting of shareholders.

11. *Notice of Meetings of the Board, Adjournment.*

(a) Regular meetings of the board may be held without notice at such time and place as it shall from time to time determine. Special meetings of the board shall be held upon notice to the directors and may be called by the president upon three days notice to each director either personally or by mail or by wire; special meetings shall be called by the president or by the secretary in a like manner on written request of two directors. Notice of a meeting need not be given to any director who submits a waiver of notice whether before or after the meeting or who attends the meeting without protesting prior thereto or at its commencement, the lack of notice to him.

(b) A majority of the directors present, whether or not a quorum is present, may adjourn any meeting to another time and place. Notice of the adjournment shall be given all directors who were absent at the time of the adjournment and, unless such time and place are announced at the meeting, to the other directors.

12. *Chairman.*

At all meetings of the board the president, or in his absence, a chairman chosen by the board shall preside.

13. *Executive and Other Committees.*

The board, by resolution adopted by a majority of the entire board, may designate from among its members an executive committee and other committees, each consisting of three or more directors. Each such committee shall serve at the pleasure of the board.

14. *Compensation.*

No compensation shall be paid to directors, as such, for their services, but by resolution of the board a fixed sum and expenses for actual attendance, at each regular or special meeting of the board may be authorized. Nothing herein contained shall be construed to preclude any director from serving the corporation in any other capacity and receiving compensation therefor.

ARTICLE IV—OFFICERS

1. *Offices, Election, Term.*

(a) Unless otherwise provided for in the certificate of incorporation, the board may elect or appoint a president, one or more vice-presidents, a secretary and a treasurer, and such other officers as it may determine, who shall have such duties, powers and functions as hereinafter provided.

(b) All officers shall be elected or appointed to hold office until the meeting of the board following the annual meeting of shareholders.

(c) Each officer shall hold office for the term for which he is elected or appointed and until his successor has been elected or appointed and qualified.

2. *Removal, Resignation, Salary, Etc.*

(a) Any officer elected or appointed by the board may be removed by the board with or without cause.

(b) In the event of the death, resignation or removal of an officer, the board in its discretion may elect or appoint a successor to fill the unexpired term.

(c) Any two or more offices may be held by the same person, except the offices of president and secretary.

(d) The salaries of all officers shall be fixed by the board.

(e) The directors may require any officer to give security for the faithful performance of his duties.

3. *President.*

The President shall be the chief executive officer of the corporation; he shall preside at all meetings of the shareholders and of the board; he shall have the management of the business of the corporation and shall see that all orders and resolutions of the board are carried into effect.

4. *Vice-Presidents.*

During the absence or disability of the president, the vice-president, or if there are more than one, the executive vice-president, shall have all the powers and functions of the president. Each vice-president shall perform such other duties as the board shall prescribe.

5. *Secretary*

The secretary shall:

(a) attend all meetings of the board and of the shareholders;

(b) record all votes and minutes of all proceedings in a book to be kept for that purpose;

(c) give or cause to be given notice of all meetings of shareholders and of special meetings of the board;

(d) keep in safe custody the seal of the corporation and affix it to any instrument when authorized by the board;

(e) when required, prepare or cause to be prepared and available at each meeting of shareholders a certified list in alphabetical order of the names of shareholders entitled to vote thereat, indicating the number of shares of each respective class held by each;

(f) keep all the documents and records of the corporations as required by law or otherwise in a proper and safe manner.

(g) perform such other duties as may be prescribed by the board.

6. *Assistant-Secretaries.*

During the absence or disability of the secretary, the assistant-secretary, or if there are more than one, the one so designated by the secretary or by the board, shall have all the powers and functions of the secretary.

7. *Treasurer.*

The treasurer shall:

(a) have the custody of the corporate funds and securities;

(b) keep full and accurate accounts of receipts and disbursements in the corporate books;

(c) deposit all money and other valuables in the name and to the credit of the corporation in such depositories as may be designated by the board;

(d) disburse the funds of the corporation as may be ordered or authorized by the board and preserve proper vouchers for such disbursements;

(e) render to the president and board at the regular meetings of the board, or whenever they require it, an account of all his transactions as treasurer and of the financial condition of the corporation;

(f) render a full financial report at the annual meeting of the shareholders if so requested;

(g) be furnished by all corporate officers and agents at his request, with such reports and statements as he may require as to all financial transactions of the corporation;

(h) perform such other duties as are given to him by these by-laws or as from time to time are assigned to him by the board or the president.

8. *Assistant-Treasurer.*

During the absence or disability of the treasurer, the assistant-treasurer, or if there are more than one, the one so designated by the secretary or by the board, shall have all the powers and functions of the treasurer.

9. *Sureties and Bonds.*

In case the board shall so require, any officer or agent of the corporation shall execute to the corporation a bond in such sum and with such surety or sureties as the board may direct, conditioned upon the faithful performance of his duties to the corporation and including responsibility for negligence and for the accounting for all property, funds or securities of the corporation which may come into his hands.

ARTICLE V—CERTIFICATES FOR SHARES

1. *Certificates.*

The shares of the corporation shall be represented by certificates. They shall be numbered and entered in the books of the corporation as they are issued. They shall exhibit the holder's name and the number of shares and shall be signed by the president or a vice-president and the treasurer or the secretary and shall bear the corporate seal.

2. *Lost or Destroyed Certificates.*

The board may direct a new certificate or certificates to be issued in place of any certificate or certificates theretofore issued by the corporation, alleged to have been lost or destroyed, upon the making of an affidavit of that fact by the person claiming the certificate to be lost or destroyed. When authorizing such issue of a new certificate or certificates, the board may, in its discretion and as a condition precedent to the issuance thereof, require the owner of such lost or destroyed certificate or certificates, or his legal representative, to advertise the same in such manner as it shall require and/or give the corporation a bond in such sum and with such surety or sureties as it may direct as indemnity against any claim that may be made against the corporation with respect to the certificate alleged to have been lost or destroyed.

3. *Transfer of Shares.*

(a) Upon surrender to the corporation or the transfer agent of the corporation of a certificate for shares duly endorsed or accompanied by proper evidence of succession, assignment or authority to transfer, it shall be the duty of the corporation to issue a new certificate to the person entitled thereto, and cancel the old certificate; every such transfer shall be entered on the transfer book of the corporation which shall be kept at its principal office. No transfer shall be made within ten days next preceding the annual meeting of shareholders.

(b) The corporation shall be entitled to treat the holder of record of any share as the holder in fact thereof and, accordingly, shall not be bound to recognize any equitable or other claim to or interest in such share on the part of any other person whether or not it shall have express or other notice thereof, except as expressly provided by the laws of New York.

4. *Closing Transfer Books.*

The board shall have the power to close the share transfer books of the corporation for a period of not more than ten days during the thirty day period immediately preceding (1) any shareholders; meeting, or (2) any date upon which shareholders shall be called upon to or have a right to take action without a meeting, or (3) any date fixed for the payment of a dividend or any other form of distribution, and only those shareholders of record at the time the transfer books are closed, shall be recognized as such for the purpose of (1) receiving notice or of voting at such meeting, or (2) allowing them to take appropriate action, or (3) entitling them to receive any dividend or other form of distribution.

ARTICLE VI—DIVIDENDS

Subject to the provisions of the certificate of incorporation and to applicable law, dividends on the outstanding shares of the corporation may be declared in such amounts and at such time or times as the board may determine. Before payment of any dividend, there may be set aside out of the net profits of the corporation available for dividends such sum or sums as the board from time to time in its absolute discretion deems proper as a reserve fund to meet contingencies, or for equalizing dividends, or for repairing or maintaining any property of the corporation, or for such other purposes as the board shall think conducive to the interests of the corporation, and the board may modify or abolish any such reserve.

ARTICLE VII—CORPORATE SEAL

The seal of the corporation shall be circular in form and bear the name of the corporation, the year of its organization and the words "Corporate Seal, New York." The seal may be used by causing it to be impressed directly on the instrument or writing to be sealed, or upon adhesive substance affixed thereto. The seal on the certificates for shares or on any corporate obligation for the payment of money may be a facsimile, engraved or printed.

ARTICLE VIII—EXECUTION OF INSTRUMENTS

All corporate instruments and documents shall be signed or countersigned, executed, verified or acknowledged by such officer or officers or other person or persons as the board may from time to time designate.

ARTICLE IX—FISCAL YEAR

The fiscal year shall begin the first day of _____ in each year.

ARTICLE X—REFERENCES TO CERTIFICATE OF INCORPORATION

Reference to the certificate of incorporation in these by-laws shall include all amendments thereto or changes thereof unless specifically excepted.

ARTICLE XI—BY-LAW CHANGES

Amendment, Repeal, Adoption, Election of Directors.

(a) Except as otherwise provided in the certificate of incorporation the by-laws may be amended, repealed or adopted by vote of the holders of the shares at the time entitled to vote in the election of any directors. By-laws may also be amended, repealed or adopted by the board but any by-law adopted by the board may be amended by the shareholders entitled to vote thereon as hereinabove provided.

(b) If any by-law regulating an impending election of directors is adopted, amended or repealed by the board, there shall be set forth in the notice of the next meeting of shareholders for the election of directors the by-law so adopted, amended or repealed, together with a concise statement of the changes made.

E.9 Waiver of Notice of First Meeting of Shareholders

WAIVER OF NOTICE OF FIRST MEETING OF SHAREHOLDERS

of

_____

We, the undersigned, being all the shareholders of the above corporation hereby agree and consent that the first meeting of the shareholders be held on the date and at the time and place stated below for the purpose of electing officers and the transaction thereat of all such other business as may lawfully come before said meeting and hereby waive all notice of the meeting and of any adjournment thereof.

Place of meeting

Date of meeting

Time of meeting

_____
_____
_____
_____

Dated:

Forms and Documents That Paralegals May Draft 375

E.10   Minutes of First Meeting of Shareholders

MINUTES OF FIRST MEETING OF SHAREHOLDERS
of
_____

SPECIMEN FORM

The first meeting of the board was held at
on the   day of   19   at   o'clock   M.

The meeting was duly called to order by the president who stated the object of the meeting.

The secretary then read the roll of the shareholders as they appear in the share record book of the corporation and reported that a quorum of the shareholders was present.

The secretary then read a waiver of notice of meeting signed by all the shareholders and on motion duly made, seconded and carried it was ordered that the said waiver be appended to the minutes of this meeting.

The president then asked the secretary to read the minutes of the organization meeting and the minutes of the first meeting of the board.

On motion duly made, seconded and unanimously carried the following resolution was adopted:

WHEREAS, the minutes of the organization meeting and the minutes of the first meeting of the board have been read to this meeting, and

WHEREAS, at the organization meeting by-laws were adopted, it is

RESOLVED that this meeting hereby approves, ratifies and adopts the said by-laws as the by-laws of the corporation, and it is

FURTHER RESOLVED that all of the acts taken and the decisions made at the organization meeting and at the first meeting of the board hereby are approved and ratified, and it is

FURTHER RESOLVED, that the signing of these minutes shall constitute full ratification thereof and waiver of notice of the meeting by the signatories.

There being no further business the meeting was adjourned.

Dated the   day of   19   .

_____
Secretary

_____
_____
_____
_____

The following is appended hereto:
Waiver of notice of meeting.

E.11 Notice of Annual Meeting

NOTICE OF ANNUAL MEETING

PLEASE TAKE NOTICE that the Annual Meeting of the Shareholders of * * * for the purpose of electing * * Directors and Inspectors of Election, and transacting such other business as may properly come before the meeting, will be held on the * * day of * * 19 * , at * * o'clock in the * * noon, at the office of the Corporation, No. * * and State of * * .

The transfer books will remain closed from the * * day of * * 19 * , until the * * day of * * 19 * .

SPECIMEN FORM

Dated the * * day of * * , 19 * .

_____
                    Secretary

E.12 Affidavit of Mailing of Notice of Annual Meetings

AFFIDAVIT OF MAILING OF NOTICE OF ANNUAL MEETING

STATE OF   )
) ss.:
COUNTY OF   )

* * * being duly sworn according to law, deposes and says:

I am the Secretary of * * * a corporation; that on the * * day of * * 19 * , I personally deposited in a post-office box in the * * *, State of * * * *, copies of the aforesaid notice, each enclosed in a securely sealed post-paid wrapper, one of said notices addressed to each person whose name appears on the annexed list, and to their respective post-office addresses, as therein set forth.

_____
                    Secretary

Sworn to before me this
* * day of * * , 19 * .

_____

Forms and Documents That Paralegals May Draft

E.13 Notice of Regular Meeting
of Board of Directors

NOTICE OF REGULAR MEETING OF THE BOARD

PLEASE TAKE NOTICE that a * * * meeting of the Board of * * * will be held at the office of the Corporation at * * * in the * * of * * on the * * day of * * 19* , at * * o'clock in the * noon, for the purpose of transacting all such business as may properly come before the same.

Dated the * * day of * * 19* .

SPECIMEN FORM

_____
Secretary

E.14 Proxy—Shareholders Meeting

PROXY—SHAREHOLDERS MEETING

KNOW ALL MEN BY THESE PRESENTS, that * * * the undersigned, Shareholder in the * * * hereby constitute and appoint * * * or either of them * * true and lawful attorney and agent for * * and in * * name, place and stead, to vote as * proxy at the * * Meeting of the Shareholders of said Corporation, to be held on * * * or at any adjournment thereof, for the election of * * * and for the transaction of any business which may legally come before the said meeting, and for * * and in * name, to act as fully as * could do if personally present; and * * hereby revoke any other proxy heretofore given by * *.

WITNESS * hand * and seal * this * * day of * * 19 * .

In presence of * * * Witness

Note: Proxy expires 11 months from date unless otherwise provided therein.

_____ L.S.

E.15 Resolution Re Execution of Lease

RESOLUTION RE EXECUTION OF LEASE

WHEREAS there has been presented to and considered by this meeting a proposed lease from * * *, as Lessor, to this corporation as Lessee, covering the premises known as * * *; and

WHEREAS said proposed lease is for a term of * * * years, commencing * * * at the annual rental of $ * * *;

NOW, THEREFORE, be it

RESOLVED, that the terms and conditions of the proposed lease presented to and considered by this meeting be and the same hereby are approved.

FURTHER RESOLVED, that the president and secretary of this corporation be and they hereby are authorized to execute said lease in the name and on behalf of this corporation and in substantially the form approved at this meeting.

E.16 Resolution Re Ratification of Shareholders' Agreement

SPECIMEN FORM

RESOLUTION RE RATIFICATION OF SHAREHOLDER'S AGREEMENT

RESOLVED, that this Corporation join in a certain agreement dated * * * between * * *, a copy of which has been presented to this meeting, and adopt and confirm all the provisions thereof; and it was further

RESOLVED, that upon the execution of said agreement by the proper officers on behalf of this Corporation the proper officers be and they hereby are authorized and directed to take all steps necessary and appropriate to carry out the terms of said agreement; and it was further

RESOLVED, that the original of said agreement, duly executed by * * * and the Corporation, be placed in the Minute Book of the Corporation.

E.17 Form of Corporate Certification of a Shareholders' Agreement

FORM OF CORPORATE CERTIFICATION OF A SHAREHOLDERS' AGREEMENT

STATE OF NEW YORK   )
) ss.:
COUNTY OF NEW YORK   )

SPECIMEN FORM

The undersigned,   , the President of   Corporation, being duly sworn, does hereby state on oath that the attached Shareholders Agreement is a true and complete copy of the fully executed Shareholders Agreement dated March 31, 1978 by and among   Corporation (the "Corporation") and all the shareholders of the Corporation.

_____, President

Sworn to and subscribed
before me this 26th day
of July, 1978

_____
Notary Public

E.18   Plan to Offer Shares Qualifying Under
        Section 1244 of the Internal Revenue Code

PLAN TO OFFER SHARES QUALIFYING UNDER
1244 OF THE INTERNAL REVENUE CODE

SPECIMEN FORM

The Corporation is a small business corporation, as defined in 1244 of the Internal Revenue Code, and is authorized to issue   shares,   par value. At the present time, none of said shares have been issued, and there is not now outstanding any offering by the Corporation to sell or issue any of its shares.

The Board of Directors wishes to offer said shares for sale, and it is deemed desirable to offer, sell and issue said shares in such manner that qualified shareholders will receive the benefits of 1244 of the Internal Revenue Code.

To carry out the wishes of the Board of Directors, the following course of action is adopted:

1. The President of the Corporation, and such other officers as he may designate, are authorized to offer for sale, sell and issue up to   shares, for a total consideration not in excess of $100,000.

2. Payment for said shares is to be in cash or other property, but in no event for stock or securities.

3. This Plan shall become effective upon adoption thereof by the Board of Directors, and shall remain in full force and effect until said shares are sold, or until the Corporation shall make a subsequent offering of any shares, or for a period of two years from the effective date, whichever shall first occur.

4. Such other action shall be taken by the Corporation as shall qualify said shares as "1244 shares," under the provisions of the Internal Revenue Code.

E.19 Form of Plan of Merger

PLAN OF MERGER

1. Mfg. Co., a Delaware corporation ("   "), all of the outstanding shares of which, consisting of 100,000 shares of Capital Stock, $1.00 par value, are owned by   , a Delaware corporation ("   "), shall be merged into Kewanee pursuant to the provisions of §253 of the General Corporation Law of the State of Delaware.

2. The identity, existence, rights, privileges, immunities, powers and purposes of   shall continue unaffected and unimpaired by the merger and the corporate existence and rights of   shall be fully vested in Kewanee as the Surviving Corporation.

3. The merger shall become effective upon the filing of the Certificate of Ownership and Merger in the State of Delaware (hereinafter called the "Effective Time").

4. The Certificate of Incorporation and By-Laws of   in effect at the Effective Time, shall remain in full force and effect, and the persons who are directors of   at the Effective Time shall continue to serve as directors of   as the Surviving Corporation in accordance with   's By-Laws.

5. (a) At the Effective Time all of the shares of Capital Stock of   then issued and outstanding shall forthwith be cancelled and all such shares shall no longer be outstanding and shall be thereupon deemed null and void and   shall not receive any consideration with respect to such shares; and (b) each share of stock of   then issued and outstanding shall continue, unaltered and unimpaired by the merger provided for by this Plan.

E.20   **Form of Letter to the
Office of the Secretary of State
Requesting Review of Decision to
Refuse Reservation of Corporate Name**

FORM OF LETTER TO THE OFFICE OF THE
SECRETARY OF STATE REQUESTING REVIEW
OF DECISION TO REFUSE RESERVATION
OF CORPORATE NAME

                , Esq.
New York Department of State
Bureau of Corporations
Albany, New York 12231

                          Re: _____, Inc.

Dear Mr.   :

    As we discussed yesterday, I am writing to request that you kindly review the decision, made by Mr.   of your bureau, to refuse reservation of the above corporate name.

                Inc. was organized in 1972 under Georgia law for the purpose of   consulting. It is presently active in several states, rendering services to a number of universities which are initiating   programs. Its New York subsidiary, the   , Inc. is a consultant to   program. A second New York subsidiary, the   Inc. is now being organized for the purpose of consulting colleges with programs to train fund-raising and development experts.

    Mr.   found that the name "The   Inc." was unduly similar to that of a New York corporation, "The   Ltd." I respectfully submit that the two are sufficiently distinct so as not "to confuse or deceive" the public, within the meaning of Business Corporation Law §301(a)(2).

    The policy of B.C.L. §302(b)(3) is also relevant here, although the provision is not literally applicable except to foreign corporations organized at least 10 years prior to qualification in New York. This statute provides that where an applicant for qualification "has engaged in business as a corporation under its . . . name for not less than 10 consecutive years . . . [and] the business to be conducted in this state is not the same as or similar to the business conducted by the corporation with whose name it may conflict [and] . . . the public is not likely to be confused or deceived," the foreign corporation should not be prevented from qualifying under its original name if it agrees "to use with its corporate name, in this state, . . . the words ' . . . (name of jurisdiction of incorporation) corporation.' " Should there be any question as to the distinctness of its name the _____ would be agreeable to the addition of the statutory suffix to its name, *i.e.*, "a Georgia corporation."

The activities of The _____ and its subsidiaries have significant social value: they provide colleges and universities with the ability to teach useful knowledge and professional skills. It is essential that the parent company be able to conduct business in New York directly, to manage its business and to coordinate its subsidiaries. As its activities continue to grow, The _____ should not needlessly be required to form a succession of New York subsidiaries.

I trust that you will give this matter your careful attention. I would of course be willing to appear in Albany at an informal hearing concerning the reservation of the subject corporation's name. Thank you for your assistance.

Sincerely yours,

E.21 Form of Letter to the Office of Secretary of State Advising Corporate Approval of the Use of a Similar Name

FORM OF LETTER TO THE OFFICE OF
SECRETARY OF STATE ADVISING
CORPORATE APPROVAL OF THE USE OF A
SIMILAR NAME

September 9, 197

Office of the Secretary of State
State of California
Department of Corporations
Sacramento, California

SPECIMEN FORM

Dear Sir or Madam:

On the 8th day of September, 197   the Board of Directors of   Corp. of California adopted the following resolutions regarding the use of the corporate name "   Corp.":

BE IT RESOLVED, that it is the judgment of this Board of Directors that the name "   Corp." does not so nearly resemble the corporate title of "   of California" as to tend to deceive or mislead the public within the meaning of Section 201(b) of the General Corporation Law of the State of California; and it is further

RESOLVED, that, accordingly, this Board of Directors hereby consents to the use of the corporate name "   Corp." in the State of California.

By: _____
, Secretary

Forms and Documents That Paralegals May Draft

E.22 Form of Letter to Office of the Secretary of State Releasing the Reservation of a Corporate Name

FORM OF LETTER TO OFFICE OF THE SECRETARY OF STATE RELEASING THE RESERVATION OF A CORPORATE NAME

Office of the Secretary of State
Name Availability Department
111 Capital Mall
Room 400
Sacramento, California 95814

SPECIMEN FORM

Gentlemen:

                California, having reserved the name   on February 20, 1976 (Certificate No.   ), does hereby release the name   to   , Inc.

                              By   , Inc.
                                     (its general partner)

                              By _____

E.23   Form of Letter to the State Franchise
Tax Department Concerning Payment of Taxes

FORM OF LETTER TO THE STATE FRANCHISE
TAX DEPARTMENT CONCERNING PAYMENT OF TAXES

July 7, 197

The Franchise Tax Department
Department of Revenue
Raleigh, North Carolina

SPECIMEN FORM

Gentlemen:

We hereby grant permission to the local representative of United States Corporation Co.,   Esq., P.O. Box 527, Raleigh, North Carolina, to receive on behalf of   Inc., a North Carolina corporation, a certificate with respect to the due and timely payment of taxes. This certificate is required in connection with the proposed sale of assets by   Inc.

_____

E.24 Form of Designation of a Limited Partnership of the Secretary of State to Act as Agent Required by Law

FOREIGN ISSUER

DESIGNATION UNDER SECTION 352-b OF ARTICLE 23-A OF THE GENERAL BUSINESS LAW OF THE STATE OF NEW YORK

SPECIMEN FORM

TO WHOM IT MAY CONCERN:

* * * * a limited partnership formed in * * * , 19* , and existing under the laws of the State of * * * and maintaining an office at * * * * * * * California, and its General Partner * * * Corporation, a corporation organized in * * 19 * , and existing under the laws of the State of * * * , hereby irrevocably designates the Secretary of State of the State of New York as the person upon whom may be served any subpoena, subpoena duces tecum, summons, complaint, notice, order, judgment or other process directed to the aforesaid and issued on any investigation, examination, action or proceeding pending or about to be instituted, under and pursuant to the provisions of Article 23-A of the General Business Law of the State of New York for the uses and purposes therein set forth.

IN WITNESS WHEREOF, the undersigned General Partner has caused this instrument to be duly executed.

By _____ CORPORATION
General Partner

By _____
President

E.25   Form of Business Certificate for Partners

Business Certificate for Partners

The undersigned do hereby certify that they are conducting or transacting business as members of a partnership under the name or designation of

at
in the County of   , State of New York, and do further certify that the full names of all the persons conducting or transacting such partnership including the full names of all the partners with the residence address of each such person, and the age of any who may be infants, are as follows:

NAME Specify which are infants and state ages.   **RESIDENCE**

....
....
....
....
....
....

SPECIMEN FORM

WE DO FURTHER CERTIFY that we are the successors in interest to

the person or persons heretofore using such name or names to carry on or conduct or transact business.

In Witness Whereof, We have this   day of   19   made and signed this certificate.

....
....
....
....
....
....

State of New York, County of   ss.:   INDIVIDUAL ACKNOWLEDGMENT

On this   day of   19   , before me personally appeared
to me known and known to me to be the individual   described in, and who executed the foregoing certificate, and   he   thereupon   duly acknowledged to me that   he   executed the same.

E.26   Form of Certificate of Limited Partnership

FORM OF CERTIFICATE OF LIMITED PARTNERSHIP

WE, THE UNDERSIGNED, being desirous of forming a Limited Partnership pursuant to the laws of the State of New York, do hereby certify as follows:

1. The name of the Partnership is   Partners.

2. The character of the Partnership's business is to engage, throughout the continental United States, in the development, manufacture and sale of medical instruments, including general purpose respirators and related accessories and products.

3. The principal place of business of the Partnership is New York, New York 100   .

4. The names and places of residence of the General Partners are as follows:

Name	Place of Residence
	New York, New York 100
Corporation	New York, New York 100

The names and places of residence of the Limited Partners are set forth on Exhibit A annexed hereto.

5. The term for which the Partnership is to exist is from the date of filing of this certificate until the earliest to occur of (i) the resignation or withdrawal of both of the General Partners, unless their functions shall be carried on by a successor; (ii) the filing of any petition in bankruptcy by a General Partner which at the time of such filing is the sole General Partner as a bankrupt, or the occurrence of any substantially similar event or (iii) January 1, 2008. The death, legal disability, bankruptcy, dissolution, withdrawal or expulsion of any Limited Partner shall not result in the dissolution or ter-

mination of the Partnership. Upon the death or legal disability of a Limited Partner, his interest in the Partnership shall pass to his legal representatives with the full power in them or his heirs or legatees to become substituted (with the consent of the General Partners) as a Limited Partner in his place.

6. The amounts of cash to be contributed by each Limited Partner to the Partnership upon admission thereto is set forth on Exhibit A annexed hereto.

7. The Limited Partners shall not be required to make any additional contribution to the Partnership.

8. The share of the profits or other compensation by way of income which each Limited Partner shall receive shall be that percentage of the Limited Partners' aggregate share of the Partnership's profits and income as the amount of such Limited Partner's capital contribution to the Partnership bears to the Partnership's total capitalization.

9. The Limited Partners may not make any assignment of their interest in the Partnership to any person other than the General Partners without the prior written consent of the General Partners. No right is given to the Limited Partners to assign or encumber either in whole or in part their interest in the Partnership.

10. The General Partners may in their discretion admit additional Limited Partners.

11. There is no right of priority as to contributions or as to compensation by way of income among the Limited Partners, either presently or hereafter.

IN WITNESS WHEREOF, we have hereunto set our hands and seals this   day of   , 19 .

                                                GENERAL PARTNERS

(Corporate Seal)

                                                By: _____
                                                                        CORPORATION

(Corporate Seal)

                                                By: _____

E.27   Form of Consent and Guarantee   SPECIMEN FORM

CONSENT AND GUARANTEE

                    Corporation, a New York corporation with offices at   Avenue, New York, New York 100   (the "Seller"), has this day sold to   , an individual, having an office address at   , New York, New York (the "Owner"), a   percent (%) undivided interest in a certain IBM System 370/148 computer and related equipment (the "Equipment"), pursuant to a Purchase Agreement of even date. The Owner has purchased said interest in the Equipment from the Seller subject to:

    (i) a security interest created between Messrs.   ,   , and   , as Secured Party, and Seller, as Debtor, pursuant to a Security Agreement, dated June   , 19 ;

    (ii) an Agreement of Lease, dated December 30, 19 , between Messrs.   ,   ,   and   , as lessors, and   , Inc. ("   "), as lessee;

    (iii) an Agreement of Lease, dated August 1, 19   , between   , as lessor, and   Corporation ("   "), as lessee, to the extent that such lease pertains to the Equipment;

    (iv) a lease (the "Underlying Lease"), between   Corporation ("   "), as lessor, and   Stores (Central Organization), Inc. ("   "), as lessee, which Underlying Lease was assigned by   to   ; and,

    (v) a first lien security interest, held by   (   ), pursuant to a Security Agreement dated   , 19 , between   , as Debtor, and   , as Secured Party, securing the obligations described therein (such obligations being referred to herein in the aggregate as the "Obligations").

    In consideration of the mutual consents and promises herein contained, and other good and valuable consideration, the parties hereby agree as follows:

1.   hereby consents to the sale, by the Seller to the Owner, of the aforesaid   % undivided interest in and to the Equipment, and hereby releases the Seller from any further liability or obligation under the Consent and Guarantee between   and the Seller, dated   ,19 . The Owner hereby agrees that it will not sell, or otherwise transfer, any interest in the Equipment without the consent of   , which consent will not be unreasonably withheld upon assurance to   that it will have a valid perfected first lien on such interest in the Equipment in the hands of the proposed transferee.

2. The Owner hereby guarantees collection by   of all monthly rental, and any Termination Payment hereafter becoming payable, by   pursuant to the Underlying Lease, with respect to the Equipment; subject, however, to the following conditions:

(a) In the event   shall fall to pay any installment of monthly rental, or such Termination Payment, then, before the Owner shall be liable for any payment hereunder,   shall take all such steps as may be necessary and proper to effect collection thereof from   , and from any person having heretofore guaranteed the obligations of   under the Underlying Lease, including, without limitation, instituting and prosecuting such legal actions or proceedings as may be necessary or appropriate, obtaining judgment therein, and levying execution thereunder, in an endeavor to collect the same, and having failed to obtain satisfaction in full;

(b) Except as provided herein,   shall not release, or reduce in any way, the obligations of any guarantor under any guarantee of the Underlying Lease, unless it shall have simultaneously therewith released or reduced the obligations of   to the same extent; and,

(c) The liability of the Owner hereunder shall not exceed in the aggregate the sum of $

Dated: , 19

By: _____
        Vice President

_____

E.28   Form of Assumption Agreement

ASSUMPTION AGREEMENT   *SPECIMEN FORM*

WHEREAS, pursuant to a Purchase Agreement of even date herewith between   Corporation, a New York corporation ("Buyer"), and   , an individual with a business address at   , New York, New York, ("Seller"), Seller is this day selling to Buyer an undivided interest in certain Equipment referred to therein; and

WHEREAS, in connection with his acquisition of said undivided interest, Seller had issued a limited recourse promissory note dated   ,19   to   Inc. in the original principal amount of $ (the "Limited Recourse Note"); and

WHEREAS, as part of the purchase price for said undivided interest, Buyer has agreed to assume all of the obligations of Seller under the Limited Recourse Note;

NOW THEREFORE, in consideration of the premises and other good and valuable consideration, receipt and sufficiency whereof is hereby acknowledged, Buyer hereby assumes and agrees timely to perform all of the obligations of Seller under the Limited Recourse Note, and agrees to indemnify Seller and hold Seller harmless against any liability, cost or expense (including without limitation attorneys' fees) which Seller may incur as a result of any failure or alleged failure on the part of Buyer so to perform any such obligation.

IN WITNESS WHEREOF, Buyer has executed this Assumption Agreement this   th day of   , 19   .

                                           CORPORATION

                              By _____
                                           President

E.29   Form of General Assignment

Know all Men by these Presents,

THAT
of

assignor(s),

in consideration of $, the receipt whereof is hereby acknowledged, has sold and by these presents does grant, assign and convey unto

of   *assignee(s)*

the following:

SPECIMEN FORM

TO HAVE AND TO HOLD *the same unto the said assignee(s) executors, administrators and assigns forever, to and for the use of the assignee(s), hereby constituting and appointing said assignee(s) true and lawful attorney(s) irrevocable, in assignor's name, place and stead, for the purposes aforesaid, to ask, demand, sue for, attach, levy, recover and receive all such sum and sums of money which now are, or may hereafter become due, owing and payable for, or on account of all or any of the accounts, dues, debts, and demands above assigned, and giving and granting unto the said attorney(s) full power and authority to do and perform all and every act and thing whatsoever requisite and necessary, as fully, to all intents and purposes, as assignor's might or could do, if personally present, with full power of substitution and revocation, hereby ratifying and confirming all that the said attorney(s) or attorney's substitute shall lawfully do, or cause to be done by virtue hereof.*

IN WITNESS WHEREOF, *the undersigned has hereunto set   hand(s) and seal(s) the* day of   19   .

SIGNED, SEALED AND DELIVERED
IN THE PRESENCE OF   ....L.S.

                                                         ....L.S.

Forms and Documents That Paralegals May Draft

E.30   Form of Bill of Sale

T 1100—Bill of Sale, Short Form.   JULIUS BLUMBERG, INC., LAW BLANK PUBLISHERS

Know all Men by these Presents,
That

party of the first part, for and in consideration of the sum of

            Dollars ($) lawful money of the United States, to the party of the first part in hand paid, at or before the ensealing and delivery of these presents, by

party of the second part, the receipt whereof is hereby acknowledged, has bargained and sold, and by these present does grant and convey unto the said party of the second part, the heirs, executors, administrators, successors and assigns thereof.

SPECIMEN FORM

To Have and to Hold the same unto the said party of the second part, the heirs, executors, administrators, successors and assigns thereof forever. And the party of the first part does covenant and agree to and with the said party of the second part, to **Warrant and Defend** the sale of the said goods and chattels hereby sold unto the said party of the second part, the heirs, executors, administrators, successors and assigns thereof, against all and every person and persons whomsoever.

Whenever the text hereof requires, the singular number used herein shall include the plural and all genders.

In Witness Whereof: the party of the first part has duly executed this bill of sale on the   day of   19   .

In Presence of

....(L.S.)
....(L.S.)
....(L.S.)

APPENDIX E

E.31 Form of General Release

To all to whom these Presents shall come or may Concern, Know That

in consideration of the sum of   as RELEASOR,

received from   ($),

                                                                                                                                           as RELEASEE,

receipt whereof is hereby acknowledged, releases and discharges

the RELEASEE, RELEASEE'S heirs, executors, administrators, successors and assigns from all actions, causes of action, suits, debts, dues, sums of money, accounts, reckonings, bonds, bills, specialties, covenants, contracts, controversies, agreements, promises, variances, trespasses, damages, judgments, extents, executions, claims, and demands whatsoever, in law, admiralty or equity, which against the RELEASEE, the RELEASOR, RELEASOR'S heirs, executors, administrators, successors and assigns ever had, now have or hereafter can, shall or may, have for, upon, or by reason of any matter, cause or thing whatsoever from the beginning of the world to the day of the date of this RELEASE.

Whenever the text hereof requires, the use of singular number shall include the appropriate plural number as the text of the within instrument may require.

This RELEASE may not be changed orally.

In Witness Whereof, the RELEASOR has hereunto set RELEASOR'S hand and seal on the day of   19   .

In presence of

                                                                                                                                           L.S.

STATE OF   , COUNTY OF   ss.:
       On   19   before me
personally came

to me known, and known to me to be the individual(s) described in, and who executed the foregoing RELEASE, and duly acknowledged to me that   he   executed the same.

If the party making payment is not the same as the party released, delete words "as RELEASEE" and add names of parties released after the word "discharges."

Index

All numerical references are to paragraph [¶] numbers.

—A—

Abell, David, 510
Adelphi University, 202.1
Age discrimination, 302.1
Altman & Weil, 106
American Bar Association, 202.1, 202.4, 404.3, 1301
American Bar Association Status Reports, 101.1
Administrative law, training, 203.8
Appeals, paralegal's role in, 704.1
Associate of Applied Science Degree, 202.2, 202.3
Avila College, 203

—B—

Bachelor of Science Degree in Paralegal Studies, 202.2, 203.3
Banking, paralegals in, 1005
Bar Association of Metropolitan St. Louis, 202.2
Billing, combined paralegal and attorney, 103
Billing paralegal's time, 703.4, 1203.5
"Blue sky" materials, paralegal preparation of, 906

—C—

Calendar specialist, 702.2
Capital University, 202.2
Certificate of Proficiency, 202.2

Client contact, 509.3
Clients, emotional support by paralegals, 102.1
Clients, interviewing, 703.2
"Cloning" of legal assistants, 305.2
Closing statements, paralegal preparation of, 807
Code of Professional Responsibility, 1301
Columbus Ohio Bar Association, 202.2
Commercial practice, 908
Communication, intra-office, benefits of, 405
Consumer protection, legal assistant's role in, 1001.3
Corporate counsel, paralegal to, 1008.1
Corporate documents, paralegal preparation of, 903
Corporate paralegal, 901
Corporate paralegal, required training for, 203.1
Cost reduction, 509
Creditors, preparing notices, 706.4
Criminal cases, paralegal's role in, 707

—D—

Dartnell Corporation Survey, 501
Depositions, paralegal's role in, 703.8
Domestic relations practice, paralegals in, 706

—E—

Employee benefit plans, paralegal assistance with, 909
ERISA paralegal, 911, 912

Estate administration, paralegal's role, 603
Estate planning, paralegals in, 601
Estate progress file, 603.1, 603.2
Ethics, ABA guidelines for paralegals, 1301

—F—

Form letters
   Acceptance letters, 304.2
   Interview, setting up, 303.2
   Rejection at application, 303.2
   Rejection of interviewed candidate, 304.2
   Universal letters, 511
   Also see Appendix E
Free-lance paralegals, 1104.1
Fry, William, 1004

—G—

George Washington University, 202.1
Government agencies, paralegal's work, 1001
Group interviewing techniques, 303, 304, 304.2
Group interviews, to save time and money, 306
Guinan, Mary, 406

—H—

Hanson, Linscott R., 510
Hiring paralegals, *see* Paralegal recruitment
"How to Create a System for the Law Office," 504, 507

—I—

Illinois Corporate System, 510
Illinois Probate System, 510
Illinois Residential Paralegal System, The, 510
Incorporation documents, paralegal preparation of, 902
Insurance companies, use of paralegals, 1007
Interrogatories, handled by paralegals, 703.7
Interview techniques for hiring paralegals, 302
Institute for Paralegal Training, Philadelphia, 202.1

—J—

Job description manual, 203.9, 302.2, 408, 408.1
Justice Department, paralegals, 1001.1

—K—

Kerr, Alexander, 701

—L—

Law office administrator, 402.2
   Paralegal as, 402.3
Law Office Economics and Management, 206
Law, practice of, how to increase enjoyment of, 107
Law Week, 1001.2
Lawyer acceptance of paralegals, 404.1
Lawyer productivity, 509.3
Lawyer responsibility, 404.3
Lawyer substitutes, 509.2
Legal Aid offices, paralegal's work for, 1004
Legal assistant, definition, 101.1
Legal assistant coordinator, 402, 402.2, 402.3, 409
Legal business, preventing loss of, 509.2
Legal clinics, paralegal staffs, 1104.3
Legal research, by paralegals, 707
Legal research training, 204.5
Legal specialist teamwork, 508.2
Litigation coordinator, 702, 705
Litigation paralegal
   Functions, 701.2
   Required training, 203.3
Litigation team, 702.1

—M—

Malpractice suits, prevention by legal assistants, 104
Manan, Barbara H., 510
Master Information List, 505.1
Matrimonial paralegals, required training, 203.5
MIL formats, 505.1, 505.2, 505.3

Index

Missouri Bar, 509.3
Mortgages, drafting by paralegals, 804

—N—

National Association of Legal Assistants, 1301
National Federation of Paralegal Associations, 1301
National Paralegal Institute, 1004
New York Law Journal, 406
New York State Bar Association, 305.2
New York University, 202.1
North Hennepin Community College, 202.2

—O—

Office management,
    Adopting a paralegal system, 301
    Communication techniques, 405
    Coordinator of legal assistants, 402.3
    Cost reduction, 509
    Improving office routines, 405
    Lawyer productivity, 509.3
    Paralegal-systems interface, 501.2
    Paralegal work assignments, 404.2
    Paralegals as professionals, 404.1
    Problem-solving methods, 406.2
    Reasons for using systems, 501
    Reduce fees and increase profits, 103
    Supervising the legal staff, 402, 402.2, 402.3, 409
    Team approaches, 403.1
    Using paralegals to increase income, 106
Office manual, 408-410
Office of Economic Opportunity, 1004
Oregon State Department of Education, 202.3

—P—

Paralegal
    Affirmation of Responsibility, Appendix D
    Associations, Appendix B
    Billing time, 703.4, 1203.5, 1204.1
    Code of Ethics, Appendix D
    Code of Responsibility, 1301
    Compensation and benefits, 204.2, 1201, 1205

Paralegal (Cont'd)
    Emotional support of clients, 102.1
    Employers, identifying, 1203.7
    Ethical uses of, 1301, 1302, 1302.1, 1302.2
    How to integrate into your office staff, 105, 404
    Limitations, 1302
    Professional status, 404.1
    Programs, evaluation of, 1101, 1206
    Public recognition of, 1303
    Rating system for, 1102
    Use of
        To reduce possibility of malpractice suits, 104
        To reduce legal fees and increase profits, 103
        To save attorney time, 101
    Recruitment, administrator of law office, 402.3
Paralegal recruitment
    Bar Associations, 201.4
    Classified advertising, 201.2
    Criteria for employees, 302.1
    Employment agencies, 201.1
    Evaluation of specialized training, 203
    Finding experienced paralegals, 201
    Group interviews save time, 303
    Hiring decision, techniques, 305
    Locating experienced paralegals, 201
    Paralegal associations, 201.4
    Resumes, how to process, 303.2
    School placement officers, 201.3
    Schools, Appendix A
    Tests for candidates, 304.1
Paralegal system
    Acceptance by lawyers, 404.1
    Establishing, 404, 408
Paralegal training programs
    ABA approved schools, 202.1, 202.3, 201.3
    Eastern U.S., 202.1
    Institutions, types of, 202
    Legal specialties, 412
    Middle America, 202.2
    Office efficiency, 401
    On-the-job training
        Benefits and pitfalls, 204
        Videotape training programs, 204.1
    Six steps to follow, 407
    West Coast, 202.3
Patent specialist, legal assistant to, 1008.1

Pension, profit-sharing and ERISA, training, 203.6
Pepper, Hamilton & Sheetz, 701
Plaintiff investigation, 703.3
Pleadings, drafting by paralegals, 703.6, 706.5
Portland Community College, 202.3, 203.5
Prentice-Hall, 509.3
Probate paralegal, required training for, 203.2
Problem-solving techniques, 406.2
Procedural Outline and Checklist, 505, 505.6, Fig. 5.16
Promotion standards, 411.2

—R—

Ramo, Roberta Cooper, 504, 507
Real estate paralegal, 801
Real estate paralegal, required training, 203.4
Reference for Better Personnel Selection, 303.1
Resumes, how to process, 303.2
Rikli, Donald C., 510
Rockhurst College, 203
Rockland County Bar Association, 201.3

—S—

Salaries for paralegals, 204.2
S.E.C. registrations, paralegal assistance in, 907
Secretarial productivity, increasing, 409.2
Secretaries
  And paralegals, 206
  Promotion to paralegals, 411
  Resentment of paralegals, 411, 411.3
Special skills inventory, paralegal, 409
Specialties of law, paralegal training, 412
St. Louis Community College, 202.2
Stock transfer ledger, paralegals maintain, 904
Strong, Kline, 510
Supervising attorney, 402
Survey of Law Firm Economics, 106
Systems binders, 408.1, 412
Systems management, 501–510
  Analysis, 502.1
  Centralized control of work, 508.1
  Documents, 502.3
  Lawyer productivity, 509.3

Systems management (Cont'd)
  Master Information List, 505.1
  MIL formats, 505.1, 505.2, 505.3
  Procedural Outline and Checklist, 505
  Universal documents, 504.2
Systems manuals, 412

—T—

Taxes, estate, computation by paralegals, 602.2
Team approach
  Hiring paralegals, 305.2
  Law office operations, 403.1, 604
  Litigation, 701.1, 701.2, 701.3
Temporary paralegals, 1104.1
Tennesee State Bar, 106
Texas Probate System, 502.4
Title companies, paralegal's work with, 806, 1006.1
Trial assistant, 702.2
Trial preparation, paralegal's role in, 704
Turner, Betsy, 304.2, 305.2
Turner, Lee, 502.4, 508.2, 702.2

—U—

U.S. Attorney's Office, paralegals work for, 1001.4
Universal documents, MIL reference system, 505.3
Universal letters, samples, 511
Universal versions of documents, 504.2
U.C.L.A. Extension Attorney Assistant Program, 202.3
U.C.L.A. School of Law, 203.3
University of Minnesota, 203
University of West Los Angeles, 202.2

—V—

Videotape
  Attorneys preparing for trial, 406.3
  Training techniques, 204.1
Visual progress charts, 406.1

Index

—W—

Westchester County Bar Association, 201.3
William Woods College, 202.2
Witness interviews, by paralegals, 706.3

Wolf, Jerome T., 206
Word processing, 404.2
Word Processors of America, 509.3
Work assignment, 404.2